DAN

D0529472

The World of Dante
PQ
4332
W6

DATE DUE

JA 8 '98 DE 17 '05			
AP 2'98			
DE 23 '99			
DE 18 99			
OC 8'02			
MR 21'03			
MR 20'04			
OC 31'00			
MO 21'05			

PQ4332
W6

RIVERSIDE CITY COLLEGE
LIBRARY
Riverside, California

OCT 1980

THE WORLD OF DANTE

THE WORLD
OF DANTE

Essays on Dante
and his Times

Edited for the Oxford Dante Society
by
CECIL GRAYSON

CLARENDON PRESS · OXFORD
1980

Riverside Community College
Library
4800 Magnolia Avenue
Riverside, CA 92506

Oxford University Press, Walton Street, Oxford OX2 6DP

OXFORD LONDON GLASGOW
NEW YORK TORONTO MELBOURNE WELLINGTON
IBADAN NAIROBI DAR ES SALAAM LUSAKA CAPE TOWN
KUALA LUMPUR SINGAPORE JAKARTA HONG KONG TOKYO
DELHI BOMBAY CALCUTTA MADRAS KARACHI

© Oxford Dante Society 1980

Published in the United States
by Oxford University Press
New York

All rights reserved. No part of this publication may be reproduced, stored in a retrieval system, or transmitted, in any form or by any means, electronic, mechanical, photocopying, recording, or otherwise, without the prior permission of Oxford University Press

British Library Cataloguing in Publication Data

The world of Dante.
  1. Dante Alighieri—Criticism and interpretation
  I. Grayson, Cecil   II. Oxford Dante Society
  851′.1   PQ4390   79-40599
  ISBN 0-19-815760-6

Set, printed and bound in Great Britain by
Fakenham Press Limited,
Fakenham, Norfolk

Preface

In November 1976 the Oxford Dante Society celebrated its centenary. It was founded by Dr. Edward Moore, Principal of St. Edmund Hall, who through his numerous studies and his basic work on the text of the *Comedy* became one of the world's leading Dante scholars. From the beginning the Society was composed of a small group of Oxford senior members of different disciplines, united by a common devotion to the study of Dante and his works. For over a century it has met regularly once a term to hear and discuss papers presented by its members, among them, besides Dante specialists such as Moore himself, Paget Toynbee, and Cesare Foligno, scholars distinguished in other fields like W. P. Ker, C. S. Lewis, Maurice Bowra, J. R. Tolkien, Edgar Wind. In 1920 Paget Toynbee, editor of Dante's *Epistolae* and second only to Moore in British Dante studies, published a Record of the Society's first forty-four years, which clearly indicates in its bibliography how the Society acted as stimulus and sounding-board for the publications of its members. It has continued to do the same in the past half-century, and some evidence may be seen in the Society's volume of *Centenary Essays on Dante* published by the Clarendon Press for the seventh centenary of Dante's birth in 1965.

In this same tradition, and in order to mark the centenary of the Society's foundation, eight present and two former members gave a series of lectures in Oxford in 1976–7, which form the basis of the present volume. They appear here not necessarily in the form or the order in which they were delivered. It seemed appropriate to group them according to area of interest: broadly speaking, history and politics, philosophy and classical learning, poetry and art. They do not, of course, represent all the constituents of Dante's world; their range, though inevitably limited, is none the less wide, and the character of the essays diverse. Together they form an introduction (as the original lecture series intended) to major aspects of Dante's works, thought, and times; individually they aim, each in its own way, to present a new view or a new synthesis or a new methodology in relation to their chosen topic. The Society is grateful to the Delegates of the Oxford University Press for accepting its proposal to give these lectures a more permanent form. It was made not only out of the desire to mark a milestone in the history of the Oxford Dante Society, but also in the belief that these essays can offer a useful and original contribution to Dante studies in general.

C. G.

Contents

Contents

Illustrations

Between pages 236 and 237

Editor's Note

All quotations in this volume from the works of Dante are taken from the following editions:

La Commedia secondo l'antica vulgata, a cura di Giorgio Petrocchi, 4 vols. (Milan, 1966–7).

Vita Nuova, a cura di Michele Barbi (Florence, 1932).

Convivio, a cura di Maria Simonelli (Bologna, 1966).

De vulgari eloquentia, a cura di A. Marigo, ed. riveduta da Pier Giorgio Ricci (Florence, 1957).

Le Rime, a cura di Gianfranco Contini (Turin, 1946).

Epistolae, ed. by Paget Toynbee, second edn. with a bibliographical appendix by C. G. Hardie (Oxford, 1966).

Monarchia, a cura di P. G. Ricci (Milan, 1965).

English translations of passages quoted in Italian or Latin are given in most instances in the footnotes.

Florence, Tuscany, and the World of Dante

JEREMY CATTO

To the modern observer the world of Dante must be seen through the window of Florentine civilization, as he embodies the first of its several phases. Yet Dante himself has eluded both his early admirers who wished to enshrine him in the pantheon of Florence's civic patriots, and the subsequent attempts of those who, abandoning the search for an enduring Florentine tradition, would place him in a 'medieval' past contrasted with his city's 'Renaissance' manifest destiny. As Leonardo Bruni, the principal spokesman of the first school, recognized, Dante combined political activity with literary study in accord with the subsequent humanist ideal, but his embarrassment that Dante should show no sympathy at all with republican independence and the notion of the city state (and had indeed placed his formidable talents as a publicist on the side of Florence's enemies in the struggle with Henry VII) is palpable in his *Dialogi*, where the derogation in the *Divina Commedia* of the republican hero Brutus to the jaws of Satan is elaborately explained away.[1] Bruni's dilemma is with us still. Dante was indisputably the founder of Florence's literary greatness, but his political opinions have either had to be dismissed as a quirk of genius, the sour consequence of his exile in 1302, or passed over as 'medieval' or romantically conservative, a faded imperial dream of an order rapidly passing from contemporary reality.

Neither of these approaches to Dante's politics will do. Both of them founder against the palpable solidity and realism of a poet explicitly of his own time who, in raising his friends and contemporaries to the mythological level, placed a unique value and significance on the political world of his generation. The *Commedia* placed otherwise ephemeral figures like the glutton Ciacco and potentates of rather limited importance like the

Angevin Charles Martel beside the great poets of antiquity, classical monsters, and the fathers of the Church; the centaurs had to share their corner of hell with the Pistoiese nonentity Vanni Fucci; and in raising the historical Beatrice Portinari to a place of theological significance in the celestial hierarchy, Dante effected an astonishing, almost Proustian conjuncture between his own personal and social world and the fixed stars of the fourteenth-century heavens. His very success has dimmed the effect for modern readers to whom the *Commedia*'s characters contemporary with Dante are as remote and mythopoeic as their classical counterparts, but to his own time it must have been startling. Only a man quite unusually receptive to the contemporary social and political scene would have dared to present so much gossip, for gossip is what it originally must have been, in so elevated, so serious a form. His neglect of Florence as a focus of patriotism and contempt for the notion of *Florentina civilitas* must therefore have deeper roots in his social attitudes than mere eccentricity or nostalgia. Not only the politics of Florence and the opinions of Dante but the experience of life in the city, the opportunities it offered and its natural groupings and affinities need fuller understanding before these attitudes can be grasped. What is attempted here is a number of observations on the society of Florence and its cultural context and on Dante's position within them, which may help to show how the poet and the political thinker can be reconciled.

At least a century of scholarly scrutiny has been lavished on medieval and renaissance Florence and her singularly rich archives, but, perhaps for that reason, the society of the thirteenth-century city has not been in recent years studied as a whole, as have those of Pisa, Padua, and even San Gimignano. The last great narrative account and the last attempt at synthesis were made by the two great 'Whig' historians of Florence, respectively Robert Davidsohn and Gaetano Salvemini, before 1914.[2] For them, it was beyond question that the period of Dante's youth was characterized by the struggle of an emerging bourgeoisie against the feudal nobility, who were finally expelled, if not from the city then from the urban polity and from government, with the enactment of the Ordinances of Justice in 1293. The outcome also marked the victory of the city over the *contado*, of commerce over agriculture. Though these pairs of opposites continue to be influential, the views of Salvemini and Davidsohn as applied to Florence have had to be drastically modified in the light of closer political analysis and further prosopographical evidence. In the political sphere, this was above all the work of Nicola Ottokar; his careful dissection of the Florentine governing class has perhaps more affinities with English historiography than with the work of Italian historians, who have found his conformity to neither materialist nor idealist general theories unsatisfying.[3] Nevertheless his critical work dissolved the mirage of a Florentine commercial class distinct from the great landed families, and though since he wrote, the 'plutocratic bourgeoisie' has frequently been invoked, a credible criterion for distinguishing specific 'bourgeois' families from their aristocratic counterparts has yet to be invented.

Above all, the study of the Florentine *contado*, the uplands of the Mugello and the Casentino, the Val d'Elsa and the slopes of Monte Albano, which encircle the middle Arno basin, has weakened the force of the traditional opposition of town and country. Though nothing of the scale of, for instance, Toubert's massive work on Southern Latium is available on the region of Florence, the pioneer work of Plesner on the topography and society of the uplands and the redistribution of the inhabitants which followed the occupation of the plain has shown that the growth of Florence was a part of the secular movement of population from the hill-communities to the plains, and a final stage of the process of *incastellamento*.[4] Only the draining of the marshlands in which the city was founded made possible its rapid expansion in the thirteenth century. Roman Florence must have been an isolated fort, built upon a *bassissima collina* in the marshes of the middle Arno. In the recession of the sixth and subsequent centuries the community may have resembled a miniature Ravenna, as its neighbour Prato, built amid a system of ditches and canals, might have been a kind of Tuscan Venice or Torcello. By Dante's time, of course, the lowlands had been almost completely drained, and the people of the hills, the 'miserrima Faesulanorum propago', as he epitomized them, had come down to cultivate them and to constitute the historical Florence. The descent of the 'Fiesolans' was to be a theme of the earliest Florentine historiography, where they had to take responsibility for the ignoble, rustic characteristics of the citizens whose better part was held to be Roman.[5] The detailed topographical and prosopographical work of Plesner has put the immigrants in a new perspective: it is no longer possible to see them fleeing from feudal oppression, since the larger rural proprietors were themselves an important element in the migration. The rulers of thirteenth-century Florence, the founders of its commercial pre-eminence, were none other than the successful lords and proprietors of the *contado* whose lands and vineyards in the hills complemented their business in the city. At a lower social level, Plesner found in the single, if well-documented, community of Passignano a large number of professional families, *judices* and notaries who had originated and prospered there, and while retaining substantial property in their home town had subsequently accumulated business and interests in Florence.[6] The descent of the Fiesolans, therefore, was partial and contingent: it was a kind of secondary transhumancy, imposing upon a population of farmers and rural proprietors a stratum of urban experience. The style of life and even the architecture of the uplands might be found again in the tower societies of Florence: for instance in the Torre dei Cattanei, where a group of interrelated families of the Mugello to whom the defence of the vital pass towards Bologna was entrusted shared a tower by the city gate nearest their own region.

Dante's Florence was a city of such towers, 'a forest of towers', as Plesner put it, 'more serried than the chimneys of a modern industrial town'. The towers might comprise one of the most elemental institutions of thirteenth-century Italy, the strong familial clan, or in some cases an association of family groups or 'tower society'. The internal cohesion of the large family group was assumed in Florence's constitution, and the family left its mark on every aspect of Tuscan life, rural or urban: no student of Dante could ignore the quarrel of the Cerchi and Donati. It was certainly not rigid, and was subject to constant division and redefinition; nor was it an inheritance from the distant Lombard past. The Italian *consorterie* seem to have taken shape during the late tenth and eleventh centuries; their emergence was evidently a result of the occupation of new lands and the establishment of *castelli*, the defensive and agricultural settlements which were the upland precursors of the communes.[7] Whether the solidarity of the family group was the phenomenon only of *domini castrorum* or *milites*, as has been suggested in the case of Latium, or whether the peasant *fraterna* with its habit of occupying contiguous property in the *castelli* had at least some cohesion, is in the present state of knowledge uncertain. But the modern Mediterranean parallel of the shepherd society of Epirus has shown that primary loyalty to a restricted circle of kindred and a system of values founded on the notion of honour and family pride need not be limited to the lords of the land.[8] In Florence, certainly, the cohesion of the family group does not seem to have been limited to the richer lineages. In its characteristic form, the *consorteria* or patrilineal family was frequently the legal owner of property in the thirteenth century, and its members tended where possible to live together in the same or adjacent houses, like the humble *fraterne* of the Latin *castelli*. Its inner discipline and code of mutual obligation was perhaps the nursery of urban experience and the wider co-operation on which city life depended. In fact the commune arose from its constituent family units through the medium of the *sesto* (district). The remarkable stability of families living within the same *sesto* can be demonstrated in innumerable cases: the Alighieri's habitation in the parish of San Martino del Vescovo within the *sesto* of Porta San Pietro from the twelfth century to the time of Dante is an example.[9] As each district formed a social unit of its own, it is not surprising that Dante should find the great passion of his life among the daughters of the Portinari, a prominent family of the Porta San Pietro; nor that Villani should often identify a Florentine by his *sesto*. Moreover, these divisions were the basis of the Florentine constitution: the representative regime of the priors after 1280 was not instituted to represent the guilds, as Ottokar showed, but the *sesti* and therefore the groups of *consorterie* which they comprised. Every election to the innumerable committees which together constituted the city government had to balance the various *sesti*. Above all, indications that the clannishness of Florence was not confined to a few great families come from the statutes of the earliest guilds. The first statutes, those of the humble retail traders (*rigattieri*) and linen workers in 1296 and of the money-lenders in 1299, made elaborate provisions for the representation of members from each part of Florence in their government. Not even for six months could one group of families, rich or poor, be suffered to have the edge on another.[10]

In this respect, town and country in Dante's Tuscany were simply two related settings for family life. Shortly before his exile indeed, the Ordinances of Justice appear to have made some such distinction between *magnati* with their interests outside Florence and *popolani* whose world lay within it; with their promulgation in 1293, the government of the city seems at last that of an independent urban commune, dominated by commercial interests. This view of the Ordinances, however, has not stood up to the careful analysis of Ottokar, who showed that the distinction of *magnati* and *popolani* made in them, and in the associated schedule of named *magnati* families, does not correspond to political reality. The same group of Guelf lineages which had dominated affairs in the past continued to do so after 1293: the Bardi, the Donati, the Cavalcanti, and others were still supplying city officers from their respective *sesti* in the fourteenth century. No modification of the basis of power can therefore be observed, as a result of the Ordinances, in the actual conduct of government.[11] Nor is it clear that Giano della Bella and his colleagues intended anything so far reaching: for the language of those clauses which deprived the *magnati* of their civil power was not the measured tone of constitutional reform, but the revolutionary rhetoric of a party, and the proscriptions made no nice distinctions between powerful men and their more remote and poorer cousins. They banned them all irrespectively, if they bore the name of a family on the list.[12] The schedule of families, in terms of wealth and social importance, is arbitrary: and as the product of a momentary factional victory, the ban was naturally ineffective in practice. The Ordinances were, of course, incorporated into Florence's political myth, and in the fourteenth century the stigma of magnate status was invoked according to convenience. Though it would be wrong to belittle the serious, and in some ways sophisticated, constitutional provisions worked out by Giano and his colleagues, their purpose in giving the term *magnati* a juridical meaning seems to have been moral rather than social: it was an epithet, like the alternative term *potentes*, used to mean something like vandals, violent men and disturbers of the peace.[13] As such, rather than as a considered social category, it was destined to survive in the political vocabulary of Florence.

If the leading families of Dante's Florence were only ephemerally *magnati* or *popolani*, they were no more distinguishable from their country cousins by the character of their affairs. The range of their interests can be assessed through the numerous surviving *ricordanze*, business and personal memoranda often kept up for several generations of the same family in the late thirteenth and fourteenth centuries: and a recent survey has emphasized the unexpectedly prominent role of agricultural concerns in the business of families better known for commercial enterprise.[14] Yet even the banking fortunes of the Strozzi or the Sassetti were founded on the hardly spectacular business of lending money to small farmers of the *contado* or rural communes struggling to pay their taxes, and whether the Cavalcanti with their estates at Brozzi or the Niccolini at Passignano were 'feudal' families who engaged in trade or 'commercial' families who bought land in the country is an artificial question the answer to which depends on perspective. Money-lending, like some other forms of commerce, was from the beginning intimately associated with the exploitation of land and livestock.[15] Exploitation naturally took many forms; but the predominance on land owned by Florentine families of the *mezzadria* or share-cropping system in which the landlord might take a variable part in the supply of the seed or other aspects of farming, implies that Florentine landowners were prepared to take a direct interest in their estates.[16]

The half-rural, half-urban world of the Florentines is typified by the Alighieri. Dante himself, who associated the influx of immigrants with declining public standards, gives no hint of being anything but a descendant of autochthonous stock. This is confirmed by the earliest record of the Alighieri, an agreement of 1189, which shows his great-grandfather Alighiero established on the same site as the Casa degli Alighieri of Dante's own time —a modest group of houses to the west of the traditional Casa di Dante. There is no reason to doubt his claim of descent from the knight Cacciaguida who had died taking part in the second Crusade.[17] Other documents, however, indicate that in the early thirteenth century the Alighieri had interests outside the walls, some complex territorial rights in the vicinity of Prato,

where Dante's grandfather and some of his uncles were active
in the 1240s. One document in the archives of Prato shows them
as proprietors in the ancient parish of San Giusto on the
shoulder of Monte Albano, with other properties below in the
'new lands' to north and south, the former marshlands of
Tavola and Limite.[18] The distribution of these residual possessions round an ancient settlement suggests (though no more)
that they were ancestral lands, with subsequent accretions in the
lowlands beneath Monte Albano. Was San Giusto, then, the
original home of Cacciaguida's ancestors, 'onde venner quivi',
whether or not they were of the Elisei?[19] This is a mere speculation, but the involvement of later generations of the family in the
immediate contado is established by the record of several transactions in Florence itself and more particularly at Prato, where
they appear as lenders of small sums and speculators in grain.
Dante himself first appears, in 1283 or 1284, as the owner of a
debt, while his sister married the money lender Lapo Riccomanno.[20] The public activities of the Alighieri were perhaps
more at the level of the *sesto* than the city itself, and it is as a
representative of the *populus* of San Martino and the Porta San
Pietro that his uncle Brunetto was made one of the *pediti del
Carrocio* in 1260.[21] Their pride of citizenship, itself the latest
of a hierarchy of loyalties to family, parish, and neighbourhood,
was wholly compatible with their interests at Prato and in the
surrounding contado.

Cacciaguida, as Dante emphasized, was a knight; and the
Florentines' participation in war is a reminder of their knightly
values and co-operation in the Guelf alliance with Tuscan,
southern Italian, and French feudatories. It has recently been
pointed out that in the thirteenth century they fought their wars
with their own infantry and cavalry: at Montaperti about 1,400
cavalry and 4,000 infantry, supported by about 8,000 rural
levies, took the field, and as late as 1323 local horse and foot
soldiers were the backbone of the city's defences.[22] The role of
mercenaries in these forces, though not negligible, was supple-
mentary: and if the professional soldiers in their service had a
wider military experience, there is no evidence to suggest that
the native Florentine forces were significantly less proficient in
war than the hired contingents, which without the counter-
balance of a strong local force would have been useless and

dangerous. The *Libro di Montaperti* and other early military records of Florence are the written remains of a government thoroughly versed in the business of war, and that more is known of the dispositions of the ill-fated campaign of 1260 than of any other aspect of the Primo Popolo is itself an indication of where its priorities lay.[23] That they had not changed in the years after 1282 is amply demonstrated by the interminable, detailed and informed discussions of military matters in the various constitutional bodies of the republic, as minuted in the *Consulte*. Brunetto degli Alighieri was one of the standard-bearers at Montaperti, and Dante himself fought at Campaldino.

As a military power, moreover, Florence was a willing partici-pant in the revived Guelf alliance after 1270, with an obligation to contribute to the Guelf *tallia* or standing army. The Guelf party was founded upon the French and more especially the Provençal connection in Italy, which centred on the house of Anjou; and it opened the door, for Florence, upon the world of southern-French and Catalan professional knighthood. The Tuscan *cavallata* found themselves under the captaincy of foreign condottieri like Amaury of Narbonne or William the Catalan, who were successively in the pay of Florence; the former commanded Dante and other soldiers in the field of Campaldino, with the battle-cry of 'Nerbona cavaliere'. The cry evokes the knightly and Provençal context of Dante's mili-tary experience, reminiscences of which abound in the *Commedia*. It is therefore no surprise to meet so many stars of the galaxy of Guelfs, together with the more notable of their opponents, in position in his celestial universe. The supreme captain, Charles of Anjou, sits in Ante-Purgatory, while Charles Martel, his high-spirited grandson with whom Dante claimed acquaintance, is in the heaven of Venus among the spirits of lovers.[24] Dante clearly felt at ease in this world, and refers to gossip no longer penetrable Guelf captains like Guido Guerra, William Marquis of Mont-ferrat, and Azzo VIII of Este; while one of the most courtly of his *tenzoni* with Cino da Pistoia was evidently written for the eyes of the former captain of the Guelfs (in 1288) and his future host, Marquis Moroello Malaspina. In these respects Dante seems to have been a typical Florentine *cavaliere*.

The military experience of Dante and his contemporaries admitted them into the fraternity of the Guelfs; and the Guelfs

shared not only a martial way of life but a literary culture which
brought them under the influence of France, and especially of
Provence. The influence of Provençal models is most obvious in
the adoption of Provençal as the language of poetry and enter-
tainment in the thirteenth-century Italian courts. It was established at Montferrat as early as the beginning of the century,
when an earlier Malaspina Marquis had taken on the Provençal
troubadour Raimbaut de Vaqueiras in a vituperative poetical
tournament or *tenzone*, redolent with ritual insults; and Provençal was the language of Sordello, the other great Mantuan
poet, a knight, wandering versifier, and amorous adventurer in
the best traditions of the Guelfs.[25] Accordingly, Dante assigned
him the appropriate role of interlocutor between himself and the
great European princes of the last generation who waited in Ante-
Purgatory, Rudolf of Habsburg, Philip III of France, Peter III
of Aragon, Henry III of England, and many others.[26] For
ordinary purposes of communication, the northern Italian
courts, under similar influences, evolved a hybrid Italianized
French; and though Tuscan dialect had already found a variety
of written forms from the third quarter of the thirteenth century
onwards in a number of accounts and *ricordanze* (among them
those of Jacopo Riccomanno, the father of Dante's brother-in-
law Lapo), the foundations of a true Italian prose, which
raised Tuscan to the level of intellectual expression, were laid by
Dante himself in *Vita Nuova* and *Convivio*.[27] For poetry, the
Siciliano illustre of the Hohenstaufen court gave way in the 1260s
to the Tuscan of Guittone d'Arezzo. The language of this
Tuscan tradition was much refined and developed by Guido
Guinizelli and his school of poetic reformers; and the refined
version or *dolce stil nuovo* was, of course, the language of Dante
himself. It was the first conscious and deliberate poetic rival of
Provençal in Italy, and it owed most of its inspiration to the
language of the troubadours; and with the *rime* of Dante, Cino
da Pistoia, and Guido Cavalcanti, it was soon established in the
courts and castles of Italy.

The character of the poetry, with its pyrotechnics of rhyme
and metre, the smart repartee of its literary jousts, and its theme
of courtly love, establishes it as the product of a sophisticated
society, like its Provençal model. Dante, of course, had read and
imitated a great number of the Provençal poets; he could turn a

Provençal *canzone* with ease, as he demonstrated with a few verses in the mouth of the great Arnaut Daniel.[28] He found himself at home in a courtly world where the values of honour and nobility held first place. But it was a world which however natural to him, could not, unaltered, satisfy his aspirations. As a literary reformer, he sought to turn Italian into the vehicle of a higher and more serious poetry than his predecessors had produced: and as a moral reformer he reinterpreted nobility and honour, the warlike and the amatory virtues of the Guelfs, constructing first a new ethical theory, and finally a poetic image of their lives, their experience, and their destinies. Citizenship was the exercise of these transformed aristocratic virtues: the most admirable and perfect knight of all the Guelfs, Charles Martel, is the spokesman of Dante's higher social ethic when he asks whether man would be in a worse condition, 'se non fosse cive'; citizenship, is the answer, united men in different ways of life, 'diversamente per diversi offici'. To be a *cive*, then, is not to be a *cittadino* or to live within a city, but to be a political man in the Aristotelian sense. The message is not delivered by the inhabitant of a commune but by a prince of unassailable nobility.[29]

Though his kindred was not among the most illustrious Tuscan lineages, Dante shared their pride of ancestry and inherited notions of honour, to which his urban background made no obvious difference. It was no civic spirit but his intellectual and moral vision which raised him from the state of nature in which their limited outlook kept them; and if, as is here suggested, Florence and other cities had no distinctive social structure or cultural values, the range and quality of Dante's highly conscious art may indicate in what their true distinction lay. The most striking characteristic of the cities was their concentration of acquired skills, arts or, to use a thirteenth-century term, *pratice*: skills and techniques, after all, not the possession of any particular natural resources, nor even an especially favourable geographical position, enabled Tuscan towns in general and in particular Florence to flourish. The origins of the Tuscan aptitude for commerce, so marked in the late thirteenth century, are obscure, but all the activities which gave them their temporary preeminence were sustained by a spirit of innovation in commerce not obvious, though not entirely absent, in Genoa or Venice. Florence's earliest powerful guild, the Calimala, was a league of men proficient in the arts of dyeing and finishing cloth; the material was largely imported from northern Europe, and the process could have been undertaken in any centre where the required skills were available. The same is true of the essentially technical contributions made by the primarily inland Tuscan towns to international commerce. These consist first of all in the art of *mercatura*, the application of special knowledge of the market encapsulated in a new genre, the *Pratica della Mercatura*, a kind of handbook of Tuscan origin, evidently kept from about 1270 by a number of Pisan and Florentine families engaged in international trade. Originally individual productions distilled from the experience of particular companies, they developed into compendious manuals, the best known example of which is the early-fourteenth-century *Pratica* of Pegolotti. For their compilers, commerce on a large scale was a skilled, almost a learned occupation.[30] A second contribution was the art of accounting, a Florentine speciality resulting from a systematic approach to business as a single enterprise and not simply a series of transactions; though not fully developed by 1300, its progress has been charted through a series of accounts of Florentine companies.[31] Thirdly, Tuscan entrepreneurs pioneered the permanent international company, which depended upon a network of agents placed in foreign centres, relaying a lively and regular commercial intelligence, and on the invention of the direct letter of credit or exchange without the intermediacy of a notarial deed.[32] On these technical foundations the bankers of Florence had established, by 1300, an astonishingly precocious system of international credit, without any of the advantages of situation enjoyed by the Italian ports, and without the backing of exceptional agricultural wealth or mineral resources. The identity of the *campsores*, Bardi, Frescobaldi, or Acciaiuoli, places them among the greatest of Florence; and the city's commercial wealth ultimately lay in the ability of members of great magnate families to acquire and develop new and often complex skills. The growing importance of the *Arti* or guilds did not mark the emergence of a new class, but the organization and husbandry of these skills by the maintenance of professional standards. Indeed the familial bond of the *consorterie* was an essential element in the success of the international companies whose agents had to rely, without effective legal redress, on one another's letters of exchange.

The acquisition of these arts or skills was the foundation of all the opportunities which Florence offered her inhabitants. Government itself, to the practice of which members of the commune made a notably original contribution, seems to have been treated as an art which could be learnt by precept or practice. Brunetto Latini, himself active in Florence's affairs, had devoted the last book of the *Tresor* to an exposition of the proper conduct of a *podestà*: and in the later thirteenth century it was possible for a Florentine citizen to serve—Lapo Saltarelli is an example—as a semi-professional *podestà* in a series of Italian cities. The technical ingenuity of Florentine constitution makers can be seen in the work of Giano della Bella's last constitutional committee, the *commissione degli arbitri degli statuti del capitano* in 1294, which attempted a systematic revision and codification of the laws.[33] It is still more apparent in the massive volumes of *Consulte* and *Consigli* of the Republic which, as more or less verbatim minutes of the various bodies of government, are unusually revealing about political processes. The various committees appear in the *Consulte* almost as political academies, where a large and constantly changing section of the citizens co-operated in perfecting a balanced constitution and working out intelligent diplomatic and military measures. The Council of the twelve greater Arti and the Council of One Hundred were the scene of Dante's own political education. His half-dozen recorded interventions were largely concerned with various methods of election, a favourite form of erudition in these bodies.[34]

However technical the arts of commerce and government were, they demanded certain moral qualities, dispositions, or habits, to use the scholastic term sometimes employed by Dante. They could not be had without a desire to co-operate, to sink purely clannish loyalties in the pursuit of the common good; and they needed a certain intellectual curiosity, a willingness to understand events beyond the horizon of the family and the horizon of Florence. Political and commercial success alike would only result from accurate and detailed knowledge of the world. Cosmopolitan interests are especially evident in the chronicle of Giovanni Villani, whose eyes were constantly raised from the immediate matter of his Florentine history to the more distant landscapes of Bohemia, Flanders, and the Orient. It is significant, therefore, that many leading intelligences of Dante's generation were engaged in various ways in propagating these new cultural or moral values, not simply to the inhabitants of Florence but to the Tuscans, to the rest of Italy and beyond. This was the burden of Latini's *Tresor*, which is a handbook of essential general knowledge and civilized behaviour for the Italian, and French, gentleman. It was also implicit in the new, more serious poetry composed by the reformers of the *dolce stil nuovo* school, whose centre was Florence and whose master was Dante's own poetic mentor, Guido Cavalcanti. This poetry was addressed to the same 'knightly' world as its Italian or Provençal precursors; its vehicle, the *volgare illustre*, its forms, the *canzone*, the *ballata*, the *sonetto*, and the *tenzone*, and its traditional theme of love were familiar in every Tuscan household with leisure for poetry and song. It was also a learned poetry, and Cavalcanti's poems, couched partly in the language of philosophy, were largely didactic. His well-known *canzone Donna mi prega* is virtually a treatise on love, seen no more simply as a human emotion, but philosophically.[35] Behind it, at some removes, was the learning of the schools. For Guido and his friends, poetry had become an instrument of moral transformation and intellectual discovery, leading the gentle 'knight' of Tuscany from his absorption in family and warfare to an awareness of his inner feelings and individual destiny.

Among the intellectual friends of Guido, of course, was Dante. His own early poetry was addressed to a coterie of like-minded friends, and as *De Vulgari Eloquentia* shows, he was even more aware than others of his school, of poetry as a learned art capable of sustaining its own critical literature. In his maturity, however, he addressed increasingly a wider public, ending triumphantly with the immediate success of the *Commedia*. The *Vita Nuova* is a poetical autobiography, but its starting-point is a widely acceptable scene of courtly love, and its theme throughout *intelletto d'amore*. As its first, Aristotelian sentence implies, the *Convivio* is a work of instruction: 'tutti li uomini naturalmente desiderano di sapere'. Dante specified its intended readers, the 'principi, baroni, cavalieri, e molt'altra nobile gente, non solamente maschi ma femmine, che sono molti e molte in questa lingua, volgari e non litterati'.[36] It is largely an attempt to refine the familiar courtly concepts of nobility and liberality through the equally familiar medium of love poetry. The often cryptic contemporary allusions in the *Divina Commedia* must have been made for a similar audience, well informed on the personalities not only of Florence but of Tuscany in general, the Romagna, and the northern Italian courts; and at least an interest in princes beyond the Alps is taken for granted. In this Dante was very much a Florentine intellectual: his face was turned firmly outward to the wider world which his compatriots had travelled, chronicled, and exploited.

Dante's attitude to Florence, therefore, was determined by the range of his vision of the contemporary scene. He was not deficient in feeling for his birthplace, 'la bellissima e famosissima figlia di Roma.'[37] But the most sustained passage on Florence in the *Commedia*, the sad speech on her derangement and luxury in *Paradiso* XV and XVI, is spoken by Cacciaguida, and consists of a retrospective muster of ancient Florentine families and a lament for their past glories. Dante regarded Florence from the perspective of his own kindred but, just as the first circle of his affection was narrower than the city, so its ultimate range was much wider. Florence was the middle term between natural ties of kin and pride of ancestry, and citizenship in the Roman Empire. The letter to the Florentines written in 1311 treats *Romana civilitas* as a moral state: the idea of a separate *Florentina civilitas*, so powerful a century later, is contemptuously dismissed.[38] Fundamentally, his cosmopolitan outlook was neither a nostalgic dream of past imperial grandeur, nor the worldly wisdom of the exile; it was shared by the compatriots whose invention and intelligence had made Florence rich from unpromising beginnings, most of all by the enlightened coterie of the *dolce stil nuovo*. It was natural that in 1311 the city state, whatever its future fortune, should hold few attractions for Florence's intellectual leading lights, and that none of them would hail as a patriotic victory the Florentine resistance to Henry VII: and there is no need to expel Dante from their company.

NOTES

1. Leonardo Bruni, *Ad Petrum Paulum Histrum Dialogus*, ed. E. Garin, *Prosatori latini del Quattrocento* (Milan, pp. 88–90).

2. R. Davidsohn, *Geschichte von Florenz* (Berlin, 1896–1927); G. Salvemini, *Magnati e popolani in Firenze dal 1280 al 1295* (Florence, 1899).

3. Nicola Ottokar, *Il commune di Firanze alla fine del Dugento* (Florence, 1926); see E. Sestan, 'Nicola Ottokar', *Rivista storica italiana* lxxi (1959), 178–84. On the 'magnates' see also Berthold Stahl, *Adel und Volk im florentiner Dugento* (Cologne, 1965), and Guido Pampaloni 'I magnati a Firenze alla fine del Dugento', *Archivio storico italiano* lxxix (1971) 387–423.

4. J. Plesner, *L'Émigration de la campagne à la ville libre de Florence au XIIIᵉ siècle* (Copenhagen, 1934): idem, *Una rivoluzione stradale del Dugento* (Acta Jutlandica X, Copenhagen, 1938); on the Florentine *contado* see E. Conti, *La formazione della struttura agraria moderna nel contado fiorentino*, I (Rome, 1965), who however does not consider its relation to Florence. On Latium see E. Toubert, *Les Structures du Latium médiéval* (2 vols., Bibliothèque des Écoles Françaises d'Athènes et de Rome, Rome, 1973), esp. i. 303–68.

5. *Epistolae*, vi. 6; see Nicolai Rubinstein, 'The beginnings of political thought in Florence', *Journal of the Warburg and Courtauld Institutes* v (1942), 198–227.

6. Plesner, *L'Émigration*, pp. 127 ff.

7. D. Herlihy, 'Family solidarity in mediaeval Italian history', in *Economy, Society and Government in mediaeval Italy, Essays in Memory of Robert L. Reynolds*, ed. D. Herlihy, R. S. Lopez, and V. Slessarev (Kent State, 1969), pp. 173–194; J. Heers, *Family Clans in the Middle Ages* (Amsterdam, 1976), pp. 36–7; Toubert, *Latium médiéval*, i, 714–34. On the early Florentine *consorterie* see also F. W. Kent, *Household and Lineage in Renaissance Florence* (Princeton, 1977), pp. 6–13.

8. J. K. Campbell, *Honour, Family and Patronage* (Oxford, 1964), pp. 106–13, 188–203.

9. R. Piattoli, *Codice diplomatico dantesco* (Florence, 1950), pp. 3, 4, 32, 35, 42–7. Ottokar lists the leading families of each *sesto* in *Comune di Firenze*, pp. 68–107.

10. F. Sartini, *Statuti dell' arte dei rigattieri e linaioli di Firenze* (Florence 1940), pp. 3–7; G. Camerani Marri, *Statuti dell' arte di cambio di Firenze* (Fonte sulle corporazioni medioevali iv, Florence, 1955), 4–8.

11. Ottokar, *Comune di Firenze*, pp. 258–9.

12. Ed. Salvemini, *Magnati e popolani*, App. XII, pp. 384–432. The schedules are ed. ibid., App. IX, pp. 376–7. See Ottokar, *Comune di Firenze*, p. 270 n. 3.

13. Ottokar, *Comune di Firenze*, pp. 132–3; see the use of the term *potentes* in G. Rondoni, *I più antichi frammenti del costituto fiorentino* (Florence, 1882), p. 10 (1283).

14. P. J. Jones, 'Florentine families and Florentine diaries in the four-

teenth century', *Papers of the British School at Rome* xxiv (1956), pp. 183–205.

15. For fourteenth-century parallels in Piedmont see J. Heers, *L'Occident aux XIVᵉ et XVᵉ siècles* (Paris, 1970), pp. 385–6 and literature there cited; for a modern example, Campbell, *Honour*, pp. 250–3.

16. Jones, 'Florentine families', p. 201, and 'From manor to mezzadria', in *Florentine Studies*, ed. Nicolai Rubinstein (London, 1968), pp. 193–241, esp. 222–5.

17. Piattoli, *Codice*, pp. 3–4; *Par.* xv. 136–48.

18. Piattoli, *Codice*, pp. 7–12.

19. *Par.* xvi. 44.

20. Piattoli, *Codice*, pp. 5–28, 51–2, 59–62.

21. Piattoli, *Codice*, pp. 32–3.

22. Daniel Waley, 'The army of the Florentine Republic from the twelfth to the fourteenth century', in *Florentine Studies*, pp. 70–108.

23. See *Il libro di Montaperti*, ed. C. Paoli (Florence, 1889).

24. *Purg.* vii. 114: *Par.* viii. 31 ff.

25. *The Poems of the Troubadour Raimbaut de Vaqueiras*, ed. J. Linskill (The Hague, 1964), pp. 109–10; Sordello, *Le poesie* ed. M. Boni (Bologna, 1954); see, on Sordello in contemporary eyes, his two *vide*, pp. 275–6.

26. *Purg.* vi. 74; vii. 91–136.

27. A. Castellani, *Nuovi testi fiorentini del Dugento* (Florence, 1952), ii. 516–55. On the use of Italian in the Dugento, see B. Migliorini, *Storia della lingua italiana* (Florence, 1960), pp. 126 ff.

28. *Purg.* xxvi. 140–7. See G. Folena, *Vulgares eloquentes. Vite e poesie dei trovatori di Dante* (Padua, 1961).

29. *Par.* viii. 116–19. The identity of the questioner rather detracts from the 'municipal spirit' of Dante seen in this passage by A. P. d'Entrèves, *Dante as a Political Thinker* (Oxford, 1952), pp. 11–12.

30. R. L. Lopez, 'Stars and spices: the earliest Italian manual of commercial practice', in *Economy, Society and Government in Mediaeval Italy*, pp. 35–42.

31. F. Melis, *Storia della ragioneria* (Bologna, 1950), pp. 480–94; R. de Roover, 'The development of accounting prior to Luca Pacioli according to the account books of mediaeval merchants', in his *Business, Banking and Economic Thought* (Chicago, 1974), pp. 119–80, esp. 123–8.

32. De Roover, *L'Évolution de la lettre de change* (Paris, 1953), pp. 38–41, and *Business*, p. 123.

33. Ottokar, *Commune di Firenze*, pp. 282–4.

34. Piattoli, *Codice*, pp. 64, 93–6, 98–100.

35. Cavalcanti, *Le rime*, ed. G. Favati (Milan, 1957), pp. 214–16.

36. *Convivio*, I. 9: 'the princes, barons, knights, and other nobility, both men and women, many of whom know the vulgar tongue but not Latin'.

37. *Convivio*, I. 3.

38. *Epistolae*, VI. 2.

2

Dante and the Popes

GEORGE HOLMES

The popes played a large part in Dante's life and works. He was exiled from Florence in 1302 partly on the ground of alleged hostility to the papacy. *Monarchia* was written to exclude the Papacy from temporal possessions. He subjected the contemporary Papacy to a thundering, apocalyptic denunciation in *Inferno* xix, in *Purgatorio* xxxii, and in *Paradiso* xxvii. Two popes are particularly prominent in the *Commedia*, as they were in the Italian politics of Dante's later life. Boniface VIII (1295–1303) was the adversary of the White Guelfs of Florence at the time of Dante's political prominence in the city. He was pope at the fictional date of the *Commedia* and is, therefore, the immediate object of its anti-papal message. He was also the victim of the French attack at Anagni, condemned in *Purgatorio* xx. Clement V (1305–14), the first pope of the Avignon Papacy, resident in France, was the pope who first supported and then rejected Dante's hero the Emperor Henry VII and he is condemned for this in *Inferno* xix and *Paradiso* xvii and xxx.

The subject of this essay is the connection between the popes and Dante's attitude to the papacy. This subject falls into two halves which have to be approached separately. Firstly there is the question of Dante's attitude to the Papacy during the period 1300–1 when he was an active politician, closely involved in political events. Secondly there is the period of Henry VII's expedition to Italy, 1310–13, when Dante was not, so far as we know, an active politician in the same sense, but was certainly, as his political letters show, deeply committed as a propagandist. These two phases present problems of quite different kinds which have to be examined in different ways. In the first case we know something about Dante's political actions but we have no ideological pronouncements from him. The problem is to guess what his attitude to politics was. In the second case the problem is to place his ideological utterances in the right political context.

The Florentine judgment on Dante and his fellow victims, dated 27 January 1302, which led to his exile, condemns them for using corruptly acquired money 'contra summum pontificem et d. Karolum pro resistentia sui adventus' ('against the pope and Charles of Valois to prevent his coming').[1] On 19 June 1301 Dante had been recorded as advising in the Council of One Hundred 'quod de servitio faciendo d. pape nichil fiat' (that no action should be taken about doing service to the lord pope).[2] Do these documents, taken together with the severe criticism of Boniface VIII in the *Commedia*, justify the conclusion that Dante in the words of Bruno Nardi 'ha dovuto certamente porsi il problema dell 'Impero e delle relazioni di esso colla Chiesa, fin dal 1300'?[3]

What happened in 1300, the year of Dante's emergence into political prominence and of the fictional date of the *Commedia*, was that a rift developed within the governing oligarchy of the city of Florence. One of the two parties was openly supported by the pope who intervened on their side. The first explicit indication of papal intervention is a letter from the pope to the Bishop of Florence dated 24 April, in which he complained of the recent condemnation by the commune of three Florentines who were at the Roman court: Simone Gherardi degli Spini, the chief representative of the Spini banking company, Cambio de Sesto, a lawyer, and Noffo Quintarelle, another merchant. The pope demanded the cancellation of the sentences imposed on them on pain of excommunication of the city officials and summoned their accusers to appear before him within fifteen days.[4] We know from another document that the three men had been sentenced in Florence on 18 April.[5] The Pope's letter said that he had already made an unsuccessful attempt to intervene. We do not know what the three Florentines at the papal court had been accused of. But the move against them was probably connected with a Florentine embassy which went to Rome in March of the same year, an impressive deputation of knights from leading Guelf families and a prominent lawyer Lapo Saltarelli who was one of the delators of the criminals.[6] We have no direct evidence of the object of the embassy or what the ambassadors discovered. We have only the report of a chronicler, Dino Campagni, who tells us that the three Florentines had influence with the pope and enlisted papal aid for some unspecified action against the Cerchi family,[7] currently the leaders of the ruling oligarchy. It seems probable that the embassy was a reaction to reports of hostile propaganda by Florentine exiles at Rome, that it was sent in an attempt to win over the pope to the ruling party in Florence, that it was unsuccessful and that, therefore, action was taken against hostile Florentines at the Roman court on its return. When his letter of 24 April had produced no response from Florence, Boniface sent another on 15 May to the bishop. He complained that his action had been misrepresented. It had been put about that his letters were sent with the intention of diminishing the city's powers of jurisdiction and liberty—this was untrue, on the contrary he wished to augment them. In particular Lapo Saltarelli, the lawyer who accompanied the Florentine embassy to Rome, had claimed publicly that the pope should not intervene in the judgments of the commune—he neglected the supreme powers of the pontiff in this case. Who should act as corrector of Tuscany if not the pope? Did not an earlier pope appoint King Charles of Sicily Vicar General of Tuscany during the vacancy of the Empire and was not the Empire now vacant since the pope had not recognized Albert of Austria? If officials of the city and the offenders did not appear to answer a charge of heresy, they would be under pain of excommunication.[8]

The division within the ruling Guelf party had developed over the past two years and by the spring of 1300 had long been a very serious rift. As presented by the Florentine chroniclers that division stemmed from the personal and family enmity between two prominent leaders of the Guelfs, Corso Donati and Vieri de' Cerchi. It was in part a family feud of the familiar type arising from the marriage of Corso with a Cerchi girl and her subsequent death. A more general political feeling against Corso Donati had been intensified after the discovery in 1299 that he had corrupted the *podestà* of Florence Monfiorito da Coderta. The result of the discrediting and banishment of Corso was that the Guelf oligarchy was divided; his enemies, the Cerchi and others, became dominant in Florentine politics and individual allegiances arranged themselves around the two parties which later became the Black and White factions of 1301 and after. Meanwhile Corso in exile had found refuge and employment at the papal Curia. In the second half of 1299 he succeeded Pope Boniface himself as *podestà* of Orvieto. He had connections with the Spini who were the most important curial bankers. It was, therefore, inevitable that Pope Boniface should be subjected to advice and pressure from people who were hostile to the existing regime at Florence, and natural that the members of the regime should expect trouble from an aggrieved exile who had such powerful friends. There was worse to follow. Soon after the papal intervention in April the internal rift in Florence itself was sharpened by the shedding of blood. On 1 May there was a scuffle in the streets of Florence in which a Cerchi had his nose cut off by a Donati follower.[9]

The papal intervention in April was then undoubtedly in part a product of the internal feud. But it has been connected by some historians with ambitious and aggressive plans for the extension of papal authority over Tuscany and, therefore, with papal–imperial relations, partly because of the claim in the letter to the bishop on 15 May, partly because Boniface was, at about the same time, demanding the cession of Tuscany from the newly elected German king, Albert of Habsburg, as the price of papal recognition. The letters which provide the evidence that Boniface put forward this idea were dated 13 May and addressed to the German imperial electors. They announced that the Apostolic See which had once transferred the Empire to the Germans intended to take back the province of Tuscany as part of its imperial inheritance and was sending an envoy to discuss the matter with them.[10] This has some superficial resemblance to the statement of papal powers in Tuscany which was included in the letter to the Bishop of Florence dated only two days later.

The context of papal relations with Germany into which the letter to the imperial electors falls was, however, to a large extent separate. Since the election of Albert of Habsburg Boniface had been consistently hostile and suspicious. He feared alliances directed against him between the powers of Europe. An *entente cordiale* between the alarmingly powerful King of France and the King of Germany was not to his liking, and his hostility was stimulated by a marriage alliance between Albert

of Habsburg and Philip the Fair of France which ripened at the
end of 1299 and was finally concluded in February 1300. He
seems to have reacted with violent animosity when Capetian and
Habsburg missions arrived together at the Curia in the spring of
1300. The date of this meeting is not known precisely. It certainly began before 21 April but probably not much before.
One of the French envoys, Guillaume Nogaret, later said that
Boniface, when receiving the ambassadors, condemned the
election of Albert and threatened that he would not recognize
him unless he ceded Tuscany to the Papacy, 'nisi daret Eccle-
siae Tusciam ex integro, intendebat quippe de Tuscia regnum
disponere'.[11]

The letters of 13 and 15 May put forward two propositions
which are obviously connected but also separate. The claim to
dispose of the vicariate of Tuscany during an imperial vacancy
which Boniface made to Florence was probably offensive but not
novel or indefensible in terms of papal claims earlier in the
century. The demand for the cession of imperial rights in
Tuscany made to the German electors was a different matter
and a more unusual claim.[12] It is impossible to know just how
these two ideas were related in Boniface's mind, but they
probably were related; he was prone to angry, exaggerated
reactions and it is quite possible that the frustration of his intervention in Florence helped to shape his reaction to the Germans.
But it is easier to see what the Florentine reaction was. Boniface's
rather wild throw in the European diplomatic game had little or
no bearing on the immediate political situation in Tuscany.
The actions of the Florentine government suggest that if they
knew of it, and they must surely have heard rumours, they did
not take it seriously. The Florentine leaders, including now
Dante, did not behave in succeeding weeks as though they were
locked in a life-and-death struggle with the spiritual power, as
Robert Davidsohn and other historians have tended to portray
them. They behaved as though they were facing a tiresome
intervention in their private affairs by a power with which they
expected in general to be on good terms. The most important
factor in events of this period as far as they affected Dante and
Florence is the assumption of a natural identity of interests
between Florence and the Papacy.

To understand Boniface's intervention we must look again

at the papal position in Italy and Europe. There has been some tendency to regard the spring of 1300, the year of the Jubilee, as a moment of great splendour in the history of the Papacy. From a strictly political point of view it was actually a moment of great difficulty. The political objective which absorbed Boniface's attention throughout his pontificate more than any other was the reconquest of Sicily for the benefit of his ally Charles II of Naples, the reconstruction of a unified, friendly kingdom of Naples. It was for this purpose that the financial resources of the papacy had been chiefly used. It was a bitter disappointment for Boniface when the ally on whom he chiefly depended, James II of Aragon, was defeated by the Sicilians at Falconaria in December 1299. At the beginning of 1300 Boniface was on all sides destitute of effective support among the major European powers: the French and the German kings had made peace, the Angevin had been beaten, the Aragonese had left him. Georges Digard, the editor of Boniface's register, said perceptively of the withdrawal of James: 'ce brusque départ laissa Boniface VIII à la merci de Florence'.[13]

The Papacy had a dual interest in the Guelf oligarchy of Florence, firstly as bankers and secondly as rulers of a state with strategic importance in central Italy. The trio on whose behalf the pope took action included a prominent member of the Spini family who must himself have been at that time effectively the most important banker at the Curia. The Spini had by 1300 acquired a clear predominance in the more speculative business of advancing money to the pope for his major political enterprises. The essence of papal finance was the imposition of taxes on the European clergy as a whole with which to pay for armies to carry out papal policy in Italy. To make this system effective the pope needed bankers who would advance large sums of cash which would eventually be repaid to them from taxes as the proceeds came in. The Spini had recently paid out large sums in anticipation of revenues. An account drawn up between the pope and the Spini on 6 May 1300 showed him as owing them 57,900 florins. No doubt Boniface hoped that they would soon be advancing large sums to his new champion Charles of Valois in advance of subsidies from the clergy of France. The virtual monopoly of large-scale lending to the pope, which the Spini had in the spring of 1300, was fairly unusual, and Boniface was, therefore, in a sense particularly dependent on them. They were dependent on him too but they would have been important enough for him to do favours and this relationship in itself goes a long way towards explaining the intervention of 24 April and after.[14] Boniface also required the support of Florence in the volatile world of central Italian politics. Between northern Romagna and the borders of the Patrimony Florence was the most powerful state and the natural leader of other Guelf powers. A hostile Florence would be very dangerous. This was a cornerstone of normal papal policy. In the summer of 1300 two events occurred which demonstrated the dangers of central-Italian politics and no doubt increased the pope's concern. On 19 July the Count of Santa Fiora inflicted a severe defeat on the Sienese allies of the Papacy at Radicofani and a few weeks earlier a Ghibelline force had unexpectedly seized control of Gubbio.[15] It is easy to imagine how a man of Boniface's choleric disposition could be persuaded by his good Florentine friends at the Curia that the Guelf allegiance of Florence was threatened by the existing regime led by their enemies. This is a plausible explanation of Boniface's actions. This advice, if it was so given, was however bad advice. The evidence suggests that the White Guelfs in Florence were driven slowly and reluctantly into a position of alienation which they had no wish to adopt.

The reaction of the rulers of Florence after the papal intervention of 24 April was to continue on the same path as before. The condemnation of the three Florentines was not revoked in response to papal threats. It was handed on—a poisoned chalice —to the new priors, of whom Dante was one, who took office on 15 June. After the riot of 1 May a *balia* was given to the priors to deal with the disorder, and on 10 May Corso Donati was sentenced to death—he was, of course, in exile anyway—possibly because of the discovery of a conspiracy of his supporters to take the city by force. In an attempt to reduce the political temperature by an even-handed rebuke to enthusiasts on both sides the priors exiled a list of prominant Donati and Cerchi supporters including Dante's friend Guido Cavalcanti. The city showed no sign of abandoning the position in international affairs which linked it with the Papacy. When Dante reappears in the records of Florentine politics for the first time for four years it is as an agent of this policy. On 7 May he was at San Gimignano where he appeared in the council of the commune as an envoy of Florence to present the case for a contribution to the *Tallia*.[16] A papal envoy was sent, probably with the same message, later in the month and San Gimignano eventually decided to take part in the *Tallia*. There is no sign that this stance in international affairs was abandoned at any point in the summer. On 6 September the council of San Gimignano heard a representative of Charles of Naples, asking for money, who came with a letter of recommendation from the commune of Florence.[17] One of the pope's later complaints about Florence was that the *Tallia* had not yet been organized. The other evidence suggests that this was a misrepresentation: the Florentines had been actively promoting it, and it was held up by the usual reluctance of the smaller communes to contribute. Boniface was either blind to or misinformed about the real aims of the Florentine government.

The pope persisted in his intervention in Florence. On 23 May he appointed Cardinal Mathew of Acquasparta legate in Tuscany and northern Italy with general powers. Acquasparta arrived in Florence early in June, hoping to heal the division in the city, and this was the main problem which faced Dante and his fellow priors when they took office on 15 June. There is some, not very secure, evidence that two days earlier the commune made an ordinance which limited the ability of the ecclesiastical power to proceed against the three accusers of the Florentine curialists as heretics. But apart from this the regime was not entirely unfriendly to the cardinal in his role as peacemaker within the city. Visits by papal legates to act as peacemakers between communal factions, though infrequent, were traditional and did not offend very strongly against the sense of civic independence. On 27 June the cardinal was granted a petition for authority to act with the assistance of the secular arm in making peace between quarrelling citizens. The provision granting these powers passed the Council of One Hundred easily by 81 votes to 12.[18] He was nevertheless totally unsuccessful in his work of pacification and an attempt was made by an unnamed individual to assassinate him. According to Dino Compagni the would-be assassin was 'di non molto senno', presumably not an agent of anyone important, but it was probably the news of this act which led the pope to issue on 22 July his most angry attack on the city of Florence up to this date, an attack which was particularly directed against the priors, of whom Dante was one. The pope attributed the cardinal's failure to the 'imissionibus factis per angelos malos, et presidentium, rectorum, priorum et aliquorum officialium civitatis'. The city was governed by 'animis induratis et ostinatis in malo'. The pope gave his legate power to proceed against the persons and the goods of the officials as well as against the city.[19] This fulmination probably represented for Dante his first—and in a sense his last—direct collision with a hostile papal authority. Nothing was achieved by the cardinal. A fortnight after the end of Dante's priorate he finally abandoned his task, excommunicated the rulers of the city, and left.

The turbulent summer of 1300 was followed by a year of greater calm. During the months before the autumn of 1300 and the autumn of 1301 there was no direct confrontation between Florence and Boniface. There was, however, increasing tension and expectation of papal aggression as Boniface supported his Guelf friends in Lucca and promoted the expedition of Charles of Valois to Italy. It was in these circumstances that Dante advised on 19 June 1301 that the commune should not give military aid to the pope. The sentence, 'Dante Alagherii consuluit quod de servitio faciendo d. pape nichil fiat', sounds dramatic, but in the political context its implications were limited. On 17 April the Council of One Hundred had agreed to pay for a contingent of 100 knights to help the pope in the Marittima.[20] The vote on 19 June was about whether that assistance to the pope should be continued after the two-and-a-half months for which it had originally been granted.[21] Dante's statement would have appeared less striking if it had taken the form of the recommendation by the next speaker but one, 'consuluit quod de servitio faciendo d. pape suspendatur ad presens', and may have meant no more than that. It meant that that particular contingent should be withdrawn from papal service, not that the papal alliance should be abandoned, still less that a general anti-papal stance should be adopted. But, in the grip of his Florentine friends and their advice, Boniface continued his policy of intervention. By early September Charles of Valois was at the papal court and nominated *paciere* for Tuscany. Boniface explained his mission in a speech in consistory as being to establish peace between the Blacks and

Whites, not to take over the vicariate of Tuscany: 'quia de vicariatu nolo, quod se intromittat, licet dicant falsi Florentini quod ego volo occupare iura Tuscie et eorum'.[22] In view of the pope's aggressive behaviour it was hardly surprising that Florentines should have entertained such a suspicion. But the Florentine White regime still hoped to stave off intervention by peaceful negotiation. There was certainly a last-minute embassy to the pope in October and there was a tradition, for which there is no reliable evidence, that Dante was a member of of it. The embassy failed to prevent the occupation of the city by Charles of Valois in November and the consequent overthrow of the White regime.

The fictional date of the *Commedia* is Good Friday to Easter week 1300. At one point in the early part of *Inferno* Dante made a specific reference to the political situation at Easter 1300 as it concerned himself. In *Inferno* vi he meets and converses with Ciacco, an unimportant Florentine citizen famous for his gluttony. Ciacco begins his speech with a comment, starting

> 'La tua città, ch'è piena
> d'invidia sì che già trabocca il sacco . . .'[23]

Dante then asks him about the future of the 'città partita', the 'divided city'.

> E quelli a me: 'Dopo lunga tencione
> verranno al sangue, e la parte selvaggia
> caccerà l'altra con molta offensione.
> Poi appresso convien che questa caggia
> infra tre soli, e che l'altra sormonti
> con la forza di tal che testé piaggia . . .'[24]

The references in this passage to the Cerchi–Donati riot on 1 May 1300 which intensified party divisions in Florence, the consequent expulsion of Black leaders in the summer of 1300, and the later expulsion of Whites including Dante in 1302, are clear. 'Tal che testé piaggia', 'he who now keeps tacking', and whose force will aid the expulsion of 1302, is probably Charles of Valois. Boniface had been trying since 1298 to entice him to Italy without success. In any case the responsibility for the troubles in 1300 is placed by Ciacco squarely on the Florentines themselves. This is indeed the general tenor of the political commentaries in the early parts of *Inferno*, which taken together make up a retrospective view of Dante's political fortunes in Florence. *Inferno* vi refers to the beginning of the Black–White split. In *Inferno* x Dante meets the shade of a great Florentine exile of an earlier generation, Farinata degli Uberti, who foretells Dante's future exile, again arising from the hatred of other citizens. In *Inferno* xv Dante meets his old mentor, the humanist Brunetto Latini, who again foretells that he will be a victim of Florentine feuds, appropriately adducing the current legend that the population of the city was divided between the good strain descended from the Romans and the bad strain descended from the native Fiesolans.

We have, of course, no direct evidence about Dante's general attitudes to either the Papacy or the Empire at this period. The purpose of the argument so far has been to suggest the probability of two conclusions. Firstly, that in his political life in 1300–1 Dante acted within the conventional framework of Florentine politics, beginning as a supporter of the papal alliance, driven later by papal aggression into a position of fear of and hostility to papal intervention in Tuscany for ordinary political, not ideological, reasons. Though it cannot be disproved, the actions of the White leaders in 1300–1 make it very unlikely that they were motivated by anti-papal or pro-imperial ideas, or that such ideas played a serious part in their thinking. The imperial question arises only in the wilder pronouncements of the pope. Secondly, that Dante probably regarded the crowning misfortune of his exile primarily and justifiably as a consequence of the factionalism of internal city politics. My argument is that the political context of the period 1300–2 and the evidence of *Inferno* make it inherently improbable that Dante was at that time much concerned with the issue of relations between Empire and Papacy. The idea that the ideology, if not the composition, of *Monarchia* might go back to Dante's confrontation with Boniface VIII is a red herring which seriously distorts the true evolution and character of Dante's ideas.

The central problem in an attempt to explain Dante's later attitude to the Papacy is the position of *Monarchia* in the evolution of his ideas, and especially *Monarchia* III, which strips the Papacy of every shred of power and jurisdiction to make it the leader of a purely mendicant, apostolic Church. When was it written? The famous clause 'sicut in Paradiso Comedie iam dixi'[25] cannot be so easily dismissed as it commonly was as an interpolation now that it has been reinstated in P. G. Ricci's edition, and must be taken into account as possible evidence for a very late date. But apart from that the text contains no chronological hints. Much effort has been expended in the attempt to relate Dante's book to other polemical writings produced by the controversies of his age. The period of his political life saw a large output of polemical literature about the powers of the Papacy inspired by the two great European crises on the margins of which Dante himself participated: firstly the quarrel of Boniface VIII and Philip the Fair, which called forth the treatises of Giles of Rome and others on the papal side, and John of Paris and others on the king's; secondly the Italian expedition of Henry VII, which produced a number of official ideological statements on behalf of the pope, the emperor, and King Robert of Naples. But the many attempts to relate Dante's book directly to other writings of this period have shown the enterprise to be entirely futile.[26] It does not appear to be inspired by or to be the inspiration of any other book or document that we know, or to stand in any tradition. It stands obstinately apart. There are only two ways of approaching its origin, both highly speculative: to relate it to other works of Dante himself or to show its appropriateness to a political situation.

The main political conclusions of *Monarchia*—the necessity for a universal Roman Empire and a Church without money or jurisdiction—are entirely in agreement with the views expressed in the *Commedia*. The Dominican defender of the papacy, Guido Vernani, who wrote a rebuttal of *Monarchia* about 1330, was entirely justified in saying that Dante undermined orthodox views not only by that book but also by the 'poetic figments and fantasies' and the 'sweet siren songs' of the *Commedia*.[27] Both *Monarchia* and the *Commedia* seem to state a final position on this matter, so that comparison in that respect does not help. The argument that *Monarchia* antedates a substantial part of the *Commedia*, put forward among others by Bruno Nardi, depends on demonstrating that some of the philosophical supports of that position in *Monarchia* are incompatible with the *Commedia*. The

most convincing evidence in favour of this view is provided by
the last chapter of *Monarchia* III, where Dante rounds off his
demolition of papal pretensions by saying that man's double
nature, possessing a corruptible body and an incorruptible soul
means that there are two beatitudes for him to follow: the
terrestrial beatitude, whose figure is the earthly paradise, and
the beatitude of eternal life. These are the domains of the
emperor, who is to rule in accordance with 'phylosophica-
documenta', and the pope who is to lead men in accordance
with revelation. Nardi argues that this view of human nature
and of the relative spheres of philosophy and theology, which
accords with the philosophical sections of *Convivio*, is incompatible with the decisive subordination of philosophy to theology which is the main theme of *Paradiso*. He, therefore, thinks
that the philosophy of *Monarchia* belongs with *Convivio* in an
earlier period of philosophical speculation which Dante cor-
rected extensively in the *Commedia*.[28]

There is no doubt that the *Commedia* corrects the philosophy of
Convivio in places. It is clearly true that the *Commedia*, particularly *Paradiso*, contains an exaltation of theological truths
which would come as a surprise if one knew only *Convivio* and
Monarchia. Moreover there is a striking absence in *Paradiso* of
any philosophical demonstration of the necessity of world
government such as is contained in *Convivio* and *Monarchia*, The
essential role of the Roman Empire seems indeed to be assumed
in *Paradiso* and it is set out historically by Justinian in *Paradiso* vi,
but it is not philosophically defended. The closest approach in
the *Commedia* to a theoretical defence of the temporal–
spiritual division of authority occurs in the speech of Marco
Lombardo in *Purgatorio* xvi. The mention in the same speech of
Gherardo da Camino and Guido da Castello as embodiments of
political virtue recalls the reference to the same men as examples of nobility in *Convivio*, IV. 16. There is therefore a
natural temptation to deduce that by the time *Paradiso* was
written Dante found the philosophical views on which the
political theory of *Monarchia* was based, distasteful, or had in
part rejected them. If, however, this argument is carried
further, as it is by Nardi, to support the view that *Monarchia*,
therefore, belongs to the period immediately following *Convivio*
and before Dante was caught up in the enthusiasm for Henry

VII—say 1308–9—it creates political difficulties as serious as the philosophical ones which it has solved.

Monarchia was written to defend the proposition that the emperor had the right to absolute power over the world in temporal affairs, a right ordained by God and subject to no limitation by the pope. Dante marshalled his argument in three books which are quite distinct and deal with subject matter of three quite different kinds. The first is a philosophical demonstration that there must be a single all-powerful ruler to promote the terrestrial fulfilment of man's potentiality. The second book demonstrates that this divinely ordained world power is the Roman Empire, by showing how the authority of Rome has developed providentially from the time of Aeneas onwards. The third book shows that the Papacy and the Church have no temporal authority whatsoever over the Empire, and does this by attacking a selection of arguments which had been used in defence of papal temporal power chiefly in decretals or in commentaries on decretals. There are three arguments drawn from the Old Testament, starting with the 'sun and moon' text in Genesis, three New Testament texts, one of which, for instance, is the grant to Peter of power to bind and loose, and three non-biblical arguments: the Donation of Constantine, the Translation of the Empire, and a philosophical argument that the pope must be the measure of all men. Dante then replaces these with his own positive arguments which are philosophical in form, though his essential standpoint is wholly defined by New Testament texts which establish the Church as a powerless, propertyless spiritual body.

Monarchia III is written in a much more polemical manner than the other two. It begins by invoking Daniel safe in the lion's den because God will ensure that his 'justitia' shall prevail against the lions. Whereas in the previous two books, Dante tells us, he had to establish truth against ignorance, he is now dealing with a subject which is disfigured by conflict rather than lack of knowledge, and he names his adversaries. They are firstly the pope and the clergy, secondly those people—unfortunately not named—who are hostile to the Roman monarch and deny the rational principles underlying this work, promoting their own interests under the guise of devotion to the Church, thirdly the expounders of the decretals.[29] There were, of course, people who corresponded to these categories throughout Dante's lifetime but there are some periods at which he is much more likely to have felt the need to do battle with them than at others. I have argued that it is difficult to believe that active Guelf opposition to the Empire, embodied in the second category of opponents, was very strongly present to Dante's mind in the Florentine period up to 1302. For slightly different reasons it is difficult to believe this of the period 1303 to 1309.

In the course of the years from 1300 to 1321 the Papacy suffered enormous changes in which its significance for Italian politicians and, to a lesser extent, the ideologies expressed in papal pronouncements changed more than once. In between the years from 1300 to 1303 and the years after 1311, in both of which periods it is possible to imagine that Dante was excited by political events to an active detestation of the Papacy, there was a long period in which he might well have regarded it as being in political terms a benevolent power. The death of Boniface VIII in 1303 after the contest with France and the outrage of Anagni was followed by the election of Benedict XI, who did his best in a pontificate of less than a year to reverse the policies of his predecessor and, in particular, to induce the Black Guelfs at Florence to allow the return of the exiled Whites. For at least part of this time Dante was actively involved with the exiles on the border of Florentine territory, and he is thought to have been the author of a letter sent by the Guelf party to the pope's legate and peacemaker, Cardinal Nicholas of Prato, promising him help in his efforts.[30] Unlike his predecessor and successor Benedict XI does not figure in *Inferno*. His death was followed by the long conclave at Perugia which ended in 1305 with the election of Clement V. Though Clement was a French pope who never came to Italy himself, there were powerful Italian figures at his court who had been responsible for his election, and who in the early years of his pontificate were able to ensure that his policy in central Italy was a continuation of the work of Benedict XI, not of that of Boniface VIII. One of these was Nicholas of Prato. Still more important was Cardinal Napoleone Orsini. Napoleone Orsini was one of the two cardinals to whom Dante particularly addressed a much later letter, probably written during the next conclave in 1314, urging them to work for the return of the Papacy to Rome.

Orsini was legate in Italy from 1306 to 1309. During that period he was the most active proponent of the policy of backing the Whites and Ghibellines in Tuscany and Romagna against the Blacks in Florence to secure a pacification for the sake of the papal state and its borders. Throughout the period 1304-9, while the Blacks in Florence proclaimed themselves to be the true Guelf allies of the pope, the papacy in fact pursued very actively a hostile policy of supporting Whites and Ghibellines, not merely with words, but with armies and money.

It is generally agreed that *Convivio* was composed during this period of rather unspectacular and confused Italian politics when the papal legate was trying in vain to rally the Ghibellines against the Guelfs. *Convivio* IV is an important stage in the evolution of Dante's political thinking because it marks a very distinct shift in his interest towards the problem of the world monarchy of the Roman Empire. Distinct at any rate in the sense that no earlier writings prepare us for it and that it appears with the force of a new enthusiasm. *Convivio* IV is a commentary on the *canzone* 'Le dolci rime d'amor' which had probably been composed a decade earlier. The *canzone* is a philosophical observation on the theme of the relationship between nobility and virtue, introduced by a remark of ultimately Aristotelian origin, attributed to an emperor in the poem, to the effect that nobility is conferred by inherited wealth and good manners, which Dante then demolished. In the *canzone* the reference to the emperor is casual and disparaging; in the commentary in *Convivio* IV it serves as the excuse for a gratuitously long disquisition on the Roman Empire in general, from which it is clear that some time in the interval between the two the Empire had become a subject of passionate interest.[31] *Convivio* IV contains much of the subject matter of *Monarchia* I and II in embryo: the arguments from philosophy for world empire and from history for the providential mission of Rome. But it contains no reference to the subject matter of *Monarchia* III, the relation between temporal and spiritual power. Why? It is, of course, possible that Dante already had those arguments concealed in his breast, but it is more likely that he had not yet needed to formulate them. He had arrived at his imperialism through association with Ghibellines and reading Virgil. He could not have arrived at it through participation in a conflict

of imperialists and papalists because there had been no such
conflict for him to take part in.

The relationship of papal policy to central Italy had not
changed radically when the new, ambitious King of the
Romans, Henry VII, began his descent into Italy to assert his
imperial power at the end of 1310, and the first stages of the
relationship between Henry and Clement would not have been
likely to stimulate Dante to anti-papal pronouncements. Considering on the one hand the ideological legacy of Boniface VIII
and on the other the present inexorable pressure of the King of
France, Pope Clement V greeted the election of Henry VII
with surprising moderation. The theory expressed in Clement's
letter of recognition on 26 July 1309 was in striking contrast to
Boniface's pronouncements. It used the image of the sun and
moon, but avoided drawing directly the implication of superiority of one over the other.[32] Henry in return promised to
accept papal jurisdiction and power in the papal state and the
grants made by emperors to popes from Constantine to Rudolf
in the thirteenth century.[33] Just before Henry crossed the Alps
the pope wrote to the states of Lombardy and Tuscany ordering
them to accept the authority of the new king for the sake of
peace.[34] The Papacy was still refusing to support Guelfs against
Ghibellines. These were the circumstances in which Dante,
probably in the autumn of 1310, composed his Letter to the
Princes and Peoples of Italy, which suddenly signifies for us his
return to the political scene after the years of obscurity but, of
course, to a totally different scene from the one he had left in
1302. Letter V contains a marvellous evocation of a new political dawn, it goes on to a powerful exhortation to the Italians
to accept the new authority, and it ends with a reference to the
pope's support for the emperor which seems to echo the sentiments and the precise imagery of the papal letter of July 1309.
'Hic est quem Petrus, Dei vicarius, honorificare nos monet;
quem Clemens nunc Petri successor luce Apostolicae bene-
dictionis illuminat; ut ubi radius spiritualis non sufficit, ibi
splendor minoris luminaris illustret.'[35] As Paget Toynbee
remarked, 'Dante here accepts the symbolism against which he
argues in the *De Monarchia* (iii. 4) and which he rejects in the
Commedia (cf. *Purg.* xvi. 107–8) . . .'[36] That is still true and it is a
decisive obstacle to any attempt to date *Monarchia* III earlier

than the autumn of 1310. The probability is that in 1310 Dante, though a Ghibelline, would not yet have found it necessary to define the limits of papal power in relation to the Empire.

The alliance of emperor and pope was a remarkable temporary phenomenon due to the influence of Ghibelline cardinals at the Curia and to the hope of creating a counter-balance to the oppressive weight of France. It could not last if the emperor were successful, and within two years of the date of Letter V it had completely broken down, the immediate cause being that the pope was forced to choose between supporting Henry VII and Henry's most powerful rival in Italy, King Robert of Naples who was supported by France. As a result, in the last year of Henry VII's life Empire and Papacy were ranged against each other supporting their incompatible claims with statements more reminiscent of the theories debated in *Monarchia*. On the day of his coronation at Rome, 29 June 1312, Henry issued an encyclical letter in which he said that the position of the emperor on earth was like that of God at the summit of the celestial hierarchy, and that God had established his principate at Rome in preparation for the incarnation.[37] Imperialist spokesmen denied the competence of the pope to interfere in the emperor's treatment of the King of Naples, whom he condemned as a rebel, one of them writing, for example:

spiritual powers are greater and more worthy as far as future beatitude is concerned and in relation to the kingdom of God, and in this sense the priestly power is greater. But between living men and so far as concerns human and mutable affairs and temporal powers, nothing is greater than the empire. And moreover the temporal power is entirely alien from the spiritual power, for the great shepherd Jesus Christ said my kingdom is not of this world . . .[38]

Spokesmen for the King of Naples on the other hand revived the argument that the Roman Empire was founded on force, not justice, and argued that the pope could and should cancel the election of an unsuitable emperor.

The nature of Dante's involvement in the politics of this period is largely obscure. What we know for certain comes entirely from the Letters and can be very quickly summarized. He was in the upper Arno valley on 31 March 1311 when he wrote a fierce letter to the Florentine enemies of Henry VII.

Next month he wrote from the same place to the emperor
advising him to advance swiftly against Tuscany, and possibly
implying that he had been present at Henry's coronation at
Milan in January. Then there is silence until the early summer
of 1314, when he wrote to the Italian cardinals in the conclave
following Clement V's death urging them to bring about the
return of the papacy to Italy.[39] From these letters we can deduce
only that Dante was in some undefined way a keen supporter of
Henry and that, at least by 1314, he had a detestation of the
Avignon papacy. The two sentiments are complementary. In
the *Commedia* there is a distinction between the denunciation of
the depravity of the contemporary Papacy in general and the
new depth of depravity reached by Clement. This distinction is
still more clearly indicated in Letter VIII. In this letter Dante
appeals to two Italian cardinals who had survived from the
College of Boniface VIII. The implication of the appeal is that
what had happened since then is much worse. Cardinal Napoleone Orsini, who had been an opponent of Boniface and
responsible for the election of a French pope, is asked to bring
about the return of the papacy to Rome 'ne degradati collegae
perpetuo remanerent inglorii'.[40] Cardinal Jacopo Stefaneschi,
who had been a supporter of Boniface VIII, is to act 'ut ira
defuncti Antistitis in te velut ramus insitionis in trunco non suo
frondesceret'.[41] The 'defunctus Antistes' is Boniface VIII.
Dante is encouraging a revival of the Bonifacian policy towards
France. Bad as Boniface was, he was nearer to the right path
than Clement. By 1314 it was possible for Dante to regard the
pontificate of Boniface with something approaching nostalgia.

Modern historians, observing the Avignon Papacy and aware
that it cannot be shown in any objective way to be more or less
corrupt than its predecessor at Rome, are in danger of under-
estimating the emotional impact upon contemporaries of its
inevitable alliance with the French monarchy. By 1312 considerable progress had already been made in transforming the
College of Cardinals and the Curia into French bodies. In the
conclave of 1305 nearly all the cardinals were Italian. In the
conclave of 1314 a majority were French or Gascon. In international diplomacy the Papacy was tied to French policy. This
had a considerable effect on political thinkers throughout the
period of the Avignon Papacy, because the popes, instead of

being the assertors of a general political supremacy like Boniface appeared to have put their Petrine authority at the service of a particular lay power. The most celebrated political thinkers of the period following Dante's death, Marsilius of Padua and William of Ockham, like Wycliffe later, wrote with the aim of stripping the Papacy of political authority in reaction against the specific circumstances of the Avignon Papacy. The Avignon Papacy inaugurated a new anti-clericalism in Italy and a new phase in the history of political thought. It is to this phase, not to the *Différend* of Boniface VIII and Philip IV, that *Monarchia*, like Marsilius of Padua's *Defensor Pacis*, belongs. The poet of *Paradiso* differed from that prophet of modern secularism in many ways, but they had a common anti-papal alignment in politics which led them both to formulate extreme anti-papal theories. Both were supporters of the imperialist anti-French party in Italy between 1312 and 1321. One of the two Italian cardinals to whom Dante hopefully addressed his political letter in 1314, Stefaneschi, recommended Marsilius for a benefice in 1316.[42] The difference between them was that Dante's anti-papalism took the form of apocalyptic religious radicalism. That religious radicalism is the hallmark of Dante's later political thought. The process by which he was converted to it is perhaps the most mysterious part of his spiritual biography, but there cannot be much doubt that it was connected with his reaction to the change of papal policy by Clement V.

Dante's son Pietro and other fourteenth-century commentators on the *Commedia* tell us that the last stage of the apocalyptic drama of the Church in *Purgatorio* xxxii represents the history of the Papacy in the time of Boniface VIII and after. After the chariot, which is the Church, has put out the seven heads, which are the seven deadly sins, there appears seated upon it a whore. This imagery is adopted from the Book of Revelation and is similar to the imagery used in *Inferno* xix: the picture of the whore seated upon the waters symbolizing the simoniacal Papacy. In *Purgatorio* xxxii Dante went further in following the practice of those religious radicals of his day who adapted biblical imagery to precise contemporary references. Beside her appears a giant, representing the French king who exchanges kisses with her, and then, because her eyes appear to be flirting with Dante, beats her. Finally, incited by the whore to overpowering anger, the giant detached the whole chariot—presumably from the griffon who had been drawing it—and dragged it off into the wood out of sight. The political interpretation receives support from the imagery of part of the Letter to the Cardinals, where the Church is 'crucifixi currum sponsae'— 'the chariot of the bride of Christ'—and 'sponsae reticulum', and the cardinals at Avignon are rebuked for taking the chariot out of its course like Ovid's Phaethon who drove the chariot of the sun too near to earth.

Dante's horrified rejection of the actions of the French monarchy is, of course, most fully expressed in *Purgatorio* xx. The general denunciation of the House of Capet, put into the mouth of its founder, Hugh Capet, culminates in the seizure of Pope Boniface at Anagni by the agents of Philip IV and his death shortly after. The ordeal of the pope is compared to the ordeal of Christ. Christ is made captive in the person of his vicar, is mocked and killed a second time, and the new Pilate then invades the temple, presumably a reference to seizure of the property of the order of the Temple which Philip IV compelled Clement V to allow. There might seem to be an awkward dichotomy in Dante's treatment of Boniface VIII. The man who is contemptuously dismissed as 'quel d'Anagni'—'he of Anagni'— in *Paradiso* xxx, where it is foretold, as in *Inferno* xix, that he will be pushed further down in the circle of the simoniacs, re-enacts Calvary in *Purgatorio* xx. But the treatment is really perfectly consistent and perfectly harmonious with the view of the papacy in *Monarchia* III. Dante had no quarrel with the claim of the pope to inherit the powers of Peter. He was no conciliarist. He fully accepted the power of binding and loosing and papal monarchy within its proper sphere. Boniface's grand gesture in proclaiming the Jubilee indulgence of 1300, which was in force at the fictional date of the *Commedia*, was clearly accepted. In *Purgatorio* ii Casella tells Dante that since the beginning of 1300 Charon has ferried across to Purgatory the souls of all who wish to come. Boniface is guilty of avarice and simony, but he is not because of that less than a full pope with all the powers of Peter. There is also no inconsistency in Dante's final statement at the end of *Monarchia* III which has puzzled some commentators. After demonstrating that the emperor is totally free of subordination to the pope in temporal matters he adds that this is not to be taken as meaning that the monarch is not subject to the pope in anything, because mortal felicity is 'in a certain way'—'quodammodo'—directed to immortal felicity, and monarch should look to pope as son to father for the light of paternal grace. This does not mean that Dante has had second thoughts about the separation of spiritual and temporal powers. It means that, as he has said earlier, 'regnum temporale non recipit esse a spirituali . . . sed bene ab eo recipit ut virtuosius operetur per lucem gratie quam in celo et in terra benedictio summi Pontificis infundit illi'.[43]

There is, of course, no doubt of Dante's general denunciation of Boniface VIII in the *Commedia*. He is expected to join the simoniacs in *Inferno* xix. He is condemned for misleading Guido da Montefeltro by promising absolution in order to secure the destruction of the Colonna cardinals' stronghold at Palestrina in *Inferno* xxvii. It is he who has usurped St. Peter's see and made his burial place a 'cloaca del sangue e de la puzza'[44] in *Paradiso* xxvii. But there is a difference between his depravity and that of Clement. Clement had committed a grave political offence against Henry VII which was not paralleled among Boniface's misdeeds. Therefore, in *Inferno* xix Clement is, 'di più laida opra, /di ver' ponente, un pastor senza legge'.[45] Therefore, in *Paradiso* xvii he is the 'Guasco' who 'l'alto Arrigo inganna'.[46] Finally in *Paradiso* xxx he is the

> prefetto nel foro divino
> allora tal, che palese e coverto
> non anderà con lui per un cammino.[47]

And, Dante adds, 'Ma poco poi sarà da Dio sofferto/nel santo officio'.[48] The fact that the deception of Clement is mentioned in Cacciaguida's prophetic account of Dante's life suggests that it was a significant turning-point in that life. For all these reasons it is an almost irresistible conclusion that *Monarchia* III was composed after the break between Clement and Henry VII became apparent. It is difficult to fix a precise date for that, but it would presumably have been quite clear to those who were at all closely associated with Henry's court, then at Pisa, by April 1312, when Clement wrote urging Henry to make an alliance with Robert of Naples[49] instead of writing to Robert ordering him to clear his troops out of Rome in preparation for

Henry's coronation. But the hostile ideological exchanges between the courts of emperor, pope, and King of Naples did not begin until after Henry's coronation. The ideal political circumstances for *Monarchia* III were offered by the situation in the autumn of 1312 and after.

Dante's conversion to anti-papalism was not just a recognition of the prevalence of simony at the Roman court or of the excessive development of papal political interference. It was a conversion to a fanatical belief that the contemporary Papacy had been degraded, and that the providential plan of history required a saviour to rescue it and the world: the 'veltro' of *Inferno* i, the 'cinquecento diece e cinque' of *Purgatorio* xxxiii, the successor to Scipio foreseen in *Paradiso* xxvii. This apocalyptic belief is most dramatically presented in *Purgatorio* xxxii. If we accept the theory of dating put forward by Petrocchi,[50] the composition of *Purgatorio* would probably have ended in the period *c.* 1312–14, when Dante turned against the Papacy. The preview of the apocalyptic vision in *Inferno* xix, which implies a knowledge of the death of Clement V in 1314, is probably a later addition to that canticle, which had been mainly composed earlier in 1304–8. The end of *Purgatorio*, the pageant of the destruction of the Church, records the impact on Dante of his intense disillusionment and his turn to a radical ecclesiology. Thereafter he saw the Papacy, not within a framework of conventional politics, as he probably saw it in 1301, but within a framework of apocalyptic prophecy. He also came to see himself as a prophet. By the time he wrote *Paradiso* xvii he had reinterpreted his own life as a part of the great papal–imperial theme of world history. Easter 1300, the beginning of his real political tragedy and the date of his fictional descent into Hell, had changed its significance in his mind. He now believed his own exile, attributed more rationally to Florentine politics in *Inferno*, to have been plotted at Rome by Easter 1300:

> Questo si vuole e questo già si cerca,
> e tosto verrà fatto a chi ciò pensa
> là dove Cristo tutto dì si merca.[51]

The evolution of Dante's political ideas can never be described with certainty. But, if the ideas are related to his political environment, some strong probabilities can be established. Dante's mature political theory is imperialist. The key to the development of that theory, however, is not his attitude to the empire but his attitude to the popes. His final view of politics, though set out in *Monarchia* in the language of rational syllogisms, is the political theory of a fanatic. It was inspired by Clement V, not Boniface VIII, and almost certainly by Clement V in his last years. Any theory of Dante's evolution which pushes his anti-papal conviction back into his early political life involves such political improbabilities that it ought not to be seriously considered.

NOTES

1. *Codice diplomatico dantesco*, ed. Renato Piattoli (Florence, 1940), p. 106.
2. Ibid., p. 96.
3. *Saggi di filosofia dantesca* (2nd edn., Florence, 1967), p. 269.
4. G. Levi, 'Bonifazio VIII e le sue relazioni col comune di Firenze', *Archivio della Società Romana per Storia Patria*, v (1882), pp. 450–2; cf. *Registres de Boniface VIII*, ii, no. 3535.
5. *Cod dipl. dantesco*, pp. 82–3.
6. Robert Davidsohn, *Storia di Firenze*, iv (Florence, 1960), pp. 138–9.
7. *Cronica di Dino Compagni*, ed. I. del Lungo (*Rerum Italicarum Scriptores*, 1913–16) pp. 62–3.
8. Levi, pp. 455–8; *Reg. Boniface*, no. 3570.
9. For these events see Davidsohn, op. cit., pp. 90–146.
10. *Monumenta Germaniae Historica, Constitutiones*, IV. i, no. 105.
11. Georges Digard, *Philippe le Bel et le Saint-Siège de 1285 à 1304* (Paris, 1936), ii. p. 26.
12. The history of papal claims of this kind in the thirteenth century is sketched by Friedrich Baethgen in 'Der Anspruch des Papsttums auf das Reichsvikariat' reprinted in *Medievalia* (Stuttgart, 1960).
13. Digard, *Philippe le Bel et le Saint-Siège*, ii. p. 9.
14. Baethgen, 'Quellen und Untersuchungen zur Geschichte der päpstlichen Hof und Finanzverwaltung unter Bonifaz VIII', reprinted in *Medievalia*.
15. On the background to these events see Daniel Waley, *The Papal State in the Thirteenth Century* (London, 1961), pp. 245–6.
16. *Cod. dipl. dantesco*, pp. 80–1.
17. Robert Davidsohn, *Forschungen zur älteren Geschichte von Florenz*, ii (Berlin, 1900), p. 251.
18. Davidsohn, *Forschungen*, iii (1901), p. 279.
19. *Reg. Boniface*, no. 3899.
20. Davidsohn, *Storia*, p. 197; *Consigli della repubblica fiorentina*, ed. Bernardino Barbadoro (Bologna, 1921), i. p. 9.

21. Davidsohn, *Storia*, pp. 197–8. The extract including the record of Dante's speech, which is printed in *Cod. dipl. dantesco*, can also be read in the context of other votes on other questions in this period in the full edition of the *Liber Fabarum* in *Consigli*, i. 14.

22. H. Finke *Aus den Tagen Bonifaz VIII* (Münster, 1902) p. xxv. For the events of this year in general the best account is in Davidsohn, op. cit.

23. 'Your city which is so full of envy that the sack overflows.'

24. 'And he said to me "after long contention they shall come to blood and the party of the woods shall expel the other with much offence. Then this must befall within three suns and the other party prevail through the force of one who now keeps tacking".'

25. 'As I have already said in the Comedy in Paradiso' (*Monarchia*, I. xii, 6), implying that *Paradiso* was written before *Monarchia*.

26. See particularly the essay by Michele Maccarone, 'Il terzo libro della *Monarchia*', *Studi danteschi*, xxxiii, 1955, and the refutation of it by Nardi, 'Intorno ad una nuova interpretazione del terzo libro della *Monarchia* dantesca' in *Dal Convivio alla Commedia* (Rome, 1960).

27. N. Matteini, *Il più antico oppositore politico di Dante, Guido Vernani da Rimini* (Padua, 1958), p. 93.

28. *Saggi di filosofia dantesca*, pp. 274–5, 297–310.

29. *Monarchia*, III. iii. 6–9.

30. *Epist.* i. On the political situation in Florence and Italy during Dante's years of exile up to 1309 see Davidsohn, op. cit., pp. 355–476.

31. *Convivio*, IV. 4–5.

32. *M.G.H. Const.* IV. i, no. 298.

33. Ibid., no. 393. Henry VII's relations with the papacy and Italy are fully chronicled in W. M. Bowsky's *Henry VII in Italy* (Lincoln, Nebraska, 1960).

34. *M.G.H. Const.* IV. i, no. 435.

35. 'This he whom Peter, the Vicar of God, exhorts us to honour, and whom Clement, the present successor of Peter, illumines with the light of the Apostolic benediction; that where the spiritual ray suffices not, there the splendour of the lesser luminary may lend its light.'

36. *Dantis Alagherii Epistolae*, p. 58.

37. *M.G.H. Const.* IV. i, nos. 799–800.

38. Ibid. IV. ii, no. 1311 (*c.* Aug. 1312–Apr. 1313).

39. *Epist.* vi, vii, viii.

40. 'That thy colleagues who have been degraded should not continue forever stripped of their glory.'

41. 'In order that the wrath of the deceased pontiff might put forth leaves in thee.' The emendation and reinterpretation of this letter suggested by R. Morghen, 'La lettera di Dante ai Cardinali Italiani', *Bullettino dell'Istituto Storico Italiano per il Medio Evo*, lxviii, 1956, have been effectively rejected by A. Frugoni, 'Dante, Epist. XI, 24–5', *Rivista id Cultura Classica e Medioevale*, vii, 1965.

42. Carlo Pincin, *Marsilio* (Turin, 1967), pp. 29–35.

43. *Monarchia*, III. iv. 20. 'The temporal kingdom does not receive its being from the spiritual . . . but it does receive from it the power to act

more virtuously through the light of grace which the benediction of the Pope infuses into it in heaven and earth.'

44. xxvii. 25 f. 'A burial ground of blood and filth'.

45. xix. 82 f.: 'Of uglier deeds, a lawless shepherd from the west'.

46. xvii. 82: 'The Gascon', who 'shall deceive the high Henry'.

47. xxx. 142–4: 'The prefect in the divine forum who openly and covertly will not go with him [Henry] on one road'.

48. xxx. 145: 'But for little time thereafter shall be suffered by God to be in the holy office'.

49. *M.G.H. Const.* IV. ii, no. 752.

50. Giorgio Petrocchi, 'Intorno alla pubblicazione dell' *Inferno* e del *Purgatorio*', *Convivium*, n.s. xxv (1957).

51. xvii. 49–51: 'So it is willed and already plotted, and soon it shall be done by him who ponders on it in the place where Christ is every day put up for sale.'

3

Dante and the Prophetic View of History

MARJORIE REEVES

It is possible—even easy—to see Dante as a profound pessimist about human nature. Even in the *Paradiso* he is still obsessed by the evil state of the world. In the harmony and sweetness which is the heaven of the Sun Dante is suddenly aware of utter contrast: 'O insensata cura de' mortali!', he exclaims, and he instantly envisions what he calls the downward beat of their wings as men of all professions, lawyers, scholars, priests, rulers, and others corrupt themselves and society by going after material gain, while he—released from all these things—is with Beatrice in heaven.[1] Even in the *Cielo Stellato*, intoxicated by the music of the hymn to the Trinity and enveloped in the glory which is like a smile of the universe, Dante again suddenly breaks the ecstasy in a harsh change of mood: Peter glows red with indignation at the evil deeds of his successors and all heaven blushes for shame. Contemporary popes are ravening wolves who devour the fold: '. . . o buon principio,/a che vil fine convien che tu caschi!'[2] And Beatrice extends the indictment to society generally: faith and innocence are found only in little children before the rot sets in; cupidity cankers all true fruit.[3] Cupidity—the inability to remain content with what God has ordained as one's own—infects all men. In *Monarchia* Dante put his finger on this as the root disease of society: 'Ad evidentiam primi notandum quod iustitie maxime contrariatur cupiditas.'[4] Men must be always reaching after something which is not theirs. This is the drive which endlessly tears human society asunder and makes for that social and political restlessness which Dante so much deplores, as, for instance, in the great diatribe of *Purgatorio* vi. It would seem that the gulf between the inherently corrupt human society that Dante knew and the divine society which he experienced in imagination was absolute. In this respect we could say that he took the Augustinian view of this world.

But Augustine carried this pessimistic view to the point of denying that there could ever be a state of real justice in human society. The more there is to be had, the more men will contend for it. The State, in the political sense, is only a human compromise permitted by God, embodying utilitarian insights which make a *modus vivendi* possible. You will recall Augustine's well-known pronouncement that the State is at bottom nothing but a robber band writ large: this rates human political organization at its lowest, but even at its highest there can be no real human fulfilment. No state of justice is possible on earth and therefore no realization of human potentiality.[5]

This is the point at which Dante parts company from Augustine. The passage I referred to in *Paradiso* xxvii about the corruption of children does not stop there. Beatrice calls Dante to reflect on the fact 'che 'n terra non è chi governi;/ onde sì svïa l'umana famiglia', and then immediately sweeps into one of the grand prophetic statements: the time so long awaited is coming when the poops (of the ships) will be turned right about, so that the fleet will steer a straight course towards its goal, and, in another figure, 'e vero frutto verrà dopo 'l fiore'.[6] The juxtaposition of these two metaphors is particularly interesting because one is revolutionary, a figure of motion (the poops turn right round), and the other evolutionary, a figure of organic growth. To anticipate a little, I may point out here that the second has, rather slenderly, been held to show the influence of imagery used by Joachim of Fiore.[7] Joachim certainly had a concept of history as an organic growth towards its climactic fruition in the future, but there was also a revolutionary element in his thought and the attitudes of some of his followers, leading to a kind of ambivalence between a revolutionary and an evolutionary expectation such as Dante expresses here.

To return to our main point, Dante, then, had a vision of the future within history which remained optimistic to the end.[8] This is surprising in view of his own tragic and frustrated experience and the deep sense of this world's corruption with which he was constantly burdened. Above all, wickedness in the high places of Papacy and ecclesiastical hierarchy weighed him down. There was that one moment of hope in 1309/10 when the Sun and the Moon of Papacy and Empire seemed momentarily to be in glorious conjunction and Dante could see prophecy coming to fulfilment. But hope collapsed with the death of the Emperor Henry VII, and the election of John XXII must have been profoundly discouraging. Italy was still the riderless horse and Rome the weeping widow beside the Tiber.[9] Whence, then, did Dante derive his strong affirmation concerning the potentiality for human achievement in a future stage of history, and how was he able to maintain it in the face of constant collapses of hope?

Can we find any clue in the Florentine political experience of his early days? Looking back later, he clearly believed that his role in politics had been a just one, making Brunetto Latini say, in assumed prophecy, that he will be exiled 'per tuo ben far'.[10] But whether he was already pursuing a political principle, ideal or hope, remains obscure. Giorgio Petrocchi has deduced, from Florentine conciliar minutes and other evidence, that Dante's political position was close to that of the White Guelf party and that he was in sympathy with the popular cause in defending the constitution against violent action.[11] But Petrocchi stresses Dante's independence of judgment and unwillingness, for instance, to involve himself in the partisan politics of the *Parte Guelfa*. Already, perhaps, the fiercely independent mind was developing which would later make him a 'parte per se stesso'.[12] It seems natural that Dante, as one of the priors in June 1300, should have attempted to restore order by exiling the heads of both factions, but this does not give us any clear indication of a developing political philosophy. In all the acts of Florentine politics in which Dante participated, our one clue to the formation of a political position lies in the conciliar minutes of June 1301, recording that when Boniface VIII asked for 100 *cavalieri* for the papal army, twice over 'Dante Alagherii consuluit quod de servitio faciendo d. pape nichil fiat'.[13] Petrocchi comments: 'È arida formula del verbalizzante, ma indubbiamente suona in noi come la voce intrepida d'un uomo politico che assume tutte intiere le proprie responsabilità.'[14] Dante lost on the vote, but this clear-cut opposition surely reveals a growing conviction that the involvement of the Church in secular politics was disastrous for the autonomy of the city. At this point we could say that negatively he had much in common with the viewpoint later expressed by Marsilio of Padua, but we still have no clue as to how he will arrive at the positive political solution which will differ so widely from Marsilio's.

Dante goes into exile as one of the leaders of a faction that had lost and as an already established poet, but not as a political philosopher. Was it during the uncharted years of his early exile that he began to turn his attention to imperial history? His interest in the Hohenstaufen first appears in one sentence of the *De Vulgari Eloquentia*,[15] but years later—perhaps many years later—he gives an autobiographical hint in the *Monarchia* concerning the growth of his political imperialism. At the beginning of Book II Dante says that he once marvelled that the Roman people had been raised to world supremacy without any resistance, thinking in a superficial way that they had gained it by force, not by right. But now that, with the eyes of the mind, he had pierced to the core, all the signs convinced him that this had been the work of divine providence.[16] These words surely convey the sense of a moment of prophetic enlightenment: he had seen with the eyes of the mind, penetrated to the core, read the signs. This is the language of the seers and, although by no means peculiar to him, we may again note that Joachim of Fiore often described his sense of prophetic vision in terms of penetrating to the marrow or the core with the eyes of the mind.[17]

So Dante became convinced, through some 'given' moment of insight, that there was a providential purpose in history, focused on the 'Roman people'. Since this doctrine appears fully articulated in *Convivio*, Book IV, we must date that moment of insight to the early years of exile, perhaps during the period when he was becoming aware of the futility of White/Ghibelline political strategy and was disentangling himself from it. If history were the arena in which God worked out His purpose, then that purpose must reach some sort of consummation in history itself. If the prophetic signs were read correctly, the pattern could be discerned. But had God's providential purpose in history already been consummated when, at the time of the Incarnation, God set His seal on the Roman people? Had history anything more to add? Much orthodox thinking followed St. Augustine in averring that the only climax within history was already past, and that the space between the First and Second Advents was a period of waiting. This was not so

with Dante. But if one root of Dante's optimism may be traced
to his conviction about God's working in history, we must look
elsewhere for another, remembering Dante's desperate plunge
into philosophy for consolation. The first clear affirmation of a
philosophical 'end' for human society which still remained to be
consummated within history, also appears in the *Convivio*,
written, it will be remembered, for lay leaders. The task he set
himself was to assist them in understanding those worthy temporal ends towards which all their activities should strive. The
Convivio, therefore, was planned as the 'philosophical initiation
for worldly folk'.[18] In his hierarchy of the sciences Dante goes
against the accepted view by placing ethics above metaphysics
and next below theology. This was not to say that metaphysics
was not qualitatively higher, just as the contemplative life was
intrinsically higher than the active. But the importance of
ethics for Dante at that moment lay in the fact that it was the
supreme science which was within the practical grasp of men
and could remedy their present condition.

Here, of course, Dante draws strongly on the other source of
his hope, the philosophical one which he derives ultimately from
Aristotle. In *Convivio* IV those two lines of hope, the historical
and the philosophical, begin to converge. Dante affirms that
the fundamental root of the imperial majesty is the necessity of
human civilization, which is ordained for one end—the *vita felice*
—and he cites 'the Philosopher' on the true 'end' of mankind.[19]
Theoretically speaking, there must be a purpose for which
human society is designed and which it ought to achieve. He
then links this philosophical necessity with God's providence in
history. To achieve this 'end' monarchy is necessary, since only
the universal monarch is free from cupidity and can therefore
create the condition of peace in which men can live in felicity.
It was divine bounty that provided in the past a moment of
realization when the Son of God descended into history 'a fare
questa concordia', precisely when the earth was best disposed
to receive Him, being at peace under one rule, that of the
Emperor Augustus and the Roman people. Dante reads the
providential pattern even more deeply by drawing a parallel or
concord between the birth of David, the root from which Jesus
sprang, and the birth of Rome in the advent of Aeneas in Italy,
events which he makes contemporary.[20] The divine election of

the Roman *imperium* is manifest in the simultaneous advent of
the progenitor of the Son of God and of the founder of the holy
city, a political actualization to accompany the divine actualization. From this past manifestation Dante looks to the future.

It is impossible to say with certainty how, during the im-
potence of Dante's early exile, this sense of future meaning in
human history was generated, nor which came first, the passionate belief in the philosophical end of man, or the conviction
that there was a providence in history working towards that
end. It seems, however, that it was first necessary for Dante to
seize on the philosophical goal, the 'end' which—theoretically,
at least—must be achieved, and then to seek for this abstract
ideal a locus in time and space appointed by God's providential
purpose. In doing so, Dante was breaking with that orthodox
view to which I have referred. For the marriage of a philosophical ideal to a providential view of history changed a utopia
into a prophecy, and the logic of both his philosophical argument and his reading of history pointed towards a second 'right
moment' in future time which would, in some sense, parallel
that first 'right moment' under Augustus. The limited, but real
earthly beatitude hoped for at the end of the *Convivio* must find
embodiment under a true Roman rule.

When did Dante begin to expect an imminent 'right moment'? Was it the extraordinarily apt conjunction of Henry VII's
ambitions with Clement V's political necessities which crystallized hope into definite shape? Was Henry of Luxemburg to be
a kind of second political incarnation, standing in concord with
Augustus? The language of Dante's three political letters at this
time seems to me clearly to go beyond the terms of conventional
rhetoric. To the Princes and Peoples of Italy he writes:

Ecce nunc tempus acceptabile, quo signa surgunt consolationis et
pacis. Nam dies nova splendescit . . . quae iam tenebras diuturnae
calamitatis attenuat; . . . Arrexit namque aures misericordes leo
fortis de tribu Iuda; atque ululatum universalis captivitatis com-
miserans, Moysen alium suscitavit, qui de gravaminibus Aegyp-
tiorum populum suum eripiet . . . Laetare iam nunc miseranda
Italia etiam Saracenis, quae statim invidiosa per orbem videberis,
quia sponsus tuus, mundi solatium et gloria plebis tuae, clementissi-
mus Henricus, Divus et Augustus et Caesar, ad nuptias properat.[21]

Again, we have the well-known passage from his Letter to the Emperor: 'Tunc exultavit in me spiritus meus, quum tacitus dixi mecum: "Ecce Agnus Dei, ecce qui tollit peccata mundi"'[22] And to the Florentines he writes: '. . . tamquam ad ipsum [Henry]. post Christum, digitum prophetiae propheta direxerit Isaias, quum, Spiritu Dei revelante. praedixit: "Vere languores nostros ipse tulit, et dolores nostros ipse portavit."'[23] In his reactions to the Italian expedition of Henry VII Dante is surely reading in his own prophetic terms a series of events which, of course, have a totally other explanation on the human level. Dante's philosophy of history was developing into a theology of history which sought to discern divine patterns by applying prophetic words from the past to the present and future.

The central question we now have to ask ourselves is how did Dante's optimism survive the disaster of Henry VII's death before the accomplishment of his mission? A philosophical ideal might well not have survived as a hope against such odds, but prophetic expectation, affirming the inevitable working out of history according to divine plan, could. If, as Ricci's edition suggests,[24] *Monarchia* was written late, even as late as 1318, then we must see it as a reaffirmation of political faith in the post-Henrician period. In this case, it is highly significant that, whereas in the *Convivio* the providential argument appears late, to buttress the philosophical, here it almost takes over. Can we say that only belief in the inevitable fulfilment of divine pattern in history could carry Dante to the peak of his prophetic vision? Such a belief was current among some of Dante's contemporaries, especially those who had come, directly or indirectly, under the influence of Joachimism. If the traditional view, stemming from St. Augustine, had been that the process of history had already been consummated in the life and death of Jesus, there had developed, particularly during the twelfth century and after, traces of a hope which, without reviving an earlier crude millennialism, expected some sort of earthly fruition before the end of time. This hope had been given its fullest embodiment in Joachim of Fiore's proclamation of an imminent Age of the Spirit. I shall return to this contemporary prophetic view shortly, but first let us consider briefly the prophetic element in the *Divina Commedia*.

I take the view that the *Commedia* is in many ways a this-

worldly poem, still concerned with all that hinders the realization of the earthly beatitude, as well as with the soul's pil-
grimage towards the heavenly beatitude. The belief in the
providential development of history is still there, and it still
has to be prophetically fulfilled within time. Time may be short
—the places in the Celestial Rose are almost filled—but something more has to happen in history, a further realization of
God's purpose on earth. So I take the enigmatic utterances concerning the *Veltro*, the symbolic greyhound, pronounced by
Virgil, and the 'cinquecento diece e cinque' (*DXV*), pronounced
by Beatrice,[25] to embody the literal expectation of a decisive
moment yet to come when, in some measure at least, the earthly
beatitude will be realized and history brought to its fruition.
Into the possible solutions of who or what Dante envisaged I
cannot plunge here: one suspects that the enigmas may have
been intentional because Dante himself was not certain of the
form the solution would take. The point I want to make is that
Dante can take on the speech of true prophecy because he
believes that there is a providential plan working throughout
history and that he can attempt, by given clues, to read the
signs set in history which point towards the fulfilment of the
whole divine plan. This is something quite different from the
art of the diviners or soothsayers whom Dante condemns in
Inferno xx. At an earlier moment, in the letter to the Florentines
in which he denounces their opposition to Henry VII, Dante
writes: 'Et si praesaga mens mea non fallitur, sic signis veri-
dicis, sicut inexpugnabilibus argumentis instructa praenuntians,
urbem diutino moerore confectam in manus alienorum tradi
finaliter.'[26] Surely, in the *Divina Commedia*, he is still consciously
exercising a similar role as prophet.

In taking on this role and declaring this hope, does Dante
draw any of his strength from the contemporary prophetic
traditions to which I have alluded? Broadly speaking, these took
two, interrelated forms. In the first place, there was an ancient
expectation of a Last World Emperor. The late Paul Alexander
put us greatly in his debt by unravelling its beginnings in a
Syriac Apocalypse, commonly known as the Pseudo-Methodius,
composed in the seventh century.[27] This had come into the
West in the late seventh or early eighth century. By the eleventh
century the prophecy of the last emperor had been incorporated

into another current oracle, that of the Tiburtine Sibyl. The
established tradition was that before the end of time there
would arise a great and glorious emperor who would conquer
all his enemies, establish his rule over all Christians, destroy or
convert the Saracens and convert the Jews. Then would ensue a
period of peace and plenty. But this time of ease would be
ended when the signs of Antichrist appeared. The emperor
would go to Jerusalem and surrender the insignia of his
authority and his life to God on Golgotha. Then Antichrist
would reign in full terror until St. Michael or Christ himself
appeared to destroy him. Second Coming and Last Judgment
would follow immediately. In the thirteenth and fourteenth
centuries this prophecy (or echoes of it) was circulating in
prose and verse throughout Western Europe. Some oracles of
this type were applied to the Hohenstaufen.[28] Alexander von
Roes expected a Second Charlemagne,[29] and so did Pierre
Dubois who put forward a programme for such a Carolingian
emperor.[30]

Was Dante influenced by the idea of a final world emperor as
expected in these current oracles? I cannot find any direct
evidence that Dante knew or used them. The use of animal
symbolism in the *Veltro* is in the style of the Sibylline oracles, but
this is a very slender link. Moreover, in my view, there is one
crucial respect in which Dante's vision of the future differs from
the earlier Last World Emperor tradition: the latter's achievement was predominantly in terms of external conquest and
material peace and well-being; there is no hint of reformation,
and his is a regime which dissolves with the onslaught of Antichrist. Although only indicated in brief allusions, Dante's vision,
as expressed in the prophetic words of the *Divina Commedia*,
involves a fundamental, internal, and spiritual transformation.
The *Veltro* will not feed on land or wealth, but wisdom and love,
and he will chase the Wolf of Avarice back to hell.[31] Again,
alluding to the accursed she-wolf in *Purgatorio* xx, Dante
exclaims: 'quando verrà per cui questa disceda!'[32] And again, it
is a spiritual revolution that is implied when the poops of the
ships shall turn right round and sail towards their true goal.[33]
The *DXV* has a political mission, but this is related to the
spiritual and concerns the internal state of Christendom: he
must overthrow the wicked combination of papal and Capetian

power and be the heir to the Eagle's true role,[34] that is, create that condition of harmony under one rule which is the earthly beatitude. This reminds us of the divine Eagle in the heaven of Jupiter and the way in which Divine Justice stoops over earthly justice.[35]

Dante, I submit, envisages a new quality of living diffused throughout human society in this climax to come. This is not the characteristic of the standard emperor prophecies. But I have argued elsewhere[36] that where these older conqueror prophecies came under the influence of Joachimist thought they acquired something of this element of spiritual *renovatio* in a new age to come. Of course such a political form for the future age is far removed from Joachim's original Age of the Spirit, which was oriented entirely towards the Church and the religious aspect. But in the pseudo-Joachimist literature of the thirteenth century a transformation took place. A political Joachimism was developing in Dante's lifetime. The programme that emerges envisages the overcoming of the great Antichrist by a holy alliance of emperor and pope and then a period of bliss before history is wound up at the Last Judgment. Under its divinely appointed leaders human society is to attain, not perfection, but at least its earthly beatitude.

Did Dante's continuing hope for a transformation of human society owe anything, directly or indirectly, to the Joachimist expectation of the Third Age in which the quality of human living would be transformed? There are arguments for and against the suggestion that Dante took inspiration from the Calabrian abbot and his disciples. Let me set out some of them. In the first place, Dante seems to make rather a special point of including Joachim among the blessed spirits in the heaven of the Sun. In introducing him, Dante makes Bonaventura use words which emphasize Joachim's prophetic gift: 'di spirito profetico dotato'.[37] Moreover, these words are a direct quotation from the Antiphon to Vespers in which the monks of Fiore were permitted to celebrate their founder. Thus Dante undoubtedly believed Joachim to have been a true prophet. But since the context of this encounter is Dante's treatment of the two great Mendicant Orders, this might signify no more than that Dante, like many others, believed that Joachim had truly prophesied the advent of the Franciscans and Dominicans.

Yet I am inclined to think that the deliberate quotation implies something more.

Secondly, there is a certain similarity between their patterns of history. Joachim's concept of three ages or *status* meant two turning-points within history: the Incarnation past and—just ahead—the full manifestation of the Holy Spirit. This was the point at which Joachim went much further than others who reflected on the pattern of history. So far as I have been able to discover, none of his contemporaries postulated fully a second 'moment' of fulfilment which was either now already present or imminent in the future.[38] In the thirteenth century the Spiritual Franciscans, it seems, adapted this idea to their own sense of unique mission, seeing the second turning-point as having been initiated in the advent of St. Francis. Making a more Christological emphasis than the abbot, some of these Joachites thought in terms of three Advents of Christ: the first, at the Incarnation, the second, a 'middle advent', His manifestation in the earthly agents of this new turning-point, the third, at His coming in glory on the Last Day.[39] If Dante really felt a parallel between the political 'right moment' of the reign of Augustus and something approaching a political 'middle advent' to be expected shortly, he could have been adapting the central Joachimist concept perhaps as he received it in the Spiritual Franciscan form. Certainly it is hard to point to any other source for this idea.

Thirdly, Dante's and Joachim's concepts of the prophetic role are similar. Although the latter in fact denied himself the title of prophet, he emphasized that by the gift of spiritual intelligence—which must be 'given'—it was possible to penetrate to the full meaning of history, reading the signs set there by God, and in the light of these insights to extrapolate the pattern of things to come.[40] I have already quoted Dante's words on his understanding of what prophecy is.[41] Both shared the sense that to those who reflected deeply on the meaning of events in time, might be given the spiritual vision to interpret their full significance and the responsibility to declare their message in prophetic terms. Both would have agreed that prophecy and soothsaying were poles apart.

Finally, we reach something firmer in the almost undoubted fact that Dante used three, at least, of Joachim's *figurae*. Joachim had summed up both his Trinitarian doctrine and his theology of history in a set of intricate figures known now as the *Liber Figurarum*.[42] In the *Paradiso* Dante seems obviously to have used two Trinitarian figures of interlinked circles.[43] These help to establish the fact that Dante was interested in Joachim's figures, but it is a third one which is specifically related to the question of Dante's prophetic vision. In the heaven of Jupiter, where the theme is divine and earthly justice, the flaming spirits form in starry writing across the heavens the words *Diligite justitiam qui judicatis terram*—'Love justice ye who judge the earth'. Then, resting in the final *M*, innumerable other spirits gather like sparks to form out of it an eagle's head and neck and to entwine the *M* with lilies. Then the Eagle utters his great discourse on justice.[44] Among Joachim's tree-figures is a formalized pair which, turned upside down, have the shape of a gothic *M*, while they also become eagles, with the head as the tree-root and the wings and tail-feathers as the branches.[45] Dante does not in the Eagle's discourse include any specifically prophetic words, but Joachim's tree-eagles have a concealed prophetic message pointing to the coming new age. This is contained partly in the fact that the twelve branches are unevenly divided into five and seven,[46] a number symbolism which is always used by Joachim to express the transition to the third *status*, a movement from outward material things to inner spiritual ones.[47] It is also expressed in the lilies which entwine the branches, the flowers of the Third Age, and in the figure of the Eagle itself which, for Joachim, is the Eagle of St. John and of the contemplative life of the coming age. The prophetic symbolism of the Age of the Spirit is certainly there; but did Dante recognize this, or was he merely attracted by the striking visual imagery of this strange, rather bizarre figure? It is impossible to be certain, yet its deliberate introduction at a moment when the relation of earthly to heavenly justice is occupying his mind creates a real possibility that he did.

Nevertheless, this very symbol of the Eagle serves to emphasize that Dante and Joachim were deeply divided in their view of the place of the Roman Empire in the divine scheme. Joachim shared the common view that the Roman Empire had been ordained by God to keep the peoples of the world within their prescribed limits. It was symbolized in the River Euphrates, the

magnum flumen created by God 'ad munimen pacis et defen-
sionem ecclesie'.[48] But this was a negative function and, moreover, Rome had not been content with this function. She had
fornicated with the nations and, drunk with pride, had become
the new Babylon. So the Sixth Angel of the Apocalypse must
pour his phial on the Euphrates which will be dried up, so that
the infidel hordes will burst through to destroy the Roman
Empire. There is no place in Joachim's Third Age for a regener-
ated Roman *imperium* or messianic emperor: the spiritual
renovatio follows after the fall of Babylon.

At one point Joachim and Dante use a very similar method of
concords, but with opposite conclusions. You remember Dante's
concord between the birth of David from whom Christ sprang
and the coming of Aeneas which was the birth of Rome.[49]
Joachim's concords depend on a more complicated number
symbolism in which the unit of forty-two generations is an
important factor. Adam had two sons, one of which killed the
other; forty-two generations later, in the days of Uzziah, King
of Israel, in pagan history Rhea Sylvia gave birth to two sons,
one of whom killed the other. From Cain sprang the first
Babylon; from Romulus sprang Rome which became the second
Babylon.[50] So the method of concords between sacred and pagan
history which gives Dante the quasi-messianic character of his
Roman people gives Joachim the identification of Rome with
Babylon, the root of evil in history. Then, by a paradoxical
inversion, we discover a second sharp contrast between them.
From another of his concords Joachim derives a parallel
between David and Constantine. David exalted the first Jerusalem and forty-two generations later Constantine the Great
exalted the New Jerusalem, that is, the Church.[51] So, in this
particular instance, but without modifying his general view of
the Empire, Joachim pays honour to the great emperor. And he
does so for precisely the reason that drove Dante, obsessed by
the evil consequences of the Donation of Constantine, to
denounce his deed in bitter terms.[52]

Gathering all these thoughts together, I am suggesting that in
the *Divina Commedia* Dante was still expecting a *renovatio mundi*
and that this unconquerable hope sprang from his prophetic
vision of history, although he had worked out its meaning for
human society in philosophical as well as religious terms. When,

however, we turn to the question of a possible source for this prophetic expectation, there is no proven answer. The Last World Emperor myth does not appear to have been used by Dante, although Professor Charles Davis has recently provided an interesting point of later evidence which may modify this conclusion.[53] In the first version of his commentary on the *Commedia* Dante's son, Pietro, identified the *Veltro* with an emperor and said he would reign, like Augustus, over the whole world. Important additions to this were made in later versions of the commentary (to be found in a Laurentian manuscript, Ashburnham 841, and in the Vatican MS Ottob. Lat. 2867). Here the *Veltro* is explicitly identified with the *DXV* and his function is stated to be to root out avarice, separate prelates from their ill-gotten gains and establish universal peace. Pietro thought that his father was intentionally vague about the identity of this saviour, but suggested that he might have been thinking of the *Rex Christianorum* prophesied by Methodius, that is, the Last World Emperor of the pseudo-Methodius. Had Pietro any real knowledge of his father's source, or had he simply turned to the current myth to explain an enigma? For Dante's full conviction concerning a spiritual turning-point shortly to come we must perforce turn to Joachim of Fiore as the source, since, I have argued, no one else prophetically placed a second turning-point in history just ahead in time. Yet there are difficulties, in particular, their diametrically opposed views on the Empire, which prevent one from calling Dante in any sense a Joachite, and there is no proof that Dante knew any of Joachim's works except the *Liber Figurarum*. All we can safely say is that a certain ambience of prophetic expectation within history had been created in the thirteenth century by Joachim's disciples and was prevalent in Dante's lifetime. Dante's prophetic vision seems to belong to this mode of thought.

NOTES

1. *Paradiso*, xi. 1–12.
2. Ibid. xxvii. 19–60. 'Oh fair beginning to what vile ending must thou fall!' (ll. 59–60).
3. Ibid. 121–41.
4. *Monarchia*, I. xi. 11: 'to prove the first point we must note that cupidity is the chief opponent of justice.'

5. St. Augustine, *De Civitate Dei*, iv. 4. See also P. Brown, 'Saint Augustine', *Trends in Medieval Political Thought*, ed. B. Smalley (Blackwell, Oxford, 1965), pp. 1–18; D. Bigongiari, *Essays on Dante and Medieval Culture* (Florence, 1964), pp. 94–7.

6. *Paradiso*, xxvii. 140–8: 'there is none to govern upon earth, wherefore the human family goes so astray' (140–1); 'true fruit shall follow flower' (148).

7. L. Tondelli, *Il Libro delle Figure*, 2nd edn. (Turin, 1953), i. 236–8.

8. Years ago Nardi, in his essay 'Dante Profeta' emphasized the strongly optimistic note in Dante's thought; see B. Nardi, *Dante e la cultura medievale* (Bari, 1942), pp. 263–4, 269–72.

9. *Purgatorio*, vi. 88–114.

10. *Inferno*, xv. 61–4: 'for thy good deeds' (l.64).

11. G. Petrocchi, 'L'impegno politico di Dante', *L'ultima dea, L' ippografo II* (Rome, 1977), pp. 11–46.

12. *Paradiso*, xvii. 69: 'a party to thyself'.

13. *Codice diplomatico dantesco*, ed. R. Piattoli (Florence, 1950), nos. 83, 84, pp. 94–6.

14. Petrocchi, op. cit., p. 26.

15. *De Vulgari Eloquentia*, I. xii. 4.

16. *Monarchia*, II. i, 2 ff.

17. For references see M. Reeves, B. Hirsch-Reich, *The Figurae of Joachim of Fiore* (Clarendon Press, Oxford, 1972), pp. 2–3, 20.

18. E. Gilson, trs. D. Moore, *Dante and Philosophy* (New York, London, 1963), p. 85.

19. *Il Convivio*, IV. 4.

20. Ibid. IV. 5. See J. Scott, 'La contemporaneità Enea-Davide', *Studi danteschi*, xlix (1972), 129–34.

21. *Epistolae*, pp. 47–9: 'Behold now is the accepted time, wherein arise the signs of consolation and peace. For a new day is beginning to break ... which even now is dispersing the darkness of our long tribulation ... For the strong lion of the tribe of Judah hath lifted up his ears in compassion, and moved by the lamentations of the multitudes in captivity hath raised up another Moses, who shall deliver his people from the oppression of the Egyptians ... Rejoice, therefore, O Italy, thou that art now an object of pity even to the Saracens, for soon shalt thou be the envy of the whole world, seeing that thy bridegroom, the comfort of the nations and the glory of thy people, even the most clement Henry, Elect of God and Augustus and Caesar, is hastening to the wedding.'

22. Ibid., pp. 90–1: 'Then my spirit rejoiced within me, when I said secretly within myself: "Behold the Lamb of God which taketh away the sins of the world".'

23. Ibid., p. 76: '... as though to him, after Christ, the prophet Isaiah had pointed the finger of prophecy, when by the revelation of the Spirit of God he declared: "Surely he hath borne our griefs and carried our sorrows".'

24. *Monarchia*, I. xii. 6 (pp. 158–9).

25. *Inferno*, i. 101–11; *Purgatorio*, xxxiii. 37–51.

26. *Epistolae*, pp. 71–2: 'And if my prophetic soul be not deceived, which announces what it has been taught by infallible signs and incontrovertible arguments, your city, worn out by ceaseless mourning, shall be delivered at the last into the hands of strangers.'

27. P. Alexander, 'Medieval Apocalypses as Historical Sources', *American Historical Review*, lxxiii (1968), 997–1018; 'Byzantium and the Migration of Literary Works and Motifs: The Legend of the Last World Emperor', *Medievalia et Humanistica*, n.s. ii (1971), 47–68; *The Oracle of Baalbek* (Dumbarton Oaks, 1967). See also K. Morawski, 'Le Mythe de l'Empereur chez Dante', *Révue des études italiennes*, xii (1965), 280–301.

28. M. Reeves, *The Influence of Prophecy in the Later Middle Ages* (Clarendon Press, Oxford, 1969), pp. 309–12.

29. Ibid., pp. 313–14.

30. Ibid., p. 320.

31. *Inferno*, i. 103–9.

32. *Purgatorio*, xx. 15: 'When will he come, through whom she will depart?'

33. *Paradiso*, xxvii. 146.

34. *Purgatorio*, xxxiii. 37–45.

35. *Paradiso*, xix, xx.

36. Reeves, op. cit. (n. 28), pp. 309–14.

37. *Paradiso*, xii. 140–1: 'endowed with the spirit of prophecy' (141).

38. I hope to support this statement in a further article.

39. Reeves, op. cit., pp. 175–210.

40. Ibid., pp. 13, 16–17; Reeves, Hirsch-Reich, op. cit. (n. 17), pp. 1–8.

41. Above, p. 47, 51

42. *Il Libro delle Figure*, 2nd. edn., ii. ed. L. Tondelli, M. Reeves, B. Hirsch-Reich (Turin, 1953). See also Reeves, Hirsch-Reich, op. cit.

43. Compare *Paradiso*, xiv. 28–33 and xxxiii. 115–20 with Pl. XXVI in the *Lib. Fig.* See Reeves, Hirsch-Reich, op. cit., pp. 317–29, for an examination of Dante's possible debt to the *Lib. Fig.*, and pp. 264–5 for a suggestion supporting Mgr. Tondelli's surmise that the Reggio MS. of the *Lib. Fig.* was produced in Florence.

44. *Paradiso*, xviii. 70–114.

45. *Lib. Fig.*, Pls. XIV, XV; Reeves, Hirsch-Reich, op. cit., pp. 160–3.

46. The branches represent tribes in the Old Dispensation and churches in the New. In order to make five and seven, two names inscribed on the tree-trunks have to be included.

47. For an explanation of this number symbolism, see Reeves, Hirsch-Reich, op. cit., pp. 13–17.

48. Joachim of Fiore, *Expositio in Apocalypsim* (Venice, 1527), fos. 190^r–192^r; Reeves, op. cit., pp. 304–5.

49. Above, p. 48.

50. Joachim of Fiore, *Liber Concordie* (Venice, 1519), fo. 134^v; see also Reeves, Hirsch-Reich, op. cit., pp. 127, 143, 185.
51. *Lib. Conc.*, fo. 134^v; *Lib. Fig.*, Pls. XVI, XVII.
52. *Inferno*, xix. 115–17; *Purgatorio*, xvi. 106–12, xxxii. 124–9; *Paradiso*, xx. 58–60.
53. C. T. Davis, 'Dante's Vision of History', *Dante Studies*, xciii (1975), 155.

4

Dante's Reading of Aristotle[1]

LORENZO MINIO-PALUELLO

When considering the presence and impact of Aristotle's works or doctrines in the Latin Middle Ages it is essential to clear one's mind of two common prejudices. The first ascribes a predominant position to the 'Arabs' as having shaped and transmitted to the twelfth–fifteenth centuries a not-so-genuine Aristotle. A threefold claim is made in this connection. (a) Most works of Aristotle came to be known in Latin[2] first of all through versions from Arabic texts often derived from Syriac translations and turned into Latin by Spanish–Jewish and Italian scholars; the products were consequently very far from the Greek originals; misinterpretations due to insufficient knowledge of languages were added to interpretations based on doctrines alien to Aristotle. (b) Eminent philosophers— Persians, Syrians, Turks, Jews, and genuine Arabs—writing in Arabic or other oriental languages had the merit or demerit of presenting as purely Aristotelian their own elaborations or original doctrines. (c) Aristotle was credited with being the author of several non-Aristotelian works preserved in Arabic texts later transmitted to Latin translators and readers. This would be particularly serious in the case of a neo-Platonic treatise on the causal structure of the universe, the *De Causis*,[3] and of an Arabic adaptation of some Plotinian teachings, the *Theologia Aristotelis*.[4] The truth of these matters is rather that (a) a large proportion of Aristotle's actual works were first available and much more permanently studied in translations made directly from the Greek; (b) 'Latin' philosophers of the thirteenth and following centuries distinguished quite clearly between Aristotle on the one hand and al-Kindi, Alfarabi, Avicenna, Maimonides, Averroes, etc. on the other; (c) the more important scholars who used the *De Causis* in their speculations and teachings, did not ascribe it to Aristotle; and (d) the

Theologia Aristotelis left hardly any pseudo-Aristotelian mark on the Latin Aristotelianism of the thirteenth–fifteenth centuries. All this must be kept in mind, particularly when dealing with Dante, because this 'Arabic' bias has been reinforced in modern times by the theory of Dante's possible acquaintance with the legends of Muhammad's ascent to heaven,[5] and by the recognition of Dante's acceptance of Averroistic interpretations of some Aristotelian doctrines.[6]

The second prejudice concerns the medieval Latin translations of Aristotle from the Greek. From the fifteenth century down to our times it has been and is still said that those translations are bad, mainly because they are too literal, and also because the translators did not know enough Greek. But literal translations are not systematically misleading for readers prepared to puzzle out the texts of Aristotle, so often difficult in themselves also in the original language. The reader was forced to learn, in the Latin versions, some features of the Greek tongue, because the structure of individual sentences and the connections between different sentences are likely to preserve in these translations their Greek nature. The terminology remains sometimes Greek, with words transliterated in full or in part, or even transcribed in Greek letters. In other cases transliterations were avoided, but complex Greek words were analysed in their component elements; each element was given a Latin equivalent, the result being a new complex Latin word. Transliteration and creation of new Latin words were used when the translator realized that any Latin term chosen from the existing vocabulary as an approximate equivalent of the Greek, would be misleading or ambiguous: it was better to force the reader to elicit from the context the meaning of a totally new word rather than leading him into pitfalls of ambiguity.

The literal translators, the good ones, followed, within limits, a simplistic philosophy of language (ultimately based on Aristotle's *De Interpretatione* 1–4), according to which things are reflected by law of nature in mental events, identical one by one for all human beings; words, on the other hand, signify, are signs made by human beings, referring to things, and different according to the choice of different men who make or accept them. Translation can consist, then, in using for each word of the original text, as far as possible, a word of the other language, provided that it is a sign for the same thing; if no word is available, then one would accept the foreign word or invent a new one. Other rules presiding over such translations would frequently be the constant use of the same word when the original would carry one and the same word with a not too ambiguous meaning, and the rendering into Latin of every single Greek word even if it appears to be of little or no consequence. Thus, the reader may often have found the Latin diction hard and clumsy. What the medieval translators lacked was the knowledge of many historical and literary aspects of Aristotle's background. Still, it may appear astonishing now how much was properly understood in the Latin texts by people such as Abelard, Albert, Aquinas, etc.; and it is not easy to find passages where scholars like Dante went seriously wrong in their interpretation of Aristotle's meanings on account of the insufficiency of literal translations. They would have probably gone more easily wrong if they had been faced with Latin circumlocutions in which additional words would have suggested concepts and backgrounds alien to Aristotle's intentions or even ability.

The good literal translators of late antiquity and of the Middle Ages were well aware of the difficulties. Boethius in the early sixth century had set a good example for the translators of Aristotle's works.[7] He was quite well trained in Greek and in the various possible ways of communicating to Latin readers the contents of Greek scientific and philosophical works. He had had to face writing in Latin, Greek treatises on arithmetic, geometry, and music, with all the problems posed by technical terminologies. He had even escaped translating treatises on syllogisms by writing his own treatises, partly in an almost pure traditional Latin, partly in a Latin remoulded on the Greek. But when he came to face texts of Aristotle which required detailed word-by-word commentaries, he had hardly any choice but to provide the reader with Latin word-by-word versions of Aristotle's treatises.[8] This was one of the reasons justifying the production of literal versions by the three main medieval translators of the Aristotelian texts which Dante may have had in his hands.

James of Venice,[9] in the first half of the twelfth century, had been an official interpreter at important meetings of Roman and Orthodox theologians in Constantinople, and must have been in touch there with the lively philosophical schools of the 'New Rome'. His translations of some of Aristotle's treatises on logic, natural philosophy, psychology, and metaphysics were at the basis of texts used for several centuries for the study of those subjects. He seems also to have translated and composed literal commentaries on some of those works.

About a century later Robert Grosseteste, bishop of Lincoln, philosopher, theologian, philologist,[10] imported from southern Italy and Greece learned men to teach him Greek and collaborate with him in translating, among other things, Aristotle's *Nicomachean Ethics* and *De Caelo*, and large commentaries on them, written between the third and twelfth centuries. He acquired a considerable lexical knowledge from his collaborators and his own investigations on the nature of the Greek language.

Shortly after Grosseteste's times a Flemish dominican, William of Moerbeke,[11] resided in Greek lands, possibly as a missionary and diplomat, and ended his life as Archbishop of Corinth. He translated with meticulous care all the works of Aristotle which had not yet been translated from the Greek, and revised carefully the other translations of genuine Aristotelian writings; he translated with equal care very extensive commentaries on Plato and Aristotle, all the available treatises of Archimedes, much of Proclus, something of Hippocrates and Galen.

The presence of Aristotle pervades Dante's *Convivio, Monarchia* and *Commedia*[12] in more ways than one: exact quotations of the philosopher's words accompanied by the titles of the relevant single works and the ordinal numbers of what we call 'the books' of those divided in this way; less exact quotations or paraphrastic renderings, with or without precise references but still ascribed to Aristotle; easily recognizable phrases coming from him but appropriated by Dante as expressing his own convictions and acquired points of doctrine; the basic concepts around which much of Aristotle's philosophy turns—'matter' and 'form', 'substance' and 'accident', the four 'causes', 'intellect' and 'senses', 'definition', 'syllogism', 'demonstration', etc.; the Aristotelian structure of logical discourse in several of Dante's own doctrinal argumentations.

If we were to attribute to Dante's direct reading of large sections of Aristotle's writings each passage, phrase, or word which call them to our mind from near or far, we might be tempted to say, with the greatest of English Dante scholars, Edward Moore, that 'Dante was acquainted, and in many cases intimately acquainted, with most of Aristotle's various works; the only important exception to this which occurs to me is the *Poetics*, of which Dante appears to have known nothing.'[13] But Dante's reading of Aristotle may well have been much less extensive than the pervasive presence of some kind of Aristotelian background might suggest.

If we extract from Dante's works the explicit quotations of, and references to, Aristotle—those that form Dante's acknowledged debt to his 'maestro'—and what sound like *direct* echoes of other Aristotelian utterances, we may sketch some kind of picture of what is common to the two of them in a more concrete sense. All this must have come to Dante mainly from his reading, searching and meditating over important sections, even short passages, of Aristotle's work; in part, perhaps, from some systematic collection of views and passages explicitly and reliably ascribed to Aristotle in writings of other philosophers and theologians nearer to Dante's times, or also in the course of lectures and discussions. The sketch might be as follows.

The universe is an integrated, ordered whole consisting of a large number of beings. One supreme being, God, regulates the functions and activities of other constituent beings: he is the highest good, prime mover never in movement, who evokes motions of things through their desire for reaching what is good. God's activity is self-intellection, self-contemplation; he is immaterial, therefore impassible. There are substances intermediate between God and nature, separate from matter, incorruptible; they, or some of them, are movers of celestial spheres which have a perpetual circular motion, and influence our world below, at the centre of the universe. Things of nature, below the sphere of the Moon, have matter and form; matter is potency, potentiality; form is actuality and finality. Movement is the passing from potency to actuality; potency can only pass to actuality through something already actual. Every thing of nature tends to its good, its own actualization. The basic material elements, i.e. earth, water, air and fire tend to their 'natural' place: earth to the centre of the universe, fire to the uppermost regions below the heaven of the moon. Man is matter and form, like all other living beings—indeed, like all beings—below the Moon. The form of man is his soul, which has different powers at different levels: the lowest is the power of self-movement which is present in all living beings; the highest belonging only to human beings, is the intellect which—though a part of the soul qua form of the body—is 'divine' and im-material. Human intellects contemplate universal truths; con-templating is man's aim, his happiness or beatitude. For the achievement of his aim man acquires, through training and choice, the actualization of potential virtues. Each man is by nature an integral part of communities of men, outside which no full achievement of the highest aim is possible; he is a 'political' animal. Almost everything in this sketch proves to come from parts of the *Nicomachean Ethics*, *Metaphysics*, *Physics*, and *De Caelo*.

All the authentic works of Aristotle as we know them now, with the exception of the *Ethica Eudemia* (parts of an early edition of the *Nicomachean Ethics*), the fragmentary *Constitution of the Athenians*, and short fragments from other works, existed in Greek–Latin translations by the time Dante devoted himself to an intensive study of philosophy for two or three years in his late twenties or early thirties. He attended lectures and dis-putations almost certainly at the Dominican convent of Santa Maria Novella, and probably at the Franciscan convent of Santa Croce.

We can form a clear idea of what kind of books[14] Dante may have had in his hands in those and later years, if we look at about twenty manuscripts of the late thirteenth and early four-teenth centuries, which used to be contained in four or five shelves in the library of Santa Croce in Florence and are now in the Laurentian Library.[15] In one of those shelves were kept the books of logic containing mainly Aristotle's writings: *Categories*, *De Interpretatione*, *Prior and Posterior Analytics* (on syllogisms and theory of science), *Topics* (on probable arguments), and *Sophisms*. Three other shelves housed volumes containing mainly Aristotle's works of natural philosophy, which had been organ-ized in one corpus in the middle of the thirteenth century; the more important of these works are: the *Physics* (on the basic general concepts and facts of nature, i.e. movement, change, place, time, vacuum, etc.), *On the Heavens* (about the structure of the visible universe), *On the Soul*, *On Coming to Be and Passing Away*, *Meteorologica* (on phenomena happening between the earth and the heaven of the Moon). In the same volumes which contain these works, or separately from them, one would find the *Metaphysics*, the books *on Animals*, the *Nicomachean Ethics*, *Politics*, and *Rhetoric*. Five of the Santa Croce volumes would, between them, contain all the works of Aristotle except the *Poetics*. The books *on Animals* would appear in them only in the Arabic–Latin version; the books *On the Heavens, Meteorologica* (Books I–III), and eleven books of the *Metaphysics* would appear in both Arabic–Latin and Greek–Latin translations; all the other works only in Greek–Latin versions.

It is impossible to say confidently which works of Aristotle contained in volumes of this or some other kind were read by Dante in full or in part. It could be suggested that the accuracy, number, and extent of his quotations are indicative of his reading. If this is so, there can be no doubt that he must have had a direct knowledge of much if not the whole of the *Nicomachean Ethics*—'la tua Etica' as Virgil calls it addressing Dante.[16] Not less than forty times Dante quotes or refers to it, adding to the title the ordinal number of the 'book' in which the relevant passages occur; quotations are taken from each of the ten 'books'; and in about a hundred other cases Dante's knowledge of this or that passage of the *Nichomachean Ethics* is clearly suggested by his words. In all instances in which more than one version of the *Ethics* exist, it is clear that Dante used that made by Robert Grosseteste.

Similarly, exact references to the *Physics*—'la tua Fisica'[17]— in sixteen passages taken from six out of the eight 'books' might show some familiarity with the actual text of the Greek–Latin translation by James of Venice. The same could be said, but in a more restricted sense, for 'books' one and two of the *Metaphysics* and *De Caelo*, and for the *De Anima*. It is, however, difficult to find any such evidence for the other works of Aristotle.

It is particularly strange that Dante never gives a 'book' reference in the seven times when he quotes explicitly the *Politics*, and in the other dozen times when he refers implicitly to it. A detailed study of all these references[18] has shown that the majority of them could, or do in fact, come from identifiable intermediate sources. The case for the *Meteorologica* is even worse. According to Moore this work is at the basis of about twenty passages of Dante,[19] but the very title of the work is never mentioned, let alone the particular 'book'. Dante gives once a specific reference to Albertus Magnus' *Meteora*, and a second time a reference to '*Meteora*' without mentioning any author: a comparison between Dante's words and those of Aristotle and Albertus suggests that, once more, Dante was using Albertus, not Aristotle.[20] It is also difficult to find through explicit quotations whether Dante had read any part of the very long nineteen books *De Animalibus*. Only twice does he refer to them, both times by the general title. This suggests that Dante derived his two references directly or indirectly from Michael Scot's translation from the Arabic (the translation from the Greek, like most of the Greek manuscripts, divides the whole work into three sections under different titles). That this is the case is confirmed by the fact that one imprecise reference would have been to 'book two of *De Partibus Animalium*'. of the Greek–Latin translation by William of Moerbeke, the reference would have been to 'book two of *De Partibus Animalium*' Many connections between Dante and Aristotle for the zoological works indicated by Moore (pp. 337–8) are too vague for establishing Dante's precise source. But *Purgatorio* xxv, where Statius expounds to Dante the theory of human generation, gives abundant evidence that Dante had detailed knowledge coming from the last chapters of *De Generatione Animalium*, Book I, and Book II, chapter 1. Book III of the same work and Book V, chapter 19 of *De Historia Animalium* provided Dante with the knowledge of Aristotle's theory of spontaneous generation. The terminology used by Dante makes it clear that he had found it, directly or indirectly, in William of Moerbeke's version from the Greek.[22]

With one minor exception—five words quoted from Boethius' translation of *De Sophisticis Elenchis*[23]—Dante never mentions Aristotle's name or exact titles of works when he uses concepts or procedures coming from the Philosopher's logical and epistemological works. In one place he refers to a work *De Syllogismis Simpliciter*;[24] this, however, suggests Boethius' own *De Syllogismis Categoricis* rather than Aristotle's *Analytica Priora*. Somewhere else he mentions a *Doctrina Praedicamentorum*; what he says there derives *somehow* from Aristotle's *Categories*,[25] but, once more, the form of reference suggests that the passage came to him not directly from that text but from some scholastic textbook.

In *Monarchia* there is plenty of evidence that Dante was quite skilled in the use of Aristotelian syllogistic forms and rules of argument. This is what he could have learnt in the course of logical studies at an elementary level. In the heaven of the Sun, among the 'spiriti sapienti', Dante is shown the 'light' of Pietro Ispano who still shines below (on earth) 'in dodici libelli'.[26]

Peter of Spain, the future Pope John XXI, had written, in the middle of the thirteenth century, what was to be for three centuries at least the most popular summary of logic, *Summulae Logicales*, divided into twelve short 'libri' containing what was considered essential in Aristotle's works of logic and in the more modern developments of that art. Dante's knowledge of logic covered a certain amount of the same field, echoing more than once the non-Aristotelian chapters of Peter's *Summulae*.

Dante never mentions names of authors or titles of books which were his indirect sources for the knowledge of Aristotle. In the course of the last hundred years it has been made clear that some Aristotelian notions had come to him from the vast collection of Albertus Magnus' encyclopedic works. This may be particularly true for Dante's knowledge of notions coming from *Meteorologica*, *De Caelo*, and *De Animalibus*, for which Dante would have found Albertus Magnus more readable than Aristotle himself. It may be significant that precisely these works were those which survived quite a long time in the Arabic-Latin versions, even after the more reliable translations from the Greek by William of Moerbeke. Again, convincing parallels can be established between Dante and Aquinas' account of Aristotelian views in the fields covered by *De Anima*, *Physics*, *Metaphysics*, and *Politics*. Some remarkable coincidences point to Giles of Rome's *De Regimine Principum* as Dante's source of knowledge for the *Politics*.[27]

No less important sources of Dante's knowledge of Aristotle may well have been his listening to teachers, attending philosophical and theological discussion, and exchanges with friends. In Circle vii, Round 3 of Hell, Dante recognizes in the features and words of Brunetto Latini

> la cara e buona imagine paterna
> di voi, quando nel mondo ad ora ad ora
> m'insegnavate come l'uom s' etterna.

Brunetto's last words to Dante, his 'figliolo', recommend to him 'il mio *Tesoro*, nel quale io vivo ancora'.[28] Brunetto's teaching, in the early eighties, of 'how man makes himself eternal', could hardly have been different from that offered by the first part of book II of his *Trésor*.[29] Brunetto starts there by saying that he is now giving the foundation of a doctrine leading to the knowledge of the highest gem of his treasure, 'the most virtuous and beautiful thing that human eye can see'. This foundation will be, Brunetto says, Aristotle's book which he 'translata de Latin en Romançe'. He goes on:

Here begins the Ethics, book of Aristotle.—All art and all doctrine and all activity aims at some good: therefore the Philosopher says well that all things desire the good. . . . There are two kinds of goods: good for itself and good for something else. Good for itself is beatitude which is the end at which we aim. Goods for something else are honours and virtues; and these are desired by man in order to obtain beatitude. . . . It is a natural thing for men to be citizens, and it would be against nature to inhabit deserts, because man, by nature, enjoys company. Beatitude is a complete, perfect thing which does not require anything beyond itself: it is the greatest good of all (la plus soveraine chose et la trés millour de tous les biens qui soient).

It would be difficult to imagine a simpler and neater summary of Dante's Aristotelian ideal than this beginning of Brunetto's 'version' of Aristotle's *Ethica Nicomachea*.

What Brunetto translated into French in fifty or so pages of 'Aristotle' was in fact mainly the *Compendium Alexandrinum* of each of the ten books of the *Nicomachean Ethics*,[30] perhaps composed in Greek at some stage before the seventh century, rendered into Arabic a couple of centuries later, and, from that, into Latin in A.D. 1244. Brunetto may have found the Latin text of this *Compendium* in France and made it part of his vocational trade to translate it during the few years of his exile there. On his return to Florence around the time of Dante's birth he may have kept it as his guide when he had the chance of initiating into a life of intellectual beatitude some promising youth. When Dante, in the middle of the nineties, being already thirty years of age, listened to the appeal of 'Donna Filosofia', he probably had already absorbed and stored from the *Compendium Alexandrinum* of Brunetto Latini what was to be the basis of his philosophical vocation and devotion to Aristotle, 'maestro della nostra vita'.[31]

The most likely philosopher whom Dante must have heard lecturing and discussing such matters in the nineties was Remigio de Girolami.[32] He was for several decades, from 1277 to his death in 1319, a 'lector' in philosophy and theology at the Dominican Convent of Santa Maria Novella. In fact, he was the only real philosopher professing in Florence in those years, whose name and works have reached us. He had studied in Paris at the time of Aquinas' activity there, and left many short and long philosophico-theological works, among them a very short introduction to the study of the *Nicomachean Ethics*.

At the time of Dante's exile, Remigio had just written or was preparing a tract *De Bono Communi* condemning the moral decay of Florence.[33] In the thirty-odd pages of this tract he quotes not less than twenty-four times the *Nicomachean Ethics*, five times each the *Politics*, *Physics*, and *De Anima*, and four times the *Metaphysics*. In the second chapter he quotes the *Nicomachean Ethics* in support of the view that the individual may have to die for his country ('gratia patrie mori');[34] in *Monarchia* II. vii. 2 Dante says that from Aristotle it is clear that 'homo pro patria debet exponere se ipsum'. A few lines before, Remigio had quoted word for word a passage from the *Ethics*[35] to the effect that, when something is good for one man and good for the city, it is 'better and more divine' to obtain and protect that good for 'gens et civitates'. Exactly the same passage is quoted by Dante a few lines after he had said that life must be risked for one's country.[36]

A few years later, when Dante was presumably writing the *Convivio* and preparing the *Monarchia*, Remigio wrote a very short tract *De Bono Pacis*,[37] where he leans strongly on Aristotle's *Nicomachean Ethics* and *Politics*, both of which he quotes several times. In this tract Remigio builds on Aristotle's concepts of man as a 'political animal', of 'operatio' rather than 'speculatio' as the proper 'finis' of politics, of self-sufficiency as an essential aim of the state, of community welfare being superior to the welfare of individuals. Each of these Aristotelian concepts are Dante's as much as Remigio's.[38] How much more may have come to Dante from Aristotle through the teaching and extensive, still unpublished, works of Remigio and through discussions with him?

In the *Convivio*, Aristotle is for Dante not only 'il maestro di color che sanno', as in the *Inferno* iv. 131; he is also 'il maestro e duca dell' umana ragione, degnissimo di fede e di obbedienza'.[39] But Dante's faith is not always unqualified or clear. For instance when he asserts that the Earth is unmovable, he hints at the possibility that knowledgeable people might expect some proofs; he does not give any: Aristotle's view must be accepted without discussion 'per la sua grande autorità';[40] but this is so only because 'la gente a cui parlo' are the 'illiterate' for whom the *Convivio* is written.[41] It is these, in this case, who must have 'fede e obbedienza'; what about the 'literate'?

Dante, no doubt, introduces most of his clear quotations by 'siccome dice Aristotele', 'secondo il Filosofo', 'Aristotele ammaestra', 'prova', 'disprova', 'vuole', etc., and the Latin equivalents. But it is not rare to find Dante saying 'il Filosofo *pare* dicere', 'pare sentire' ('*seems* to say, to think'), as when he enlists Aristotle's approval for the view that the tenth Heaven, the 'Empireo', is the heaven of the 'spiriti beati, secondo che la Chiesa vuole che non può dir menzogna, ed Aristotele pare ciò sentire a chi ben lo intende, nel primo *Di Cielo e Mondo*':[42] Aristotle is in fact speaking of one heaven only and he has no 'spiriti beati'. Here Dante shows faith in and obedience to the Church 'which cannot lie', but not so unreservedly in and to Aristotle 'who seems to think'. Elsewhere Dante says that a passage of the *Politics*[43] 'innotescit', 'becomes clear' from what he, Dante himself, has presented as a basis of Monarchia, i.e. the practical activity of the intellect. The words of Aristotle paraphrased by Dante are in fact far from meaning what Dante expects: in this case Dante has faith in himself before granting it to Aristotle. Dante's attitude to Aristotle can become even more extreme, as when he condemns him for following the ancient stupidity, 'l'antica grossezza', of the astrologers, and for believing as true 'la erronea sentenza che può vedere chi vuole' in *De Caelo* III, to the effect that, in the order of the universe, the Heaven of the Sun follows immediately after the Heaven of the Moon.[44]

An inquiry into what Dante read in Aristotle and used for his own aims would be more important than going through the variations on the theme of 'fede e obbedienza'. This inquiry would take us very far: we shall give two examples.

With the two exceptions already mentioned, Dante does not cite any titles of Aristotle's works, or give Aristotle as his authority for statements or explanations in the *Commedia*. In some cases it seems obvious that, had he written in prose instead of poetry, he would have acknowledged openly his debts: a case in point concerns the theory of language. In the eighth heaven Adam gives some satisfaction to Dante who wants to know what language he (Adam) had made and used. In the course of his answer[45] Adam gives Dante a quick lesson on the nature of human language, basing himself on a few words of the latinized Aristotle. In the *Politics*[46] Aristotle says that nature has given man the power of speaking ('sermo') in order for him to express what is useful or harmful, just or unjust. In the *De Interpretatione*[47] Aristotle says that nouns, verbs, sentences, etc. are 'significant' and (according to Boethius' translation) 'secundum placitum'. Whatever the exact meaning of the Greek word translated by 'placitum', it is clear, both in Greek and in Latin that words are *made* by human beings. The Latin word 'placitum' was interpreted in various ways, but it is obvious that it could be translated by 'giving pleasure'. Dante may have known the *De Interpretatione*, but he would have found the relevant phrases in any elementary text of logic. It is also possible but by no means certain that he knew directly Aristotle's statement in the *Politics*. It is, however, clear that he had read, directly or indirectly, absorbed, and repeated in *Paradiso* xxvi those notions from a short passage in Giles of Rome's *De Regimine Principum*.[48] After referring explicitly to the *De Interpretatione* and to the *Politics*, Giles draws the inference that 'loqui est naturale', but ('autem') speaking in this or that way ('sic vel sic') is 'secundum placitum'. Dante translates literally from Giles's text: 'naturale è ch'uom favella,—ma, così o così, secondo che v'abbella' ('according to your liking, taste, pleasure'). But neither Aristotle, nor Boethius in his translation and commentaries, nor Giles in his treatise had added, in connection with 'pleasure', the concept of mutability, historical transformation, of language. Dante says that pleasure makes language 'new and new again in the course of time' ('seguendo il cielo'), and he gives the cause of this mutability: language is a product of reason ('effetto razionabile'), and human pleasure interferes with all products of reason in that it does not allow them to be permanent for all time:

> ... nullo effetto razionabile,
> per lo piacere uman che rinnovella
> seguendo il cielo, sempre fu durabile.
>
> (*Par.* xxvi. 127–9)

The reader who recognized the genuinely Aristotelian elements in these lines might well have ascribed to Aristotle also the historical, temporal mutability due to the nature of pleasure which accompanies the rational character of human free will. If Dante had not known Boethius' translation of the Greek term 'syntheke' but the more literal and more exact translation by William of Moerbeke, 'confictio',[49] he would not have found in the important passages of the *De Interpretatione* any mention of 'pleasure'.

Writing the *Monarchia* Dante reserved for himself the onus and glory of widening beyond the Aristotelian boundaries the philosophical field of knowledge: he was thus bringing out of the darkness the 'notitia utilissima' of temporal monarchy, the universal Empire.[50] But he did not, in fact, exclude Aristotle from contributing to the accomplishment of this task. When, in *Convivio* IV. iv, Dante was laying the basis of his new science, he borrowed from the Philosopher some of the foundation stones on which to raise his edifice.

'The roots of imperial majesty', Dante says, 'lie in the need of the "umana civilitade" which is ordered to one end: "happy life".' 'Civilitade'—which is not properly translated by 'civiltà', 'civilization'—is a word which Dante would have found, e.g. in the *Nicomachean Ethics*, in the sense of 'political organization', for the Greek 'politeia'.[51] 'Order to one end' is the Aristotelian basic concept for the structure of compound things or activities, on which stands the doctrine of forms as achievements, actualizations of what is in potency for each being and combination all along the ladder of beings to include the whole universe. 'Happy life' is, in Aristotle's view, what we are here for.

Dante proceeds with the Aristotelian definition of man in the *Ethics* and *Politics*: 'e però dice il Filosofo che l'uomo naturalmente è compagnevole animale'[52] ('man by nature requires company'). It is man's nature, Dante goes on, that he is led to wider and wider associations: home or family, clan, city, as Aristotle details in his *Politics*, and 'regnum'. But for Dante this progress to wider communities cannot stop as long as peace is not achieved, and this requires overcoming greed of property, which in its turn cannot stop as long as property is divided.[53] In this, Dante is no longer following Aristotle, but he does not say so; his exposition of this doctrine proceeds smoothly as if he was continuing his faithful copy of the Aristotelian plan. Only when he has dwelt a little longer on the necessity of having one owner of all possible property in the world, and on the consequent universal peace under 'uno principe in uno solo principato', does Dante give a hint that he has added something new to Aristotle's teaching. Just a hint though, because Dante says, in fact, that his argument is implicit in Aristotle's own words: 'a queste ragioni si possono reducere le parole del Filosofo ch'egli nella *Politica* dice', i.e. 'when more things are ordered to one single end, one of these things must be regulating or ruling, all the others ruled or regulated by it.'[54]

Dante's quotation, however, does not come from the *Politics* itself. It was taken by him, without acknowledgments, from the first four lines of Aquinas' prologue to his commentary on Aristotle's *Metaphysics*. Aquinas did not intend there to quote Aristotle's own words, as Dante did, but Aristotle's teaching: 'sicut *docet* Philosophus in *Politicis* suis'. And, what is more important, Aquinas was not referring here to the *Politics* for politics' sake, but for an analogy between this and metaphysics. In that prologue to Aristotle's *Metaphysics* he wanted to show that all sciences, not all human beings, are ordered to one end, 'humana beatitudo'; sciences—not men—form here one whole body of human knowledge, and there must be one of them which dominates all other sciences. This science is metaphysics, because science, any science, is primarily concerned with causes, and metaphysics is concerned with *first* causes. Aquinas also finds that metaphysics is, more than all other sciences, concerned with knowledge acquired by intellect rather than by senses, and that it is intellectual knowledge that leads men to 'beatitudo'. While Aquinas had found something in the text of the *Politics* that could be applied to his argument in favour of metaphysics, and elaborated Aristotle's words to fit his aim,

Dante took Aquinas' elaboration as being a literal quotation fit to promote his exalted view of a political organization which leads in its way to 'beatitudo' for the whole human race.

That quotation alone was not sufficient for Aquinas to go beyond a generic superiority of metaphysics over all other sciences. He also found in Aristotle's *Politics*[55] another passage which, properly reshaped, provided him with the Philosopher's support for the view that intellect has the dominating *vigour* required for metaphysics to rule over all other sciences. Here again—in Aquinas' prologue to his commentary on the *Metaphysics*, not directly in the text of Aristotle's *Politics*—Dante finds the Aristotelian key to the intellect's function, not in metaphysics but in the monarchy.[56] In William of Moerbeke's translation, the relevant Aristotelian passage reads: 'Quod quidem enim potest mente previdere principans natura et dominans natura . . .'. Aquinas quotes it after transforming it: 'quod potest' becomes 'homines vigentes'; 'mente previdere' becomes 'intellectu'; 'principans' and 'dominans' become 'rectores' and 'domini'. Dante repeats Aquinas' 'homines intellectu vigentes'. At one point, however, Dante had to part company with Aquinas. For the latter the essential feature of 'intellectus' is its being the instrument for the knowledge of universals, which transcends the knowledge provided by the senses; but Dante at this moment is concerned with politics which all along deal with particulars, and he must pass from the main feature of 'intellectus' to its commitment in this other direction, without endangering the 'oneness' of this part of the soul. In this he is helped by a formula, common in his time ('solet dici'), partly based on a misreading of a Greek word ('epitathentos' instead of 'epitattontos') :[57] 'speculative intellect *by extension* becomes practical'. There is no danger of a duality of intellects if one and the same speculative intellect extends into a practical, and consequently particularized function.

In the same chapter[58] Dante had just referred to Averroes' commentary on Aristotle's *De Anima* as the authority for the doctrine of the unity and uniqueness of the human intellect, a doctrine which was regarded as scandalous by such people as Albertus Magnus and Aquinas. It was on this doctrine that Dante based the claim for the unity and uniqueness of the Empire, the ruling power over the whole human race, the 'universitas humana'. But Aristotle had provided, with the *De Anima*, the starting-point for this doctrine.

Thus 'Aristotle' appears to accompany and inspire Dante, offering him the tools necessary for building his new theory. Would those readers of the *Monarchia* who were not experienced in Aristotle's philosophy, realize that he was in fact very far indeed from conceiving or supporting that theory?

Four chapters further on, Dante, who had read the first lines of Aquinas' *Commentary on Aristotle's Metaphysics*, shows that he also knew the very last lines of the *Metaphysics* as it stood in a number of manuscripts, including the one used by Aquinas for his commentary, and two of the three in the Santa Croce collection mentioned above, i.e. lacking the last two books.[59] In that section Aristotle concludes his excursion through the grand, magnificently ordered universe in which the First Mover regulates and provokes the movements of every thing. At that highest of levels there must be, Aristotle says, one principle only, if the universe is to enjoy a good rule. Beings, 'entia', do not want to be badly treated and organized, but multiplicity of principles, of 'principalities', is not good: there must be 'unus princeps'. Aristotle uses the metaphor of a man who rules over a society of human beings, whatever its level and size, and transfers the validity of this rule to God, first principle, first and only Ruler. Aquinas stresses Aristotle's 'theological' view of this principle: 'unus princeps *totius universi*, scilicet primum movens et primum intelligibile et primum bonum, quod Aristoteles supra dixit Deum'. For Dante this last Aristotelian simile reverts to its original and literal meaning: the 'princeps' is a man, the Emperor; the 'universe of beings' which do not want to be badly ruled is a universe of *human* beings. Thus, that man and this 'universe' are vested with a quasi-divine dignity in the political field by Dante's adoption of Aristotle's metaphysical concepts.

With these adoptions and adaptations we see Dante at work with Aristotle's texts, in a pure or derivative form, in order to lead the reader to the highest levels of philosophy, now endowed with the new realm, the Monarchy, revealed by reason's inquiry. In doing this Dante shows that he read not only Aristotle and *in* Aristotle, but also *into* Aristotle.

NOTES

1. For a survey of Dante's knowledge of Aristotle see Edward Moore, *Studies in Dante*, 1st Ser. (Clarendon Press, Oxford, 1896, repr. 1969), pp. 92–156, 334–43, 359–94. See also Bruno Nardi, *Saggi di filosofia dantesca*, 2nd edn. (Florence, 1967); *Dante e la cultura medievale* (Bari, 1942); *Nel mondo di Dante* (Rome, 1944); *Dal Convivio alla Commedia* (Rome, 1960); *Saggi e note di critica dantesca* (Milan–Naples, 1966). For the Latin Aristotle of the Middle Ages see George Lacombe *et al.*, *Aristoteles Latinus, Codices*, 3 vols. (Rome, 1939; Cambridge, 1955; Bruges, 1961), and editions of texts by various editors: vols. i–vi, xi, xvii. 2, xxv. 1–2, xxvi, xxvii. 1, xxxii, xxxiii (Bruges, Leiden, 1961–78). See also Martin Grabmann, *Mittelalterliches Geistesleben*, vol. iii (Munich, 1956), pp. 50–219, and L. Minio-Paluello, *Opuscula: the Latin Aristotle* (Amsterdam, 1972).

2. The remarks which follow refer to Aristotle's texts; it remains true that the 'Arabs' contributed extensively in the twelfth and thirteenth centuries to the general interest in Aristotle and knowledge of some of his doctrines among the 'Latins'.

3. See O. Bardenhewer, *Die Pseudo-aristotelische Schrift über das reine Gute bekannt unter dem Namen Liber de Causis* (Freiburg, 1882).

4. See 'Plotiniana Arabica' (in English translation by Geoffrey Lewis) in *Plotini Opera*, edd. P. Henry and H.-R. Schwyzer, vol.. ii (Paris–Brussels, 1959).

5. See M. Asín Palacios, *La escatologia musulmana en la Divina Comédia* (Madrid, 1919; 2nd edn. 1943); and E. Cerulli, *Il 'Libro della Scala' e la questione delle fonti arabo-spagnole della 'Divina Commedia'* (Vatican City, 1949).

6. e.g. the doctrine of the 'intellectus possibilis' in *Monarchia*, I. iv. 7–9.

7. See his translations of *Categoriae, De interpretatione, Analytica Priora, Topica*, and *De elenchis sophisticis* in *Arist. Lat.*, texts, vols. i–iii, v–vi.

8. Cf. Boethius' translations of *Cat.* and *De int.* with his commentaries on them (*P.L.*, vol. lxiv, and, for the second, ed. Meiser, Leipzig, 1877–80).

9. See L. Minio-Paluello, 'Iacobus Veneticus Grecus, Canonist and Translator of Aristotle', *Traditio* viii (1952), 265–304 (also in *Opusc.* (cit.), pp. 189–228).

10. See E. Franceschini, 'Roberto Grossatesta e le sue traduzioni latine', *Atti del R. Istit. Ven. di Sc., Lett. ed Arti* xcviii (1933), pp. 1–138; and Grosseteste's translation of the *Nicomachean Ethics* in *Artist. Lat.*, texts, vol. xxvi. 3.

11. See M. Grabmann, *Guglielmo di Moerbeke O.P., il traduttore delle opere d'Aristotele* (Rome, 1946), and M. Clagett, *Archimedes in the Middle Ages*, ii. 1 (Philadelphia, 1976), pp. 3–73; also his translations of *Cat., De int., Post. Anal. El. Soph., Gen. Anim., Pol. Imp., Rhet.*, and *Poetics* in *Arist. Lat.*, texts, vols. i, ii, iv, vi, xvii, xxix, xxxi, xxxiii.

12. See Moore, pp. 334–43.

13. Ibid., p. 93.

14. No adequate study of the possible connections of some of these manuscripts with Dante seems to have been carried out. Cf. C. T. Davis, 'The Early Collection of Books of S. Croce in Florence' in *Proc. of the Amer. Philos. Soc.* cvii (1963), 399–414, where no Aristotelian manuscript of the thirteenth century is recorded as having been in that library.
15. Cf. *Arist. Lat., Codd.* ii. 931–48.
16. *Inferno*, xi. 80.
17. Ibid. xi. 101.
18. Allan H. Gilbert, 'Had Dante Read the *Politics* of Aristotle?', *Publications of the Modern Language Association of America*, xliii. 3 (1928), 602–13.
19. Moore, pp. 335–6.
20. Ibid., p. 13.
21. *Convivio*, II. viii. 10.
22. See L. Minio-Paluello, '*Antomata* (*Purg.* x. 128) e i testi latini della biologia di Aristotele', *Studi danteschi* l=50 (1973), 111–50.
23. *Mon.* III. iv. 4; *El. Soph.* xviii, 176^{b}29.
24. *Mon.* III. vii. 3.
25. Ibid. III. xiv. 9.
26. *Paradiso* xii. 134–5.
27. See p. 73
28. *Inf.* xv. 23–124 (especially 83–5, 119–20).
29. *Li Livres dou Trésor de Brunetto Latini*, ed. F. J. Carmody (Berkeley and Los Angeles, 1948); cf. ii. 2–5, pp. 176–8.
30. See C. Marchesi, *L'Etica Nicomachea nella tradizione latina medievale* (Messina, 1904), and 'Il compendio volgare dell'*Etica* aristotelica e le fonti del vi libro del *Trésor*', *Giornale storico della letteratura italiana*, xlii (1903), 1–74.
31. *Conv.* IV. xxiii. 8.
32. See L. Minio-Paluello, 'Remigio Girolami's *De Bono Communi* . . .', *Italian Studies* xi (1956), 56–71; C. T. Davis, 'Remigio de' Girolami and Dante: a Comparison of the Conception of Peace', *Studi danteschi* xxxvi (1959), 105–36, and 'An Early Political Theorist: Fra Remigio de' Girolami' in *Proc. of the Amer. Philos. Soc.* civ. 6 (1960), 662–76.
33. MS. Florence, Bibl. Nazion. Centr., Conv. Soppr. C.4.940, fos. 97r–106v. Cf. M. Grabmann, 'Die italienische Thomistenschule des xiii und beginnenden xiv Jahrhunderts', in *Mittelalt. Geistesl.* i (Munich 1926), 361–9.
34. *Eth. Nicom.* IX. viii, 1169^{a}17–19.
35. Ibid., I. i, 1094^{b}9–10.
36. *Mon.* II. vii. 3.
37. See above, n. 32.
38. Cf. C. T. Davis, 'Remigio . . . Conception of Peace', p. 110.
39. *Conv.* IV. vi. 8.
40. Ibid. III. v. 7.
41. Ibid. I. vii. 12.
42. Ibid. II. iii. 10.

43. *Mon.* I. iii. 10.
44. *Conv.* II. iii. 3.
45. *Par.* xxvi. 124–8.
46. I. ii, 1253^{a}9–18.
47. ii, 16^{a}19, 27; iv, 17^{a}2.
48. Ed. princ. 'sine loco', 1473, III. ii. 24; Italian version of 1288, published in Florence, 1858, III. ii. 20.
49. See Moerbeke's text in *Arist. Lat.* ii. 41–3.
50. *Mon.* I. i. 5.
51. II. i, 1103^{b}6, III. v, 1113^{a}8.
52. *Pol.* I. ii, 1252^{b}13, 1253^{a}3, 28–30.
53. *Conv.* IV. iv. 4–5.
54. *Pol.* I. v, 1254^{a}28.
55. Ibid. I. ii, 1252^{a}31–3.
56. *Mon.* I. iii. 10.
57. *De Anima* III. ix, 433^{a}1; cf. L. Minio-Paluello, 'Tre note alla *Monarchia*' in *Medioevo e Rinascimento . . . in onore di Bruno Nardi* (Florence, 1955), pp. 277–85.
58. *Mon.* I. iii. 6–9.
59. Ibid. I. x. 5–6; *Metaph.* XII. x, 1076^{a}3–4.

5

Dante's Reading of the Latin Poets and the Structure of the *Commedia*

ALAN ROBSON

Dante's attraction to the late classical world, his oft-expressed love and reverence for the heroes and scholars and poets of the late republic and early empire—Cato, Cicero, Virgil, Statius—is one of the most vital elements found in his work. His yearning for the past is Petrarchan in spirit, although his technique and his achievement are curiously different. Dante's classical learning, circumscribed as it is by the tastes of the mid-thirteenth century, which he inherited in full measure, and by the intensity and narrowness of his philosophic interests, is none the less unique in his own age. For Dante as for Petrarch the sense of the Roman past was bred in the bone. With his idealization of the shallow urban culture of Florence, he felt the old family tales 'of the Trojans, of Fiesole, and of Rome', which the good wife told as she laid her hands to the spindle and her hands held the distaff, to be his inalienable heritage, a tenuous, unbroken link with a fabulous past.

Even if Dante had never written the *Commedia*, we should still remember him among the earliest pre-humanists, men like Lovato de' Lovati who sought to reassemble the scattered remains of scholarship. His fascination for the Roman Empire led him to Virgil and Lucan; his love of ethics to Cicero; his neo-Platonist and Averroist cosmology to Ovid's *Metamorphoses*, which he was almost the first to allegorize systematically, before the *Ovide moralisé* and the *Fulgentius metaforalis*. Greek mythology, available in endless profusion in the pages of Ovid, became one of the main structural elements in the *Commedia*: and Dante's riddling epigrammatic style, with its circumlocutions and suppressions of proper names, is probably due to the influence of Hellenistic techniques exemplified by both Ovid and Statius.

Renucci made the important observation that *Convivio* and

De Vulgari Eloquentia, both begun and left unfinished in the early
years of Dante's exile, appeal to the authority of the four Latin
poets, each represented by a single book: Virgil's *Aeneid*,
'Ovidius major', the *Metamorphoses*, Statius' *Thebaid*, and
Lucan's *Pharsalia*. The final schematic account of the Four
Ages of Man, in *Convivio* IV. xxiv–viii (see Table I), is built
round blocks of quotations from these books: Statius, Book i,
illustrates the virtues of awe and reverence, modesty and the
sense of shame at wrong-doing which are appropriate to
adolescence; Virgil's hero, Aeneas, provides instances of the
duties of early manhood ('youth'); the character of Aeacus, in
Ovid's Book vii, fulfils the duties of maturity ('old age'); and
the episode of Cato and Martia in Lucan, Book ii, symbolizes
the return of the soul to God in man's declining years. The same
four appear as the *regulatos poetas* of *De Vulgari Eloquentia*, ii. 6.
These four works were the prescribed books of the Bologna arts
syllabus.[1] Although Dante may well have had contacts with
Bologna in the 1290s, in the days of Taddeo Alderotti (cf. *Par.*
xii. 83) and Dino del Garbo, who commented on Cavalcanti,
there are sound reasons for believing that Dante deepened his
knowledge of the classics by following the arts course in
Bologna in the early, optimistic days of the *fuorusciti*, and that
he might even have equipped himself to become a teacher of
versification and the *auctores*. This would make it easier to
understand why Giovanni del Virgilio, who was teaching the
same books in the year of Dante's death, had urged him to
return to Bologna and receive a kind of honorary degree in
front of his pupils:

> promere gymnasiis te delectabor ovantum,
> inclita Peneis redolentem tempora sertis.
>
> *Ecl.* i. 37–8

Starting out from his thirteenth-century background,
inherited from Brunetto Latini and the Bolognese arts teachers,
we see Dante gradually transforming this scholastic culture of
auctoritates and *exempla* by his personal study of Ovid, and then
by a systematic excerpting of Virgil, Ovid, Statius, and Lucan.
The poetic images—between 120 and 144 in number—which
he culled from the forty-eight books of the four poets (*Aeneid*,
Books i–xii, *Thebaid*, Books i–xii, *Pharsalia*, books i–ix, omitting

Book x, and 'Ovidius major', Books i–xv) were combined and regrouped to form the scaffolding of the *Commedia*.

The excerpts which he embodied in his greatest work were not simply *auctoritates*, or 'tags', although each retains enough verbal similarity with the source to enable it to be unequivocally identified; they form part of a continuous cycle illustrating the Greek myths of the gods and heroes, the story of Thebes, Troy, and Rome, and the geography of the Augustan Empire. Above all, they were *imagines*, in the sense defined by Frances A. Yates, of the kind cultivated by the exponents of the artificial memory as developed and applied to ethical teaching by Albertus Magnus and his successors at Bologna in the mid-thirteenth century.

The remains of this preparatory work are still to be descried in the text of the poem: the classical *imagines* are still contained in only sixty of the cantos, the remaining forty cantos being in this special sense 'non-classical'. But Dante did not even compose the whole of the 'classical' cantos in the first place: he appears to have begun by embodying the excerpts from Virgil and Ovid, already arranged in a triadic system, in passages of 36–48 lines, sometimes adding further allusions to Statius and Lucan—and it is these passages which form the nucleus of the entire work. Some of them survive intact in the later cantos (xii–xxxiii) of both the *Inferno* and the *Purgatorio*; examples are quoted and discussed below. But the triadic system only allowed for thirty such passages, and many of these were broken up and combined with other material, so that the nucleus is now distributed over the sixty 'classical' cantos. The examination of this small corpus of poetry, saturated with images of the Latin poets, throws some light on problems such as the organization of the sins in the *Inferno*, but raises further problems about the development of the *Paradiso*, where the poet has largely expanded, if not wholly abandoned, the original classical frame.

II

Dante's familiarity with a wealth of quotations and anecdotes from classical literature is very striking; his continual use of *auctoritates* enables us to trace the gradual maturing of his knowledge of classical poetry, and at the same time initiates us into an aesthetic technique by which large bodies of quotations, arranged in an intricately interwoven pattern, like the rhymes of a medieval lyric, are used by the poet to form the groundwork of entire sections of the *Commedia*.

References to the text of Ovid were often suggested by the prose summaries of Lactantius Placidus: thus, in *Monarchia* there are scarcely any verbal citations of Ovid, and when Dante quotes two separate lines of Ovid, Book iv:

> Coctilibus muris cinxisse Semiramis urbem
>
> iv. 58

and

> Conveniant ad busta Nini, lateantque sub umbra
>
> iv. 88

this use of the fable of Pyramus and Thisbe as an allusion to the Assyrian empire is based on the summary, which covers nearly forty lines (55–92) in a few words:

Pyramus et Thisbe urbis Babyloniae, quam Semiramis regina muro cinxerat, et aetate et forma pares, cum in propinquo habitarent, rima parietis et colloqui et amoris initia inter se pignerati sunt. Constituerunt itaque, ut a matutino ad monumentum Nini regis sub arborem morum convenirent ad amorem perficiendum.

This was associated in Dante's mind with the chapter on Ninus and Semiramis in Orosius, I. iv, which he also cites in *Inf.* v. 52–9.

In many cases Dante's tags are taken from intermediate sources, and reflect the medieval habit of using the classics as a quarry for maxims and moral stories. Excerpts from the classics and scripture were assembled into compilations to illustrate the virtues and vices. Brunetto Latini's *Tresor* contains a great wealth of citations on moral topics, borrowed from works such as the *Moralium Dogma* of William of Conches, the *Summa Aurea* of Peraldus and the *Ars Loquendi* of Albertano of Brescia. These compilations ranged very widely and included citations from Terence, Juvenal, Horace, Seneca, and the Latin Fathers, which are very rare in Dante. It seems that Dante gradually moved away from the heterogeneous miscellany of quotations towards a more disciplined use of a few books he knew well: a

few treatises of Cicero, Boethius, Aristotle, the Christian scriptures, and the four Latin poets.

The habit of using *auctoritates* in the traditional manner meant
that great thoughts of great men were continually being cited
out of context; the whole of literature tended to be broken up
like scripture texts into isolated 'verses' and used to illustrate or
prove a point. This could lead to absurdities and anomalies, at
least in modern eyes, when Dante moved into a field which he
knew very superficially, such as Roman republican history, and
used a battery of Virgilian, Ciceronian, and scriptural exerpts
to support a political thesis, as he does in the *Monarchia*. One
auctoritas could be played off against another, as when Dante
says that champions may trip each other up in wrestling or
fighting, but runners in a race may not; however Virgil, in
giving the palm to Euryalus (cf. *Aen.* v. 334–8) appears to differ,
so it is better to follow Cicero, *De Officiis*, III.x.42 (*Monarchia*, II.
vii). It is even possible for the medieval debater to twist the
meaning of a tag to the opposite of what the author intended, as
when Dante in the same book (II. iii) adduces Virgil to show
that Dido was the second of Aeneas' three noble wives:

> Nec iam furtivum Dido meditatur amorem:
> coniugium vocat: hoc praetexit nomine culpam.
>
> *Aen.* iv. 171–2

The quotation of a passage out of context seems to have
played Dante false when, in his letter to the Emperor Henry VI
he produced the tag, *illa Curionis in Caesarem*:

> Dum trepidant nullo firmatae robore partes,
> Tolle moras; semper nocuit differre paratis:
> Par laboi atque metus pretio maiore petuntur.
>
> *Phars.* i. 280–2

It is puzzling that Dante should cite these words as late as 1311,
when he afterwards placed Curio in Hell for uttering them. In
his exhortation to the emperor to invade Tuscany, he appears
to have ignored the character and motives of the man whose
words he made his own, very much as people cite

> There is a tide in the affairs of men
> Which taken at the flood leads on to fortune,

without remembering that the words were spoken by Brutus

before Philippi. No doubt Dante believed that the crossing of the Rubicon was foreordained, and that the campaigns of Caesar and Augustus brought the whole world into a celestial harmony (*Par.* vi. 55–6); but if he came to regret his vengefulness against Florence, did he not also feel mortified when he came to read, or re-read, the bitterly ironical panegyric on Curio at the end of Book iv of the *Pharsalia*, itself so Dantesque in tone? Deeper absorption in the spirit of Lucan's work, and perhaps also a return to Augustine, may have modified his view of the glories of Roman imperialism. In putting Curio in the depths of the *Inferno* he seems to reprove his former self: 'I could have bitten my tongue out for uttering it.'

III

Another feature of Dante's inherited culture was the use of Greek myths, especially in Ovid's *Metamorphoses*, as a collection of exempla to which various moral and even physical interpretations could be attached. But Dante's enthusiasm for the myths was unusual, for he not only had a systematic way of interpreting the tales of the gods, he also knew the stories in a number of sources, and he shows a striking ability to fit together allusions of widely differing provenance. Thus he knew the tale of Alcmaeon and Eriphyle from an allusion in the *Nicomachean Ethics*, where Aristotle, in a discussion of voluntary and involuntary acts, says 'the things that "forced" Euripides' Alcmaeon to slay his mother seem absurd'. Dante was quite at home with this story from the *Metamorphoses*, and in *Par.* iv he conveys the gist of Aristotle's argument, including the reference to Alcmaeon, imitating Ovid's antithetical style with a paradox of his own:

> Ultusque parente parentem
> Natus erit facto pius et sceleratus eodem
>
> *Met.* ix. 407–8

> Per non perder pietà si fé spietato.
>
> *Par.* iv. 105

But the poet had already planned to use the story as an example of pride in *Purgatorio*; there he falls back on Statius, and the symbol which emerges is that of the *dirum monile*, the necklace of the gods, which was the cause of Eriphyle's temptation.

Dante's study of the *Metamorphoses* was a large part of his preparatory work for the *Commedia*, and there are traces of it in the *Convivio* and the letters. Among the Ovidian manuscripts now preserved in Florence, in the Laurenziana and the Riccardiana, we can distinguish three main types which Dante might have known:

(a) large manuscripts of the eleventh-twelfth centuries, sometimes containing the prose summaries of Lactantius Placidus, as in Laur. cod. Marcianus 225 (M); the text is very clearly set out, and headings giving the gist of the principal fables stand out in the margin in red capitals, or are even placed in red boxes as in Laur. XXXVI. 12 (L):

> ### PIRÁMI ET THISBES CRUOR IN ARBOREM MORUM

CALISTO ET ARᶜ/AS IN SIDERIBUS;

(b) smaller thirteenth-century copies, such as Laur. cod. Marcianus 238 and Laur. XXXVI. 5 (to which a later hand has added, at the end, Giovanni del Virgilio's epitaph on Dante); here the hand is much smaller, and the summaries are broken up in a mass of marginal notes, to which further notes are added;

(c) a more advanced type of commentary occurs in a group of thirteenth-fourteenth-century manuscripts, represented by Ricc. 622 (R), closely related to Ambros. N 254 (A^1); this is on an encyclopedic scale, containing clear, succinct explanations, historical, grammatical, allegorical, and scientific, less vast than Ghisalberti's 'vulgate' commentary, which appears in Ricc. 624 + 2795 (R^1) and Ambros. P 43 sup (A). The former usually contains elaborate lists of contents for each book:

In secundo volumine continetur: domus Solis descriptio, Phetontis petitio, Phebi dissuasio, Phetontis fulminatio, Clymenes et Elyadum lamentatio . . .

Et in hoc septimo volumine continetur: adepcio aurei velleris, repatriacio Jasonis, rejuvenescere Esonis et mutacio Bachi . . .

together with condensed versions of Arnulfus of Orleans's allegories.

It seems that Dante not only made use of commentated copies of these types, but might even have made a workbook of his own in which he noted passages of Ovid omitted by Lactantius, and used them in his later writings. It is noticeable that the passages he quotes from book vii are precisely those which the summarist omits. After describing in some detail Medea's aerial flight and her nefarious activities at Athens down to l. 452, Lactantius appears to lose interest in Ovid's framework, and simply retails the two main stories: the story of the Myrmidons and Cephalus' account of his loss of his wife Procris owing to her devotion to Diana and his to the dawn goddess, Aurora. He omits the whole of the link-passage (453–511) which introduces Minos of Crete, Aeacus of Aegina, and his alliance with Athens against Minos, and although he does say that the stories were exchanged by Aeacus and the Athenian ambassador, Cephalus, he does not mention Aeacus' son Phocus, to whom Cephalus in fact tells his unhappy tale while Aeacus himself is asleep. The summarist also omits the central part of Cephalus' narration (747–808) about Themis' monster and the hound Laelaps who changed into stone in mid-pursuit.

In the *Convivio*, the character of Aeacus is singled out as a perfect model of the virtues of maturity or 'old age'; his proffer of military help to Athens is translated verbatim (507–11), and Dante also reproduces a marginal note found in manuscripts of type (b):

Esopus fuit pater Egine cum qua concubuit Iuppiter et inde natus est Eacus; et iste concubuit cum Sarmace et inde nati sunt Phocus et Peleus et Telamon. Peleus fuit pater Achillis, Telamon Aiacis, Procus autem caruit filio

(Laur. Marc. 238, fo. 62ᵛ, cf. Laur. XXXVI. 5, fo. 90ʳ).

E perché più memorabile sia l'essemplo che detto è, dice di Eaco re che questi fu padre di Telamon [di Peleus] e di Foco, del quale Telamon nacque Aiace, e di Peleus Achille.

Conv. IV. xxvii. 20
(text as ed. Busnelli–Vandelli; cf. ed. Simonelli, p. 214, n. 10–11.)

It was from marginalia of this sort that medieval readers

refreshed their memories of the complex genealogies of the gods and heroes, which we can now find neatly tabulated in the alphabetic index to the Loeb edition.

Dante returns to the second omitted passage (759–64) in Beatrice's speech in *Purg.* xxxiii. 46–51 about the obscure riddles of Themis and the Sphinx and their resolution by the Naiads. Once more it is a link-passage, and a corrupt one at that, which has retained Dante's attention, no doubt because of the mass of commentary which had accumulated around it. Ovid's simple lead-in to his story—after the Sphinx was overthrown by Laiades (Oedipus), another monster was sent to the Thebans—was transformed by the commentators into a very complicated story, on which almost the last word has been said in an important article of Ghisalberti.[2] Dante must have known the tradition that Themis and the Naiades [*sic*] were competing to solve a riddle posed by Diana, or the Sibyl, relating to the petrifaction of the monster and the hound. But he probably had a manuscript, such as R, in which the riddle of the Sphinx is cited as well. He combines the purely verbal elements of text and gloss without attempting any overt logical connection, and makes a delightfully arcane poetic allusion out of a rambling mass of commentary.

The supposition that Dante is keen on explaining non-Lactantian link-passages finds support in his letters, as in *Ep.* iii. 4, to Cino da Pistoia, a fellow-exile, where he places the story of Leucothoe in its context in *Met.*, Book iv; and again in the letter to Can Grande: 'velut Austri regina Hierusalem petiit, velut Pallas petiit Helicona, Veronam petii', Athena's journey to Helicon being a mere link in Ovid between the story of Perseus and Medusa and that of the Pierides (*Met.* v. 254). The allusion to Venus and Cupid in *Conv.* II. v. 14 and the opening line of *Par.* xvii:

> Qual venne a Climenè, per accertarsi . . .

probably come from the same set of notes.

IV

A much greater interest for the critic of Dante's poetry attaches to his use of massed citations interwoven in a curiously ingenious way to illustrate an argument, or even to mark out the structure of large sections of the *Commedia*.

Although the *Convivio* is somewhat confused and digressive, the final tableau of the Four Ages of Man in Book IV is symmetrically planned; everything goes by fours and sixes. There are Four Ages, and each age has four characteristic virtues. There are ten sets of *auctoritates*, four devoted to the general introduction and adolescence (chs. xxiv–v), four to 'youth' and 'old age' (chs. xxvi–vii), and two to extreme old age (ch. xxviii). Each age is illustrated by a group of quotations from one of the four poets: Virgil and Ovid have six quotations each, Statius and Lucan have three each, with a further prose quotation from Cicero and Seneca respectively, constituting the characteristic arrangement 3 + 1. The central miscellany on prudence also has six quotations, as does the first section on extreme old age; the remainder have four, and the arrangement 3 + 1 reappears several times. The entire pattern consists of

$$(4 \times 6) + (6 \times 4) = 48.$$

Similar proportions appear when we cross-classify the quotations in terms of the *auctores*: the four poets have $6 + 6 + 3 + 3 = 18$; leaving aside the central miscellany, Cicero has twelve ($3 + 1 + 1 + 3 + 2 + 2$), and Aristotle, Seneca, and the ethical books of Scripture (Proverbs and Epistles) also have twelve. The miscellany is deliberately different: Aristotle is cited once from the *Politics*, the scriptural quotations are from the historical books (Kings and St. Matthew), and there is a supernumerary quotation from the *Pharsalia*, the famous line on Cato: 'nec sibi sed toti genitum se credere mundo) (ii. 383). The total of forty-eight is thus reached in a different way (see Table I):

$$(18 + 6) + (12 + 12) = 48.$$

TABLE I

The Classical *Auctoritates* in *Convivio* IV. xxiv–xxviii

xxiv.   Four stages of life: *De Sen.* (3) + *De Off.* (1)

       Four virtues in Adolescence; Obedience: Prov. (3) + Col. (1)

xxv.   Gentleness: *Eth. Nic.* VIII (2) + Prov. (2)

       Awe and reverence, delicacy and sense of shame: Statius, *Theb.* i (3) + *De Off.* (1)

       Comeliness in physique and dress [no authorities cited]

Table I—*contd.*

xxvi.   The prime of life ('Youth'); temperance, fortitude, love and courtesy, and the punctual performance of duties: Virgil, *Aen.* iv–vi (6)

xxvii. Maturity ('old age'). miscellany on prudence from *De Sen.* (1), Aristotle (2), *Phars.* (1), and I Kings (1), Matt. (1)
Justice, generosity, sociability: *De Sen.* (2), *Eth. Nic.* (1), *De Off.* (1)
The virtues of Maturity further illustrated from the behaviour of Aeacus: Ovid, *Met.* vii (6)

xxviii. The duties of extreme old age; return to God, preparation of death, retirement, religious life: *De Sen.* (2) + Arist. *Juv. et Sen.* (1), *De Sen.* (2) + Rom. (1)
The return of his estranged wife, Martia, to Cato allegorised as the return of the soul to God in old age: Lucan, *phars.* ii, ix (3) + Seneca (1).

Monarchia II. iii–ix, Dante's argument in favour of the divine right of the Roman Empire, also embodies a long string of mainly poetic quotations, eighteen from the Aeneid and eighteen from other sources. The pattern can be shown by numbering the quotations from the main *auctores* cited:

		Virgil	Lucan	Ovid	Cicero	Others
iii–iv.	Aeneas and Roman rule	1–10	1			Homer
v–vii.	Justice of Roman heroes; divine right shown by contests	11–16	2	1	1–4	
viii–ix.	The contest won by Rome	17–18	3–6	2		Boethius; Ennius; Scripture 1–3

The total is thus $3 \times 12 = 36$; but to this Dante has added, at the beginning of chapters vii and ix, two miscellanies from Aristotle, Cicero, and Scripture, containing twelve quotations in all, which again make the total of forty-eight. The above analysis excludes the string of historical links from 'Livy' (Orosius and others) and the argumentative prologues to chapters iii–vi which are in a different style.

There is an extremely mature and very beautiful development of the miscellany technique in *Par.* xxii–vii, xxix–xxx, and xxxii, where the whole argument is strung on a catena of—once more —forty-eight scriptural quotations. To appreciate the pattern, we have to realize that Dante has classified the books of Scripture into five groups:

(a) historical: Genesis, Exodus, and Acts:
(b) prophetic books and psalms;
(c) the three synoptic gospels;
(d) the epistles;
(e) the writings of St. John (the fourth gospel and Revelation), to which
    are added (in canto xxiii) two quotations from the Song of Songs and
    the Psalms.

Once we are provided with this key, the quotations can be shown to be arranged in three cycles (1) cantos xxii–iii (St. Benedict, triumph of Christ and Mary); (2) cantos xxv–vii (catechism of St. James and St. John; St. Peter's condemnation of the modern Papacy); (3) cantos xxiv (catechism of St. Peter) + xxix–xxx, xxxii (Crystalline Heaven, Empyrean) each of which covers the five groups. Thus in (2) we have:

canto xxv, St. James:	James	Ps.	Heb.	Job	Ps.	Ps.
	d	b	d	b	b	b

cantos xxv–vi, appearance of St. John, his catechism:

Rev.	John	John	John	Acts	Rev.	Exod.	John
e	e	e	e	a	e	a	e

cantos xxvi–xxvii, Adam in Paradise; St Peter's speech:

	Gen.	Gen.	Matth.	Matth.
	a	a	c	c

If we consider the above pattern as if it were a rhyme-scheme, it falls into two parts: four *b*s interwoven with two *d*s at the beginning, and six *e*s interwoven with four *a*s at the end, concluding with two *c*s, making eighteen quotations in all. The two other cycles are as follows:

(1) a b c a b c   d d e e d e
(3) e c d d   d d e c —
     a a b c b e   b c a c

All these quotations are cited by Edward Moore in his Index to Quotations (*Studies in Dante*, 1st Ser. (Oxford, 1896), pp. 359 ff.), and he only gives one quotation supernumerary to the pattern (the cry 'Holy, Holy, Holy' at the end of Dante's last catechism in canto xxvi). Taken together, the three cycles form a larger pattern, in which *a, b, c,* and *d* appear nine times each and *e* appears twelve times: $4 \times 9 + 12 = 48$.

Systems of this kind prepare us for the vast system of Virgilian and Ovidian quotations which Dante drew up for the *Commedia*. Dividing the *Aeneid* into four sections, *a, b, c, d,* and the *Metamor-*

phoses into three, *a, b, c,* Dante arranged his Virgilian quotations in pairs, forming cycles of the type

c b c b   d a d a;

there are three such cycles, for the three *cantiche*, with *a—a,* *b—d, c—c* as further pairs. The Ovidian quotations are in triads, all on the rotation *a, b, c.* Allowing for variants, there are thirty-six quotations from Virgil and fifty from Ovid, and these form the core of the entire system (see Table II).

TABLE II

	Virgilian Pairs	Ovidian Triads
Inferno		
Keepers of the under-world	*c* Charon/Minos	—
Hapless lovers	*b* Dido and Sychaeus	—
Monsters	*c* Cerberus	*a* Furies—*b* Medusa—*c* Minotaur
Half-human creatures	—	*a* Chiron—*c* Nessus—*b* Harpies
Suicides	*b* Polydorus/birth of Jupiter in Crete	—
Geryon: seducers	—	*c* Geryon—*a* Phaeton—*b* Jason
Soothsayers	*d* Manto—*a* Eurypylus	*a* Tiresias+Cadmus
Thieves	*d* Cacus	*b* Arethusa
False counsellors	*a* Palladium/Trojan Horse	*c* Ulysses and Circe
Depths of hell	*a* Sinon—*a* Antenor	*b* Myrmidons—*a* Athamas and Ino —*c* Myrrha/Hecuba
Purgatorio		
Guardian of purgatory	*d* Cato	*b* +Calliope and the Pierides
Spiritual ascent	*b* Rape of Ganymede	—
Pride	—	*a* Giants—*b* Niobe/Arachne—*c* Eriphyle
Envy	*b* +Circe's swine	*a* Aglauros
Anger	*d* Lavinia and Amata	*b* Procne and Philomena
Sloth	*b* Companions of Aeneas left in Sicily	—
Avarice	*c* Fabricius—*a* Pygmalion and Sychaeus —*a* Polymestor and Polydorus	*c* Midas

Table II—*contd.*

	Virgilian Pairs	Ovidian Triads
Gluttony	—	*b* Erysichthon/Meleager— *c* Centaurs
Lustfulness	*c* Pasiphae	*a* Callisto
Chariot of the Church	*b* Urania—*d* Roman triumphal chariot	*b* Proserpine/Pyramus and Thisbe—*c* Venus and Adonis *a* Chariot of the Sun
Beatrice	—	*c* Eurydice—*a* Argus and Mercury+Argus' eyes— *b* Pyramus & the mulberry
Paradiso Images of Paradise	—	*a* Apollo and Daphne—*b* Apollo and Marsyas—*c* Glaucus *b* Bulls of Colchis—*a* Narcissus *c* Iphigenia
Roman heroes	*d* Pallas—*c* Silvius *c* Decii—*d* [Camilla/ Nisus and Euryalus]	—
Images of Paradise	*a*+Dido and Ascanius	*b* Sirens—*a* Echo—*c* Hippolytus
Roman heroes:	*c* [Brutus]—*c* Shade of Anchises	*b* Ariadne and Bacchus
Images of the Divine	*b* Death of Anchises— *a* Rhipeus *a* [Aeneas]—*b* Sibyl's leaves	*a* Semele+Europa *c* Leda and Gemini

V

So far the excerpts of the medieval compilers have been considered as *auctoritates*: maxims, quotations, allusions, tags, or
sacred texts. But the Virgilian pairs and Ovidian triads are not
simply textual allusions: each stands for a vividly imagined
character, usually identified with a particular scene or episode,
and as such they can be compared with the mental images cultivated in the artificial memory of the ancient rhetoricians.
This system, explained technically in the rhetoric *ad Herennium*,
was undergoing a great revival in the generation before Dante,
especially at Bologna, and it was commented on by both Albertus Magnus and Aquinas. As Miss Frances A. Yates explains in
her highly relevant work, *The Art of Memory*,[3] the elaborate
framework of Dante's other world—its pockets and coffers, its

cornices, its heavenly spheres—was ideally suited to supply the *loci* of the artificial memory—the background against which the *imagines* were placed in the mind's eye.

A further aspect of the 120–44 *imagines* which Dante drew from Virgil, Ovid, Statius, and Lucan, and which he then rearranged according to a scheme of his own, is that they may provide us with a key to an early draft of the poem, cartoon, maquette, or blueprint, which Dante drew up before embarking on his greatest work.

These *imagines* can be envisaged in three different ways: they are designed as mnemonics to keep the virtues and vices in the memory, and so they must be sharply visualized and memorable in themselves; they form part of a complete repertory or cycle illustrating classical mythology and the history of Thebes, Troy, and Rome; and, finally, they are also *auctoritates*, or tags, inasmuch as they retain verbal similarities with a specific passage of one of the Latin poets. The example of Eriphyle is a simple illustration: the image of a princess receiving a necklace of the gods is memorable enough in itself, and as it led her to betray her husband Amphiaraus to his eventual death before the walls of Thebes, for which she was slain by her son Alcmaeon, various morals can be elicited from it. Secondly, Eriphyle, the sister of Adrastus, who initiated the war of the 'seven against Thebes', is related in various ways to the other Theban and Argive heroes, including Polynices who tempted her with the necklace. And, last but not least, the allusion made by Dante is not to the story as such, but to a precise passage in Statius containing the words *dirum monile* = *lo sventurato adornamento*, the symbol of Eriphyle's vanity, *Purg.* xii. 50–1. When the story reappears in *Par.* iv. 105 from the point of view of Alcmaeon's vow, the link is with a different passage, this time in Ovid (see p. 86 above), which emphasizes Alcmaeon's 'impious piety'. There is thus a one-to-one relationship between Dante's *imagines* and the source-passages in the Latin poets.

Identification of the *imagines* in the *Commedia* has to be pursued on the lines laid down by Moore in the first volume of his *Studies in Dante* (cit.), pp. 166–97, 206–55 (sources in the four Latin poets). On pp. 45–6, Moore explains his method, which is to list (*a*) cases of direct quotation acknowledged or at least intended as such by Dante, and placed as it were in quotation

marks; (*b*) quotations which are not verbal, but are unmistak-
ably related in form or content to a specific passage in the
source; and (*c*) cases of stylistic adaptation and literary allusion,
again relating to a specific passage. The criterion is: 'Would
Dante's language or thought have been likely to take this precise form, but for the influence exercised on them by the
recollections of such and such a passage?'

   In a few cases, as with the description of the Furies in *Inf.* ix.
37–51 (cf. especially 40–2) and with that of the Giants in
Purg. xii. 28–33, the allusion has been borrowed from Ovid and
further elaborated from Statius; Moore correctly attributes both
passages, on grounds of verbal similarity, to Statius (pp. 245,
250–2), and it is only the system of grouping the Ovidian allusions in threes:

> *a* Furies — *b* Medusa — *c* Minotaur
> *a* Giants — *b* Niobe/Arachne — *c* Eriphyle

which leads us to suppose that the passages belonged to Ovid in
the original draft of the poem. The Furies and the Giants still
'count' as Ovidian, whereas Eriphyle has been transferred to
Statius, the Ovidian allusion being transferred to *Par.* iv (see
pp. 86, 95, above).

   The application of Moore's criterion enables us to eliminate
references to classical characters lacking any specific link with a
poetic text, as, for example, Phlegyas in *Inf.* viii. 17–24. But we
are bound to apply still further restrictions and exclude from
consideration all the stylistic imitations and echoes of Virgil,
and a few of Ovid, which do not embody a specific *imago*. This is
perhaps the most difficult part of our task, most of which has
already been performed by Moore; for Virgilian phrases and
allusions abound in *Inf.* i–iii, vii–viii, x, and *Purg.* i–vii—not
only expressions such as *livida palude* = *vada livida, dolenti case* =
tristes sine sole domos, secreto calle = *secreti calles* (see the list in
Moore i. 178–9) and *il tremolar de la marina* = *tremulo sub lumine
pontus,* and the similer of the doves in the Francesca episode, but
even imitations of scenes, gestures and situations, such as the
very beautiful scene of the Valley of the Kings in *Purg.* vii,
which is inspired by the picture of the Elysian fields in *Aen.* vi.
637–83 (this would be a *locus* rather than an *imago* in the artificial memory). No *imago* emerges from these cantos except the

mighty figures of Charon and Cato, the latter being tied to
Virgil (as well as to Lucan) by a single memorable phrase:
his dantem iura Catonem, Aen. viii. 670. All the above-mentioned
cantos have to be regarded as 'non-classical' in the special
sense used here, except *Inf.* iii and *Purg.* i and iv (the latter containing an astronomical tag from Lucan).

A special place must be made for indirect allusions and poetic
adaptations of precise passages: thus, although Polydorus is not
mentioned by name in *Inf.* xiii, the episode of the sensitive and
bleeding branches and of the souls imprisoned in trees is clearly
an allusion to his fate in *Aen.* iii; similarly the descent of the
mysterious messenger from heaven in *Inf.* ix is modelled on the
descent of Mercury in *Theb.* ii (see Moore, pp. 182, 246). The
indirect allusion to the parting of Orpheus and Eurydice in
Dante's parting with Virgil in *Purg.* xxx. 49–51 (the threefold
repetition of the name of Virgil) is perhaps a borderline case
between the image and stylistic imitation, but I have ventured to retain it as an Ovidian symbol, although it is stylistically elaborated from Virgil (cf. the cases of the Furies and
Giants, above), since the pattern of Dante's borrowings from
John of Garland (see below) points to it as a structural element
in his Ovidian repertory.

We must also ignore lists of names, such as that of the heroes
and sages in Limbo, *Inf.* iv. 121–44, and that of Statius' Theban
characters in *Purg.* xxii. 109–14; but here we must make two
important exceptions. The allusion to Dido's infidelity to her
former husband, Sychaeus, is far more pointed in *Inf.* v. 61–2:

colei che s'ancise amorosa,
e ruppe fede al cener di Sicheo

(cf. *Aen.* iv. 552), than when it recurs in *Par.* ix. 97–8; hence,
although it occurs in a list of hapless lovers, it belongs to the
original sequence of *imagines*. Dante has a special fondness for
another heroine, Hypsipyle, whom he mentions three times
from Statius and once from the *Heroides*: the reference to her as
'quella che mostrò Langia' (*Purg.* xxii. 112) is a typical *imago*—
the Queen of Lemnos pointing out a spring of water to the
Argive warriors, although in the extant text it is buried in a
list. It was probably intended in the first place to illustrate the

purgation of gluttony, by withstanding thirst, and properly belongs to cantos xxiii–v.

A special problem is created by the Virgilian heroes whom Dante appears to have eliminated from his original design; several of them survive in *Par.* vi. 35–54 (Pallas, Silvius in Alba Longa, and probably Torquatus and the Decii, cf. *Aen.* vi. 763–6, 824–5). Moore accepts the mention of Pallas as a precise allusion to his death in Book x. 479 ff., but rejects the rest as mere 'commonplaces of Roman history'. However, I believe that they 'mark the spot' in an earlier plan in which Dante intended to give fuller treatment to the blameless heroes of *Monarchia*. The same applies to the famous lines in *Inferno*:

> Di quella umile Italia fia salute
> per cui morì la vergine Cammilla,
> Eurialo e Turno e Niso di ferute.
>
> *Inf.* i. 106–8

The deaths of Camilla and of Nisus and Euryalus fill important gaps in Dante's plan of excerpts from the *Aeneid* (representing Books ix and xi), and they also must have been intended for some kind of place in the first draft of *Paradiso*.

Yet another borderline case is the passage in *Inferno*, where Dante mentions specific episodes and even names his sources, but does not develop the theme:

> Taccia Lucano omai là dov' e' tocca
> del misero Sabello e di Nasidio,
> e attenda a udir quel ch' or si scocca.
> Taccia di Cadmo e d'Aretusa Ovidio . . .
>
> *Inf.* xxv. 94–7

Here Arethusa is necessary for the Ovidian triad, and the two other *imagines* are needed to complete the images from Ovid and Lucan which make up the final total of forty-eight for *Inferno*. Dante has eventually left them in the form of mere references by a highly original variant on the well-known rhetorical device of preterition.

VI

The reader will find on pp. 104–7 a general tabulation of the 144 *imagines* extracted by Dante from the four Latin poets, which he no doubt had before him when he began work on the *Commedia*; read vertically, the tables show the position of the borrowings in the source-books, but I have also cross-classified them, placing them in three parallel columns to show their distribution between the three *cantiche* of the *Commedia*.

There is obviously a high degree of symmetry both in the method of excerpting and in the redistribution of the material in the *Commedia*. Dante began by dividing the four poems, the prescribed works of the Bologna arts syllabus, with their forty-eight books (omitting *Pharsalia*, Book x), into eighteen sections: three from Ovid, four from Virgil, five from Lucan, and six from Statius. These I have indicated by the letters *a, b, c . . .* In some cases we find a fixed allocation from each of the sections to each of the three *cantiche*. Thus the basic pattern for Ovid is:

	Inferno	Purgatorio	Paradiso
a	5	5	4
b	5	5	4
c	5	5	4

The total is forty-two, corresponding to the fourteen Ovidian triads, but minor variants and additions bring the total up to forty-eight (or fifty, see details below).

In Statius there are three quotations for each of the six sections (Book iii is passed over, but there is a section devoted to the *Achilleid*), and there are a few allusions which do not occur in the *Commedia* but in the *Convivio*, as well as some tags which are not *imagines*, bringing the total to twenty-four. Lucan also has twenty-four quotations, of which twenty occur in the *Commedia*, and these are fairly evenly distributed between the five sections. But the balance between the three *cantiche*, beautifully preserved in the case of Ovid, is not found in the excerpts from the other three poets, who figure very little in *Paradiso*. This seems to indicate some change of plan on Dante's part when he finally came to compose *Paradiso* in its present form.

The divisions of the books between the sections is straightforward in the case of Statius and Lucan:

	a	b	c	d	e	+f
Statius, *Thebaid*	i	ii	iv–vi	vii–ix	x–xii	*Achilleid*
Lucan, *Pharsalia*	i	ii	iii	iv–viii	ix	

In Virgil there is a minor oddity in the division between *a* and *b* which runs through Book iii: Polymestor and Polydorus belong to *a*, but the story of Polydorus and the bleeding branches belongs to *b*. The division is more complicated in Ovid, and this can be most easily seen from the table itself.

Practically every book of every poem is represented (apart from *Thebaid*, Book iii, which appears to be compensated for by the *Achilleid*, Book i). The allusion to the migration of birds (ll. 832–4) has to count for *Pharsalia*, Book vii (see Moore, i. 239 n.). In the *Thebaid* the death of Amphiaraus, which overlaps between Books vii and viii, counts for the former; the 'twofold affliction' of Jocasta (*Purg.* xxii. 55–6) refers to the strife of Eteocles and Polynices in Book xi (omitted by Moore) and the divided flame on their funeral pyre counts for Book xii.

Dante has made a remarkably thorough and systematic use of Lucan, from a peculiar point of view: he builds up carefully selected passages into a summary guide to the geography of the Mediterranean in the time of Caesar and Augustus.

The key to Dante's method of excerpting from Lucan is his division of Books i, ii, iii, and ix of the *Pharsalia* into sections of 180 lines (these are counted back from the end of the book in the case of Book ix); he then chose one extract from each of the four sections of i, ii, and iii and from each of the five sections of Book ix:

i.	41–2	Siege of Perugia and Modena	*Par.* vi
	269–82	Caesar and Curio at Rimini	*Inf.* xxviii
	399–464	The six rivers of Gaul	*Par.* vi
	586	The soothsayer Aruns in the Carrarese and the caves of Lunigiana	*Inf.* xx

and so on. He also chose four passages from Books v–viii, and with the help of supernumerary passages (including Hercules and Antaeus in Book iv) brought the whole scheme to twenty-four passages. Of these, four are used in *Mon.* II. iii–ix, and twenty in the *Commedia*, where they are introduced at regular intervals throughout *Inferno*, *Purgatorio*, and the first eleven cantos of *Paradiso*. The purpose of this planned series is to serve as a brief gazetteer of the Roman world: Italy is defined by the range of the Apennines, Gaul by its six rivers, the Var, the Rhine, the Isère, the Loire, the Seine, and the Rhone. The south-west of Europe is covered by allusions to Caesar at Marseilles and Lerida; Folquet of Marseilles is made to insist on the fact that his home town is on the same longitude as Bougie in Algeria. A second series of places begins on the eastern frontiers of Thrace: Hellespont, Bithynia, the Troad, and then, leaving out the lands of the Bible, on to Alexandria and the Nile and back by the Libyan desert to Bougie. There are two gaps: the Greek world, which Dante regarded as beginning on the eastern frontiers of Hungary, and the Bible lands, which are fully represented by the Greek mythology and the scriptural allusions in the *Commedia*. This gazetteer delimits the frontiers of the Empire, perambulated by the Roman eagle in the campaigns of Caesar; Augustus is represented by his campaigns against Mark Antony and his brother at Modena and Perugia. To complete the series Dante added, in his supernumerary passages, a 'pseudo-Lucan' anecdote: the taunt 'Queen of Bithynia' referring to Caesar's behaviour as a very young man at the court of Nicomedes; this, like the forced allusion to Bougie, is simply part of the geographical pattern. These vivid incidents are also worked into the ethical pattern of the *Commedia*: Lucan supplies soothsayers and witches for the *Inferno*; Curio is a warning against sowing discord, Bithynia against lechery, Caesar's swiftness of action is a good example against sloth, Amyclas symbolizes poverty, and the Hellespont, 'still a bridle to all human pride', stands for the river surrounding the Earthly Paradise.

Dante's use of John of Garland's *Integumenta* as a foundation for his numerous borrowings from Ovid is surprising, since he knew Ovid very well at first hand; but this little epitome of 520 lines, in elegiac couplets, is a storehouse of sharp epigrammatic phrases; it allegorizes, giving physical as well as ethical interpretations, and it seems to have provided what Dante was looking for: a firm framework for his poem. The concision of the *Integumenta* is astounding; thus it reduces the whole of Book vi of the *Metamorphoses* to eight stories and summarizes them in eighteen lines;

De Aragne.   Ne quis maiori certet persuadet Aragne
                Que sub pauperie viscera viva trahit.
De nomine   Athanatos grecum sonat immortalis, Athenas
  Athenarum.   Nominat hinc Pallas famaque vivit adhuc.

De Niobe.	Proprietas saxi Niobe datur hoc quia durum, Hec quia dura riget firma tenore mali.
De sathiro.	Certans cum Phebo satyrus notat insipientis Impar certamen cum sapiente trahi.
De ranis.	Rusticus infelix est rana loquax lue plena, Ventris amica tumens, livida, mersa, minax.
De Pelope.	Per Pelopem lacerum signantur tempora quorum Fertilitas rapitur huic reparata tamen.

De Thereo.	Historiam tangit describens Terea de quo
	    Musa sophocleo carmine grande canit.
	Commentatur aves doctrina poetica quippe
	    Devia poscit avis, devia poscit amor.

De Zeto et
   Calay.
	Sunt acies ale Zeti Calaisque paterne
	    Quarum subsidio Iasonis arma valent.

(277–94)

Dante borrowed four of these stories (later adding two more from his own stock, the conflict of Neptune and Minerva, cf. 279–80, and Latona on Delos). He also used the structure of the first eight lines as the basis for a beautiful passage in *Purg.* xii (see the text, p. 112 below).

When I first noticed the debt of Dante to John of Garland,[4] I believed that Dante must have known him of old, that he and Arnulf of Orleans were used in schools. But allegory was probably a quite new fashion in early fourteenth-century Italy, and after examining a representative range of Ovidian manuscripts of the period, I do not think that Dante could have found what he needed in the marginalia. Manuscripts of type (*b*), such as Laur. Marc. 238, do not contain extracts from the allegorists, and when they do appear, in type (*c*), represented by Ricc. 622 (R), they are buried in such a quantity of material that they could not have served Dante as an outline. He must therefore have used a manuscript of the type found in Bodleian, Digby 104, which contains both John of Garland and the prose allegories of Arnulf, copied separately from the text of Ovid. This Dante could have obtained in Bologna, and it was presumably a copy of this type which Giovanni del Virgilio used for his *Allegoriae* in the 1320s.

At first sight the Ovidian *imagines* of the *Commedia* correspond neatly to the fifteen books of Ovid as summarized in the *Integumenta*, and I have argued that Dante took four stories from each of the first nine books and two each from the remainder: $(9 \times 4) + (6 \times 2) = 48$. There is ample confirmation for this type of system in Dante; but I now think he approached the matter in a more devious way. Eliminating provisionally Book xiii, he began by taking groups of four stories from each of Books i–vii, and groups of two stories from each of Books viii–xii, xiv–xv: A $(7 \times 4) + B (7 \times 2) = 42$, which corresponds to the fourteen Ovidian triads of the *Commedia*. But he allowed for variation on the basic pattern, in such a way that forty myths could be raised to forty-two by the adoption of alternative pairs of variants, one of which (Ariadne and Iphigenia) is not drawn from John of Garland at all. Combinations of these, together with additions to Books i–iii, v (marked by a + in the tables), bring the total up to forty-eight, or, with the addition of the two myths not in John of Garland, to fifty.

The Virgilian images provide a different kind of problem, because of their relative scarcity, especially in *Paradiso*. There are thirteen images in *Inferno*, and eleven in *Purgatorio*, and these are drawn from various parts of the *Aeneid*; Books ix and xi, however, are not represented. In *Paradiso*, apart from the passage, vi. 35–54, discussed on p. 98 above, there are only five *imagines* from Virgil: Dido and Ascanius; the shade of Anchises appearing to Aeneas in the underworld; the death of Anchises in Sicily; Rhipeus, the good Trojan warrior; and the Sybil's leaves. Since there is nothing at all from Books ix and xi, it is practically certain that Camilla as well as Nisus and Euryalus belonged to the original plan, and that they were to be mentioned in *Paradiso*; and Aeneas and one more Roman hero (possibly Brutus, as in *Aen*. vi 818–23, cf. *Mon*. II. v) are needed to complete the pattern of thirty-six *imagines*, approximately twelve for each *cantica*. For arithmetical reasons connected with the total of images in the entire work, I have also included Priam and Dardanus who figure at the beginning of the discussion in *Mon*. II.

The problem of the Virgilian heroes is part of a wider problem affecting *Paradiso*: non-Ovidian images are generally rare, Statius hardly appears, Lucan not after canto xi. It seems that Dante has freed himself from the system of classical references in the course of writing *Paradiso*, although much of the Ovidian colouring remains. I have ventured to include some of the *imagines* which belong to the symmetrical pattern of excerpts from Statius and Lucan in my plan of *Paradiso*, but these, like the hypothetical Virgilian *imagines*, are placed in square brackets.

TABLE III

The twenty-four *imagines* from the Thebaid and Achilleid of Statius

Thebaid books	Inferno	Purgatorio	Paradiso
a i	*Furies		[Adrastus and the prophecy of Apollo —daughters of Adrastus—parentage of Polynices]
b ii	The descent of Mercury —Briareus	The necklace of Eriphyle—*Overthrow of Giants	
c iv–v		Hypsipyle at the fountain of Langia	
		Hypsipyle saved from death	[Hypsipyle's lament for Archemorus]
vi			**Similes of the rowers and of the cypress tree in *Par.* xxv–vi
d vii–ix	Amphiaraus— Menalippus and Tydeus		
		Bacchic orgies near Thebes	
e x–xii	Capaneus		
		Jocasta's dual affliction	
	Funeral pyre of Eteocles and Polynices	*Statius follows Virgil	
f *Achilleid* book			
i	Achilles and Deidamia	Achilles borne away to Scyros	Apollo crowns Caesar and the bard
ii		*Achilleid left incomplete	

[   ] Cited in *Conv.* III. xi and IV. xxv, but not retained in the extant text of the *Commedia*.

*Decorations of Ovidian *imagines* and tags in the Statius episode.

**Survive as similes, not *imagines*, in *Par.*

TABLE IV

The Twenty-Four *Imagines* from Lucan's *Pharsalia*

Pharsalia, books	Inferno	Purgatorio	Paradiso
a i	Curio at Rimini —Aruns in the Carrarese		Perugia and Modena [Caesar and Pompey] —the six rivers of Gaul
b ii		Caesar and Martia —the Appenine range—Xerxes at the Hellespont	[The Samnite war]
c iii		Caesar opening the public treasury —shadows in the southern hemis- phere—Caesar at Marseilles and in Spain	Sea battle off Marseilles
d iv	Antaeus and Hercules at Bagrada		
v–viii	Erichtho	Migration of cranes	Caesar and Amyclas —[Tomb of Alexander]
e ix	Cato in the Libyan desert— snakes in the desert—Sabellus and Nasidius		[The sacred shield of Numa]—Caesar in the Troad
'ps.-Lucan'		'Queen of Bithynia'	

[ ] Cited in *Mon.* II. iv, vii-ix, but not retained in the extant text of *Paradiso*'

TABLE V

The forty-eight myths of Ovid based on John of Garland

Metamorphoses	Inferno	Purgatorio	Paradiso	Garland, Integ.
a i	Phaeton	Giants—Argus and Mercury+ Argus' eyes	Apollo and Daphne	93–116
ii	Chiron	The Chariot of the Sun—Callisto— —Aglauros	+ Europa	129–52
iii	Tiresias + Cadmus		Semele—Narcis- sus—Echo	153–68

Table V—*contd.*

Metamorphoses	Inferno	Purgatorio	Paradiso	Garland, Integ.
iv	Furies—Athamas and Ino			
				181–94
b		Pyramus and the mulberry/Pyramus and Thisbe		
v	Medusa—Arethusa	Proserpine+ Calliope and the Pierides	Muses and Sirens	227–30 253–76
vi		Niobe/Arachne—Procne and Philomena	Apollo and Marsyas	277–92
vii	Harpies—Jason and Medea—Myrmidons		The Bulls of Colchis	295–314
viii		Erysichthon/Meleager	*Ariadne and Bacchus*	321–38
c	Minotaur			
ix	Geryon—Nessus and Dejanira	Alcmaeon and Eriphyle		357–82
x	Myrrha/	Venus and Adonis		413–20
xi		Midas—Orpheus and Eurydice		421–32
xii		Centaurs	Leda and Gemini	445–52
xiii	/Hecuba		*Iphigenia*	457–8
xiv	Ulysses and Circe		Glaucus	469–78
xv			Hippolytus	507–8

Names *italicized* are not in John of Garland.
/ Variants pairs needed for completion of Triads.
+ Later additions forming total of forty-eight.

TABLE VI

The Thirty-Six Virgilian *Imagines*

Virgil, *Aen*	Inferno	Purgatorio	Paradiso
a i	Antenor	Pygmalion and Sychaeus	[Aeneas]—Dido and Ascanius
ii	Sinon—Eurypylus—the Palladium/the Trojan Horse		Rhipeus

Table VI—*contd.*

Virgil, *Aen*	*Inferno*	*Purgatorio*	*Paradiso*
iii		Polymestor and	
		Polydorus	8+2
b	Polydorus/Crete		The Sibyl's leaves—
	birthplace of Jove		Death of Anchises in
			Sicily
iv	Dido and		
	Sychaeus		
v		Rape of Ganymede—	
		companions of	
		Aeneas who stayed	
		in Sicily	
vii		Urania and the	7+2
		Muses—Circe's swine	
c vi	Charon's bark/	Pasiphae—	The shade of Anchises
	Minos—	Fabricius	—Silvius—[Brutus the
	Cerberus		consul]—the Decii and
			Torquatus 8+1
d viii	Cacus	Cato—the Roman	
		triumphal chariot	
ix			[Deaths of Euryalus
			and Nisus]
x	Manto		Death of Pallas
xi			[Death of Camilla]
xii		Lavinia and Queen	
		Amata	7+1

VII

The underlying plan of the *Commedia* seems remarkably simple when viewed in terms of the patterns formed by the Virgilian and Ovidian images. The original system of Virgilian pairs and Ovidian triads is fused into a series of patterns of which some specimens are given in Table VII. If we assume a division of each *cantica* into five sections, each with two sub-sections, we find that there is normally a triad from one poet, followed by a second triad, containing one further borrowing from the same poet and two from the other:

	Virgil	*Ovid*
sub-section 1	—	3
sub-section 2	2	1

This pattern occurs almost throughout the *Inferno*, in sections (*b*), (*c*), (*d*), and (*e*). It is possible to intervert the two sub-sections, the proportions assigned to the two writers being the same:

	Virgil	Ovid
sub-section 1	2	1
sub-section 2	—	3

and this is the characteristic pattern of *Purgatorio*, where it occurs in sections (*a*), (*c*) and (*e*).

By yet another variation on the pattern, Virgil and Ovid change places:

	Virgil	Ovid
sub-section 1	3	—
sub-section 2	1	2

and this pattern appears in *Inferno* (*a*).

TABLE VII

The Ovidian and Virgilian Triads

Pattern I Example: *Inferno* (c)

	Virgil	Ovid
sub-section 1 (*Inf*. xvii–xviii)	—	Geryon—Phaeton—Jason and Medea
sub-section 2 (*Inf*. xx)	Manto—Eurypylus	Tiresias

Pattern II: Example: *Purgatorio* (a)

	Virgil	Ovid
sub-section 1 (*Purg*. i, ix)	Cato—Rape of Ganymede	Calliope and the Pierides
sub-section 2 (*Purg*. xii)		Giants—Niobe—Arachne

Pattern III: Example: *Inferno* (a)

	Virgil	Ovid
sub-section 1 (*Inf*. iii, v)	Charon's bark—Minos Dido and Sychaeus	—
sub-section 2 (*Inf*. vi, ix)	Cerberus	Furies—Medusa

If the first two patterns are adhered to, Ovid will have twice as many images as Virgil, say, in five sections of a cantica, Virgil ten, Ovid twenty, and this is the basic proportion in *Purgatorio*. But by introducing the third pattern the proportions can be varied, and so we find Virgil twelve, Ovid eighteen (*Inferno*), Virgil fourteen, Ovid sixteen (*Paradiso*, hypothetical early draft).

The additions of images from Statius and Lucan does not affect the general outline of three *cantiche* divided each into five sections; but, together with additions to the Ovidian material, which I have italicized in the final tables (see Appendix), it brings up the total of images in each *cantica* to forty-eight. This is only a hypothetical number for *Paradiso*, where (on the above calculation) six images of Virgil and ten of Statius and Lucan have been omitted.

The general conception of the number system appears to have developed somewhat as follows. Dante began with his excerpts as shown in the tables of the four poets:

	Virgil	*Ovid*	*Statius*	*Lucan*	
	36	48	18	18	=120
projected	+6	+6	+6	+6	=144
expansions					

However, he does not appears to have pursued the idea of expanding Virgil, and the expansions were transferred to Ovid: Lucan was expanded to twenty-four as foreseen, but Statius shared his addition with Virgil and Ovid, thus:

Virgil	*Ovid*	*Statius*	*Lucan*	
36	48	18	18	=120
	+6+6		+6	
+2	+2	+2		
38	62	20	24	=144
				—16=128

Allowing for the sixteen images omitted from *Paradiso*, this is the present state of the *imagines* in the *Commedia*.

TABLE VIII

The Groundplan of the *Commedia* as revealed by the Distribution of the Classical *Imagines*

Inferno
cantos

(a)	iii, v–vi, ix	The entry to the Underworld—Minos and the unhappy lovers—monsters
(b)	xii–xiv	Half-human creatures—the violent against themselves and against God
(c)	xvii–xviii, xx	The descent to the lower Hell on Geryon's back: the seducers—the soothsayers
(d)	xxiv–vi	Thieves—false counsellors
(e)	xxvii–xxxiii	Howling of sinners in Hell—traitors; the giants in the lake of ice, scenes of horror in Antenora

Table VIII—*contd.*

Purgatorio
cantos

(a)	i, iv, ix, xii	The entry to Purgatory—the purgation of Pride
(b)	xiv–xv, xvii–xviii	The purgation of Envy—of Anger
(c)	xx, xxiii–v	The purgation of Avarice—of Gluttony
(d)	xxii, xxvi–viii	The purgation of Lustfulness—the vision of Beatrice across the stream surrounding the Earthly Paradise
(e)	xxix–xxx, xxxii–xxxiii	The Chariot of the Church—reconciliation

Paradiso
cantos

(a)	i–v	The entry to heaven—the Sphere of the Moon: broken vows
(b)	vi	The Sphere of Mercury: warriors who sought earthly glory
(c)	viii–ix, xi–xii	The Spheres of Venus and of the Sun: the teaching of St. Francis
(d)	xiii, xv, xvii, xix–xxi	The Spheres of Mars and Jupiter—Cacciaguida prophesies Dante's exile
(e)	[xxv–vi], xxvii, xxxiii	The Sphere of Saturn: just rulers—the ascent to the heaven of the fixed stars—vision of the heavenly intelligences in the prime mover.

As I remarked at the outset of this article, the oldest discernible drafts of the *Commedia*, which are saturated with classical imagery, consist of passages of 36–48 lines; the system of triads explained above allows for only thirty such passages, one for each sub-section, ten for each cantica. It ought to be fairly easy to reconstruct this small number of passages, but in many cases the materials have been dispersed and the text completely rewritten. The classical material is scattered through sixty cantos, although there are in addition forty cantos which contain no classical *imagines*.

The three accompanying passages are samples of what I believe to be Dante's earliest work, occurring in cantos xii–xxxiii of *Inferno* and *Purgatorio*. In Purg. xii. 25–60, which corresponds to the second sub-section of *Purgatorio* (*a*), the central element in the text is based on four distichs of John of Garland, in which the second and fourth Ovidian myths are replaced by Scripture texts (see the passage on p. 101–2 above). Further elements are borrowed from Statius. The five *terzine* containing the classical *imagines* are interwoven with seven others from Scripture and Orosius, and the anaphoric repetition of *Vedea* . . . , *O Niobe* [etc.] . . . , and *Mostrava* binds the whole passage together into three sets of four *terzine* = 36 lines.

The passage from *Inf.* xx (*Inferno* (*c*), second sub-section) contains the five soothsayers, the Virgilian–Ovidian triad being supplemented from both Statius and Lucan. The characters are accorded 3, 2, 2, 2, and 3 *terzine* respectively, making up once again $(3 \times 2) + (2 \times 3)$ *terzine* = 36 lines. But there is a long archeological digression, on the origins of the name of Mantua, occupying sixteen *terzine*, and so we have $36 + 48 = 84$ lines, which form the main body of the canto (l. 57, which I have omitted, is a link-up with the new passage: 'onde un poco mi piace che m'ascolte').

In *Purg.* xx, the first sub-section of *Purgatorio* (*c*), the classical triad of the avaricious is interwoven with a triad from the Old Testament, the New Testament, and Orosius (an anecdote concerning Crassus). But this whole passage is brought into a kind of accidental relation with the theme of Latona upon Delos, the floating island: the passage itself appears to have 'floated' from its moorings in cantos xxv–vi, for it must have originally formed a triad with Callisto and Pasiphae, examples of the loves of Jove. Other examples of passages of 36 lines containing classical allusions and expanded to 48 lines can be found in *Purg.* xviii. 91–138 (interpolation of the Abbot of San Zeno into the three final images of *Purgatorio* (*b*), from Virgil, Statius, and Lucan) and in *Inf.* xxx. 1–48 (Gianni Schicchi interpolated into and interwoven with a triad from Ovid).

> Vedea colui che fu nobil creato
> più ch'altra creatura, giù del cielo
> folgoreggiando scender, da l'un lato.
>   Vedea Brïareo fitto dal telo
> celestïal giacer, da l'altra parte,
> grave a la terra per lo mortal gelo.
>   Vedea Timbreo, vedea Pallade e Marte,
> armati ancora, intorno al padre loro,
> mirar le membra d'i Giganti sparte;
>   Vedea Nembròt a piè del gran lavoro
> quasi smarrito, e riguardar le genti
> che 'n Sennaàr con lui superbi fuoro.

O Nïobè, con che occhi dolenti
vedea io te segnata in su la strada,
tra sette e sette tuoi figliuoli spenti!

O Saùl, come in su la propria spada
quivi parevi morto in Gelboè,
che poi non sentì pioggia né ruggiada!

O folle Aragne, sì vedea io te
già mezza ragna, trista in su li stracci
de l'opera che mal per te si fé.

O Roboàm, già non par che minacci
quivi 'l tuo segno; ma pien di spavento
nel porta un carro, sanza ch'altri il cacci.

Mostrava ancor lo duro pavimento
come Almeon a sua madre fé caro
parer lo sventurato addornamento.

Mostrava come i figli si gittaro
sovra Sennacherìb dentro dal tempio,
e come, morto lui, quivi il lasciaro.

Mostrava la ruina e 'l crudo scempio
che fé Tamiri, quando disse a Ciro:
'Sangue sitisti, e io di sangue t'empio'.

Mostrava come in rotta si fuggiro
li Assiri, poi che fu morto Oloferne,
e anche le reliquie del martiro.

(*Purg.* xii. 25–60)

Drizza la testa, drizza, e vedi a cui
s'aperse a li occhi d'i Teban la terra;
per ch'ei gridavan tutti: 'Dove rui,

Anfïarao? perché lasci la guerra?'
E non restò di ruinare a valle
fino a Minòs che ciascheduno afferra.

Mira c'ha fatto petto de le spalle;
perché volse veder troppo davante,
di retro guarda e fa retroso calle.

Vedia Tiresia, che mutò sembiante
quando di maschio femmina divenne,
cangiandosi le membra tutte quante;

e prima, poi, ribatter li convenne
li due serpenti avvolti, con la verga,
che rïavesse le maschili penne.

Aronta è quel ch'al ventre li s'atterga,
che ne' monti di Luni, dove ronca
lo Carrarese che di sotto alberga,

ebbe tra' bianchi marmi la spelonça
per sua dimora; onde a guardar le stelle
e 'l mar non li era la veduta tronca.
    E quella che ricuopre le mammelle,
che tu non vedi, con le trecce sciolte,
e ha di là ogne pilosa pelle,
    Manto fu, che cercò per terre molte;
poscia si puose là dove nacqu' io;

                                (*Inf.* xx. 31–56)

    Allor mi disse: 'Quel che da la gota
porge la barba in su le spalle brune,
fu—quando Grecia fu de maschi vòta,
    sì ch'a pena rimaser per le cune—
augure, e diede 'l punto con Calcanta
in Aulide a tagliar la prima fune.
    Euripilo ebbe nome, e così'l canta
l'alta mia tragedia in alcun loco:
ben lo sai tu che la sai tutta quanta.

                              (*Inf.* xx. 106–14)

    Noi repetiam Pigmalïon allotta,
cui traditore e ladro e paricida
fece la voglia sua de l'oro ghiotta;
    e la miseria de l'avaro Mida
che seguì a la sua dimanda gorda,
per la qual sempre convien che si rida.
    Del folle Acàn ciascun poi si ricorda,
come furò le spoglie, sì che l'ira
de Iosüè qui par ch'ancor lo morda.
    Indi accusiam col marito Saffira;
lodiamo i calci ch'ebbe Elïodoro;
e in infamia tutto 'l monte gira
    Polinestor ch'ancise Polidoro;
ultimamente ci si grida: 'Crasso,
dilci, che 'l sai: di che sapore è l'oro?'
    Talor parla l'uno alto e l'altro basso,
secondo l'affezion ch'ad ir ci sprona
ora a maggiore e ora a minor passo:
    però al ben che 'l dì ci si ragiona,
dianzi non era io sol; ma qui da presso
non alzava la voce altra persona'.
    Noi eravam partiti già da esso,
e brigavam di soverchiar la strada

> tanto quanto al poder n'era permesso,
>   quand' io senti', come cosa che cada,
> tremar lo monte; onde mi prese un gelo
> qual prender suol colui ch'a monte vada.
>   Certo non si scoteo sì forte Delo,
> pria che Latona in lei facesse 'l nido
> a parturir li due occhi del cielo.
>
> (*Purg.* xx. 103–32)

Even without pursuing these reconstructions any further, we can get some inkling of what this *Ur-Commedia*, as I fear we must call it, was like. The lengthy prologues to the main business of *Inferno* and *Purgatorio* did not exist, nor consequently the punishment of the sins of incontinence in various sordid ways outside the city of Dis. The traveller descends rapidly through the entrance to the underworld, braving the monsters and crossing the stream in Charon's bark; he encounters further half-human creatures, and then the violent against themselves and against God. Descending on Geryon's back into the lower hell he encounters various types of fraud—seduction, sooth-saying, theft, false counsel, outright treason, but there is no evidence that the final canto of Judas and Brutus existed. In *Purgatorio* the episodes of the Ante-Purgatory—Casella, Sordello, and the Valley of the Kings—are lacking; at the end of the purgations we have a scene of reconciliation, but Beatrice was perhaps only a child, like Matelda in the present poem, not the august and even maternal figure we now recognize. It is difficult to grasp what Dante originally intended for *Paradiso*, but it was probably much simpler, contained far more Roman heroes, and did not progress far beyond the sphere of Saturn—the just rulers—whence Dante rose to the heaven of the stars to obtain a glimpse of the heavenly intelligences in the first mover.

NOTES

1. P. Renucci, *Dante* (Paris, 1958), pp. 83–5; *Dante, disciple et juge du monde gréco-latin* (Paris, 1954), pp. 70–3.
2. 'L'enigma delle Naiadi', *Studi danteschi*, xvi (1932), 105–25.
3. London, 1966.
4. *Centenary Essays on Dante* (Oxford, 1965), pp. 1–38.

APPENDIX:

The 128 [144] *Imagines* of the *Commedia*

APPENDIX: The 128 [144] Imagines of the Commedia

		The Imagines of the Inferno from Virgil and Ovid			The Imagines of the Inferno from Status and Lucan	
	cantos	VIRGIL	OVID	STATIUS	LUCAN	
(a)	iii, v	Charon's bark—Minos—Dido and Sychaeus				
	vi, ix	Cerberus	Furies—Medusa	6 The descent of Mercury	Erichtho	8
(b)	xii		Minotaur—Chiron—Nessus and Dejanira			
	xiii-xiv	Polydorus—Jupiter born on Crete	Harpies	6 Capaneus	Cato in the Libyan desert	8
(c)	xvii-xviii		Geryon—Phaeton—Jason and Medea—*Jason and Hypsipyle* [*Heroides*]			
	xx	Manto—Eurypylus	Tiresias	6+1 Amphiaraus	Aruns in the Carrarese	8+1
(d)	xxiv-xxv	Cacus	*The Phoenix*		Serpents in the Libyan desert—Sabellius and Nasidius	
	xxvi	The Palladium—The Trojan Horse	*Hermaphroditus and Salmacis*—Cadmus—Arethusa; Ulysses and Circe	6+2 Eteocles and Polynices—Achilles and Deidamia		10+2

(e)				Curio at Rimini
xxvii–xxviii	*Phalaris and Perillus [Ars Amat.]*			
xxix–xxx	Myrmidons—Athamas and Ino—Hecuba			
xxx–xxxiii	Sinon—Antenor	Myrrha	6+1	Briareus—Menalippus and Tydeus	Antaeus and Hercules at the Bagrada	10+1

		The Imagines of the Purgatorio from Virgil and Ovid			The Imagines of the Purgatorio from Statius and Lucan	
	cantos	VIRGIL	OVID		STATIUS	LUCAN
(a)	i, iv, ix	Cato—Rape of Ganymede	Calliope and the Pierides		Achilles borne away to Scyros	Cato and Martia—shadows in southern hemisphere — 6
	xii		Giants—Niobe—Arachne — 6		The necklace of Eriphyle	Caesar opening the public treasury—the Apennine range continued by Pelorus in Sicily — 6
(b)	xiv-xv	Circe's swine	Aglauros—contest of Neptune and Minerva			
	xvii-xviii	Lavinia and Amata—Companions of Aeneas who remained in Sicily	Procne and Philomena	5+1	Bacchic orgies near Thebes	Caesar at Marseilles and in Spain — 8
(c)	xx	Fabricius Pygmalion and Sychaeus—Polymestor and Polydorus	Midas			
	xxii				Hypsipyle at the fountain of Langia	
	xxiii-iv		Erysichthon—Centaurs and Lapithae-6			
	xxv		Meleager	7		— 8

(d)	xxv–xxvi	Pasiphae	Latona on Delos*—Callisto	*Jocasta	Migration of cranes—'Queen of Bithynia'	6
	xxvi–viii		Pyramus and Thisbe—Proserpine—Venus and Adonis; Hero and Leander [Heroides] 5+2	Hypsipyle saved from death	Xerxes at the Hellespont 6
(e)	xxix	Urania and the Muses—the Roman triumphal chariot	The Chariot of the Sun—Argus' eyes		
	xxx, xxxii–xxxiii		Orpheus and Eurydice—Argus and Mercury—Pyramus and the mulberry; Themis' monster 7+1		8

*now displaced before the preceding sub-section (canto xx)

*now displaced before the preceding sub-section (canto xxii)

The *Imagines* of the *Paradiso* from Virgil and Ovid   The *Imagines* of the *Paradiso* from Statius and Lucan

	cantos	VIRGIL	OVID	STATIUS	LUCAN
(a)	i		Apollo and Daphne—Apollo and Marsyas—Glaucus	Apollo crowns Caesar and the bard	8
	ii–v		Jason and the Bulls of Colchis—Narcissus—Iphigenia—*Alcmaeon and Eriphyle* [from *Eth Nic.*] 6+1		
(b)	vi	Pallas—Silvius Decii and Torquatus [Camilla—Nisus and Euryalus—Brutus]	6[-3]		The rivers of Gaul—Caesar in the Troad—siege of Perugia and Modena [Tomb of Alexander in Egypt] 10[-4]
(c)	viii–ix	Dido and Ascanius	*Typhoeus under Etna* *Phyllis and Demophoon* [*Heroides*]		Sea battle off Marseilles
	xi–xii		Muses and Sirens—Echo—Zephyrus 4+2		Caesar and Amyclas 8
(d)	xiii, xv, xvii	Aeneas and Anchises	Ariadne and Bacchus—*Phaeton and Clymene*—Hippolytus	[Hypsipyle and Archemorus—the daughters of Adrastus—the parentage of Polynices]	
	xix–xxi	Death of Anchises in Sicily—Rhipeus	Semele 6+1		10[-3]

(e)   [xxv–xxvi]   [Aeneas+*Priam*+*Dardanus*]

                                                 [The repose of the rowers—the cypress tree in the gale]

       xxvii,   The Sibyl's leaves   Europa—Leda and Gemini 4[–1]   [Adrastus and the
       xxxiii   prophecy of Apollo]

                                                        [Caesar and Pompey—the Samnite war—the sacred shield of Numa Pompilius] 12[–9]

6

Dante's 'Mirabile Visione' (Vita Nuova xlii)

COLIN HARDIE

It is generally agreed that Dante's promise at the end of *Vita Nuova* to write a poem about Beatrice 'such as had been written for no other' after 'some years' when as a result of further studies he could treat of her in a worthier manner, was eventually fulfilled by the *Comedy*. But disagreement is widespread on what the vision which occasioned this promise was like, what were the things in it which made Dante decide to say no more of Beatrice for the present, what kind of further study he contemplated for what kind of poem (a *canzone* or something of epic scale like the *Comedy*?), and whether he kept this purpose always in view until he carried it out (nineteen years later, from 1292 to 1311 on my view; about thirteen from 1294 to 1307, as others maintain), and never deviated from it, was never 'estranged' from Beatrice (*Purg.* xxxiii. 92) and his obligation, or even vow, to her. That he never displaced Beatrice from her central place in his soul (*anima*) is the prevalent view, in which the allegorical *canzoni* for the 'Donna Gentile', Philosophy, and even the 'Pietra' poems are seen as necessary developments and conscious preparation for the symbolic significance of Beatrice in the *Comedy* and its consummate technique. The *Convivio*, incomplete in the four books out of the fifteen intended, represents the further studies, and is the connecting link, the centre of Dante's trilogy,[1] between the *Vita Nuova* and the *Comedy*. There is in Dante's life, on this view, no change in direction, but substantial, if not unwavering, continuity of preparation for the fulfilment of the promise, and the vision is the nucleus of the *Comedy*.[2]

There is, of course, also much disagreement about the interpretation of both *Vita Nuova* and the *Comedy* in themselves, as well as about their relationship, and I must indicate briefly where I stand with regard to the current views, and why I offer a different view of Dante's development, with a rather different interpretation of the reference in the *Comedy, Purg.* xxx. 115, to the *Vita Nuova* as a specific work, not merely to Dante's youth, and of Beatrice's rebukes in *Purg.* xxx to xxxiii, not for moral, doctrinal, or theological errors but for his failure to fulfil his promise, and for his writing poems for other ladies. In my view the *Convivio* does 'derogate' from the *Vita Nuova* (*Conv.* I, i. 16), since it ignores the promise and turns the vision into a mere superfluous proof of immortality (II. viii. 13–16). This interpretation is borne out by *Epistle* iii to Cino da Pistoia, expounding the sonnet, 'Io sono stato con amore insieme' (with which the other sonnet to Cino (Contini ed. 52) must be taken).

The *Vita Nuova* has been much examined and reinterpreted in the last thirty years,[3] and these studies are usefully described and evaluated in the *Enciclopedia dantesca*.[4] The point of disagreement has shifted: opinions are no longer divided between a positivistic interpretation of the work as an external biography and an allegorical or a deliberate mystification for the adherents of some quasi-heretical sect. There is now general agreement that a real woman and a series of real events have been transfigured by poetic imagination into something that transcends the traditional themes of courtly love, by prolonging adoration of the beloved beyond her death and by instituting an analogy with the life of Christ. The division of opinion instead now lies between emphasis on the mystical exaltation of Beatrice as the transformation of 'amor' into Christian 'caritas', a hagiographical *Vita Sanctae Beatricis* on the model of near contemporary and Florentine saints, such as Giuliana Falconieri, and so an anticipation of the developed and more explicit doctrine of the *Comedy*, on the one side; and on the other, insistence on the work as a *Vita Dantis poetae*, primarily interested in his poetic originality and progress, especially the discovery of the 'nova matera', the 'stile de la loda', the rapture of disinterested love and praise without thought of return or reward, an end in itself, independent of such recognition as Beatrice's salutation, and resistant even to mockery, independent of even her life. The final chapter looks forward to further experiment in a yet 'newer' poetry, even more original. The biblical quotations and parallels are a bold procedure of rhetorical intensification or metaphor, within a theory of poetry, a 'poetica di forte impegno intellettuale'. J. A. Scott quotes the first printed edition of 1576 which, regarding the Christian analogy as blasphemous, altered 'salute' to 'quiete', 'gloriosa' to 'gratiosa', etc., and persuasively restates that view.[5] The beatitude and ecstasy that Beatrice diffuses is a substitute for Christian blessedness, as in *VN* xxvi. 10–13: 'Vede perfettamente onne salute'; and in 'Donne ch'avete intelletto d'amore', *VN* xix, vv. 27–8, this is actually said by God in Heaven, as if Hell would not be hell for one who had seen Beatrice, 'la speranza dei beati'. This is clear also from the canzone, 'Lo doloroso amor' (*Rime* 68. 27–8):

> ricordando la gioia del dolce viso,
> a che niente par lo paradiso.

Dante excluded this *canzone*, as also 'E' m'incresce di me' (*Rime* 67), from the *Vita Nuova*. But in the *Comedy* Dante is careful to make Beatrice herself correct this error, recalled in *Par.* xiv. 132 and xv. 34–6, in *Par.* xviii. 21: '. . . ché non pur ne' miei occhi è paradiso'. The correction is anticipated by the bystanders' comment on *Purg.* xxxii. 1: 'li occhi . . . fissi e attenti', and eight lines later 'Troppo fiso!'.

But the two interpretations of the *Vita Nuova* do not exclude each other, if there is a real contradiction in it. *VN* iii. 3–7 and xii. 3–8, 'almost certainly'[6] imply Dante's belief in the prophetic character of these visions, dreams, and 'forti imaginazioni'. Indeed the whole plot of the action turns on their genuineness as prophecies. The *canzone*, 'Donna pietosa', in *VN* xxiii. 17–28, is designed as prophecy, though it may have been added at the time when the *Vita Nuova* was composed, since it is absent from the manuscript tradition before the *Vita Nuova* as a whole. More probably the whole of chapter xxv is an afterthought, not integrated as 'Donna pietosa' is, and in its intellectual pride it denies the prophetic character of 'Amor' by declaring him, in Aristotelian rationalistic language, to be 'an accident in substance', not the 'deus' of *VN* ii. 4 nor 'the immortal part' which *Conv.* II. viii. 13 lays down as required for divinatory dreams. This access of Cavalcantian scepticism and poetic theory destroys the coherence of the *Vita Nuova*, and incidentally destroys the plot of the *Aeneid* in so far as Virgil based it on belief in prophecy.[7] Apollo is degraded to an inanimate thing, his cauldron, in language borrowed from the Epicurean speaker in Cicero's *de natura deorum* i. 36 (names of gods given 'rebus inanimis atque mutis'). There is no suggestion in the *Vita Nuova* that Dante felt it to be youthful and immature, quite the reverse: he had attained to a developed theory of poetry and seems set to develop on these lines 'for some years', but his complacency was soon undermined by his discovery of the greater world of philosophy, which, however rationalist it was, drew him away from Guido Cavalcanti's sceptical detachment from religion and politics. If Dante came to think that in the *Vita Nuova* he saw a few ideas 'as in a dream', he cannot have read Cicero's *Laelius, de Amicitia* or Boethius' *Consolation of Philosophy* before he wrote the *Vita Nuova* (not therefore to be sub-titled *Beatrix, de Amore*). If in the *Vita Nuova* Dante had advanced to as developed a theory of Christian *caritas* inwardly transforming and superseding courtly love, as Singleton would have it, he could not so soon have fallen away from it, and 'Amor' would not be 'an accident in substance', but on the road to becoming, with Apollo, what they are in the *Comedy* (e.g. *Par.* i. 13), a pagan and poetic figure for the Holy Spirit, or at least for Christian poetic inspiration.[8]

If the literary rather than the mystical element is dominant in the *Vita Nuova*, and if ch. xxv is later than the final chapter with the vision and the promise, the probable direction of Dante's mind in the next few years, in literary studies leading to new experimentation in poetry, is indicated. But was this a direction that could carry Dante across the rough country of Florentine politics, into exile, to the joining with the other White exiles and earlier Ghibelline exiles in attempting to get back by force, to the withdrawal into renewed literary studies of the *de Vulgari Eloquentia* and *Convivio*? Out of *Convivio* IV came the return to active politics, represented by the three *Epistles* and the *Monarchy* and the impassioned participation in Henry VII's '*in*faustissimus cursus' in Italy, and it was ended by the *Comedy*, and by total absorption in it, ché a sé torce *tutta* la mia cura' (*Par.* x. 26), 'tutta' apart from the *Letter to the Italian Cardinals*, and the dubious *Epistle to Cangrande* and *Quaestio de aqua et terra*.

Any answer to this problem must depend on whether the *Comedy* is interpreted as primarily mystical or literary, Truijen[9] concludes his discussion with the words: 'si deve oggi ritenere prevalente la tesi della "visio" [in the sense of *Par.* xvii. 128, "tutta la tua vision", the whole poem] come *fictio poetica'* (the view of the 'vision' as a *poetic fiction* must now be regarded as predominant), quoting Sapegno on how the poem was conceived 'con la vigile coscienza di costruire una fictio poetica' ('acutely aware that he was creating a poetic fiction'). Quite so, but fiction based on mystical experience, visions and dreams, for which Dante also went back to the mystical and prophetic element in the *Vita Nuova*, strengthening it with new experience (especially in the final vision, the beginning and end of the *Comedy*, its germ and its goal) and with a new study of the mystics, above all St. Bernard, Richard of St. Victor, and Bonaventura. It may be impossible to say where 'resoconto di un vero raptus' ('an account of a true visionary experience') passes into poetic rehandling or poetic intervention, but there is surely much material from dreams and visions in the *Comedy*. After an examination of *all* Dante's accounts of visions, dreams, and 'forti imaginazioni', I am convinced that, if in the *Vita Nuova* he naïvely accepted (for literary purposes only?) dreams and visions as 'prophetic' in the sense of foretelling the objective future, in the *Comedy* he thought of them as revelatory of the subjective latent movements in the mind of the dreamer, 'the unconscious' or preconscious as we call it. Nardi's pugnacious defence of the idea of 'Dante profeta'[10] in the *Comedy* stresses his mission to the world, his message about the two providential institutions, Church and Empire, his revelation about the imminence of a new age when Veltro and DXV restore them to their rightful functions. But if the prophecies of the Veltro, DXV, and the nine-year-old at the court of Cangrande in Verona are interpreted as *post eventum*, applying to Dante himself as the poet of the *Comedy*, future events in the world are not prophesied, except for the faith that the Church would be reformed and purified, expressed by Folco at *Par.* ix, 142 and by Beatrice at *Par.* xxvii. 142–8 (which glosses Folco's 'tosto', i.e. soon, as before some 4,000 years pass!). It is true that at *Purg.* xxvii. 93 Dante speaks of sleep as 'knowing the news before the fact' ('anzi che 'l fatto sia, sa le novelle'). But the dream of Lia and Rachel is a subjective anticipation of the figures from Dante's Florentine experience, Matelda and Beatrice. So the 'Veltro' is an element in the psyche, in the sensitive soul that man shares with animals, that will develop into a man, 'messo di Dio', and take over from Dante the lost pilgrim of *Inf.* i. at Verona before July 1312.[11]

Dante had no prophetic mission to the world, but he had found his vocation as poet, as Beatrice's poet once again, and the *Comedy* is an account of how he had found the true path to his essential self,[12] and he needed the revelations of visions, dreams, and imaginations (of himself as a second Aeneas and as a second St. Paul), given to him by Grace. This, I suggest, is what he means by the 'poema sacro al quale ha posto mano e cielo e terra'. *Par.* xxv. 1–2, where 'terra' is Dante's work on earth as a poetic artist (all that he had learnt of the art between the *Vita Nuova* and the *Comedy*) on his given 'materia' (*Par.* i. 12 and 17; x. 27; xxx. 31–6; cf. *Purg.* ix. 70–2 and elsewhere). At least the final vision in *Par.* xxxiii is 'un vero raptus', if only because its geometric abstractness, so bare and 'Byzantine', as Singleton[13] says on *Par.* xxxiii. 133–5, seems unlike a poetic fiction, even an austere Dantesque one, more like a mandala; and Singleton notes that 'fantasia' is an 'image-receiving', not an 'image-making' faculty. Furthermore, this vision is certainly not the 'mirabile visione' of Beatrice in *Vita Nuova* xlii, but far beyond it and her. If, then, the *Comedy* is not just, or even primarily, 'fictio poetica', it is again, like the *Vita Nuova*, the *De Vulgari Eloquentia* and the *Convivio* a literary self-analysis, a study of Dante's poetic development from 'Donne ch'avete intelletto d'amore' (*VN* xix; quoted at *Purg.* xxiv. 51 ff.), including the deviation of 'Voi che 'ntendendo il terzo ciel movete' (*Conv.* II and *Par.* viii. 37) and of 'Amor, che ne la mente mi ragiona' (*Conv.* III and *Purg.* ii. 112) from Beatrice to celebrate 'quella donna in cui errai' (sonnet *Parole mie*, Contini 31). But, as we shall see, the *De Vulgari Eloquentia* and *Convivio* are quite incompatible with the *Vita Nuova* and the *Comedy* on the source of Dante's inspiration.

But, first, on the evidence of the *Vita Nuova* alone without hindsight of the later works, we must touch on four questions: what did Dante mean by the 'new life', what probably was the nature of the 'mirabile visione', what kind of poem did Dante contemplate, and what studies 'for a number of years' were to nurture the proposed poem, however vaguely conceived?

Nobody without the *Convivio* would have imagined that 'vita nuova' meant youth, the first twenty-five years of life which Dante calls 'Adolescenz(i)a' in *Conv.* IV. xxiii. 12 and xxiv. 1. He mentions his 'puerizia' and 'gioventudine' in *VN* ii, but his 'new life' began in his ninth year, and only in his eighteenth did his 'vita nova' inspire him to 'canticum novum',[14] the sonnet of *VN* xxiii. 17 (cf. *Le dolci rime d'amor*, 105 = *Conv.* IV. xix, 9–10 asking for its interpretation. The word 'nuovo' occurs fourteen times in the *Vita Nuova*, but never means young, but always new, or novel, recent, original, strange, unusual, miraculous, unexpected, surprising, exceptional, or merely different and other. Its uses in all of Dante's works are tabulated and discussed by Antonietta Bufano (cf. n. 4), who adds to her main categories: 'furthermore it is said of a person, perhaps with reference to age', quoting two uses in the *Rime* 34. 1 and 44. 7, where this meaning cannot be wholly excluded. The nearest to this in the *Vita Nuova* is in the *canzone* 'Donna pietosa e di novella etate', *VN* xxiii. 17 (cf. *Le dolci rime d'amor*, 105 = *Conv.* IV. xix. 9–10 and *Inf.* xxxiii. 88 where Dante uses 'età' rather than 'vita'). The one undoubted example for A. Bufano is *Purg.* xxx. 115: 'è l'età giovanile di Dante'. Certainly Dante's youth is meant, as the references to his mature age, 'barba', *Purg.* xxxi. 68 and 74, and the simile of the 'novo augelletto', ibid. 61, show. But the question is whether in this rebuke she does not *also* with sharp irony mean the *Vita Nuova* and its unfulfilled promise to her, fulfilled for other women. She speaks of the 'inspirations which she obtained for him, recalling him in dream and otherwise'. But he paid no attention. Her point is that in the *Convivio* he dismissed the *Vita Nuova* as merely youthful, outdated, and superseded by better inspirations, which Beatrice, now inspiring the *Comedy*, dismisses as 'altre vanità' or 'novità'. But in the *Vita Nuova* the new life means not only a new understanding of love, such as no previous poet had risen to, but a new style to express it, the 'dolce stil *nuovo*', which was inaugurated by the *canzone* 'Donne ch'avete intelletto d'Amore'.

Secondly, what can we think or guess the nature of the 'mirabile visione' to have been? Clearly, it was something that went beyond the thought of the preceding sonnet 'Oltre la spera', however marvellous that quality was (xli. 7), however 'spiritual' the ascent was, to imagine 'a lady honoured there in heaven above'. It was direct vision, an anticipation of her glory that he hoped to see more fully after his death, but in the *Comedy* is privileged to see in this life in a series of visions of Beatrice, none of which can be identified with the 'mirabile visione'. His final view of Beatrice in the *Comedy* perhaps, as has been suggested,[15] in the 'candida rosa', seated next to Rachel (*Inf.* ii. 102, *Par.* xxxii. 8–9), whence she looks with a smile (*Par.* xxxi. 92), comes nearest to what we may guess at: the words 'la quale gloriosamente mira ne la faccia di colui *qui est per omnia secula benedictus*' becoming in *Par.* xxxi. 93: 'poi si tornò a l'etterna fontana'. But there Beatrice seems too distant, 'sì lontana come parea', too much in company that belongs to the scheme of the *Comedy*, Matelda as the active life paired with Beatrice as the contemplative, anticipated by Lia and Rachel in the dream of *Purg.* xxvii. 100–45. Cecco d'Ascoli simply seizes on the contradiction in 'Oltre la spera' that Dante both does and does not understand his 'new intelligence', but Dante seems to have confided to his friend Cino da Pistoia that it often caused him to feel enraptured, in ectasy, since Cino in his canzone 'Avegna che el m'aggia più per tempo',[16] of consolation to Dante in his persistent grief at Beatrice's death, seems to know more details than ch. xli provides, e.g.

> come fu ricevuta
> Dagli angeli con dolce riso e canto.

Where Dante says only (xli. 7) that he hears Beatrice's name 'often' in his thought, Cino says:

> Gli spiriti vostri rapportato l'hanno
> Che *spesse volte* quel viaggio fanno,

which Dante echoes at *Conv.* II. vii. 6: 'onde io pensando *spesse volte* come possibile m'era, me n'andava quasi rapito'. If the thought almost caused rapture, the 'mirabile visione' would seem to have been truly rapturous, and perhaps the fulfilment of what is in Cino a question:

> Lasso me! quando e come
> Veder vi potrò io *visibilmente*?,

though less than the seeing of her glory by his soul after death. But in the *canzone* 'Voi che 'ntendendo' of *Conv.* II Dante attributes this sight of her glory, 'ove una donna gloriar vedea', to the thought of 'Oltre la spera', and says nothing about the 'mirabile visione' except that it was proof of the immortality of the soul, *Conv.* II. viii. 13. This playing down has to be looked at further in its context.

The reason for it, I suggest, was that Dante had written the kind of poem that he contemplated in *VN* xlii, but for another woman or figure, a *canzone* for the 'donna gentile', whom the *Convivio* represents as Philosophy, though connecting her with the sensuous, not rational, attractions of Beatrice's rival in the *Vita Nuova*, simply reversing the relations of 'appetito–cuore' and 'anima–ragione' of *VN* xxxviii, 5–6. Later, furthermore, as we shall see, he composed yet another 'novelty' in a *canzone* for the Pietra. As it was the *canzone* 'Donne ch'avete intelletto d'Amore' that had made Dante famous, and inaugurated his 'dolce stil nuovo', it was to be expected that a grander canzone should be in view, and the *De Vulgari Eloquentia* assumes the primacy of the *canzone* in the high tragic style.

If this, then, was the programme, what studies did it entail? Presumably such as are implied in *VN* xxv, literary and rhetorical studies of Latin love poetry and its revival in Provençal, 'lingua d'oco'. He does not mention the French romances (though he doubtless read them; cf. 'Arturi regis ambages pulcerrime', *DVE* I, 10, 2) because they were best in prose, and if he cites the epics of Virgil and Lucan, it was their 'figure e colori rettorici' rather than their epic scale that he aspired to. He mentions the *Ars Poetica* of Horace, his 'Poetria', and doubtless read the medieval poetics that Faral has made available,[17] but more especially Brunetto Latini's *Rhetoric*; and it was probably at this time that he came to know Brunetto himself (cf. his 'cara e buona imagine paterna', *Inf.* xv. 83) who taught him how a man can win eternal fame ('come l'uom s'etterna') that is, as a poet, in this world (cf. *Purg.* xxi. 85; like Virgil, *Inf.* ii. 59–60, who encourages Dante, *Inf.* xxiv. 47–8, with this thought cf. *Par.* ix. 41–2, Folco da Marsiglia, and Dante poet of the *Comedy* in *Par.* xvii. 98: 's'infutura la tua vita'). Also in *VN* xxviii, 2, Dante excuses himself from treating of Beatrice's death because his power of expression, 'la mia lingua', not his philosophy, would not yet be sufficient.

When Dante, in 1304 or so, retired from political strife, leaving allies who were as bad as enemies, both hungry for his blood (*Inf.* xv. 71), he had nothing to fall back on except his fame as poet (*Conv.* I. iv. 13), and even that tarnished by his homeless poverty (*Conv.* I. ii. 4–5). He began by writing up his theory of poetry in the *De Vulgari Eloquentia*, and interrupted it when he had reached the highest point of his poetic achievement, the *canzone* on the Donna Pietra with which he had won his spurs as a knight of poetry, in order to embark on a more ambitious project, the *Convivio* in fifteen books, to rehabilitate the philosophical poetry that his thirty months of concentrated philosophical study had led to, because they were underrated in comparison with the *Vita Nuova*. He had to build on it, even if his philosophical *canzone* 'Amor che ne la mente mi ragiona' had been set to music and, as an 'amoroso canto', been much appreciated for its 'dolcezza' (*Purg.* ii. 106–17). It is this interpretation of it (and of 'Voi che 'ntendendo') as celebration of a sensuous love that Dante is at pains to deny (*Conv.* I. ii. 15–17, III. i. 11. III. iii. 12), with only partial success. He deprecates the disrepute of having yielded to so great a passion ('l'infamia di tanta passione avere seguita'), and insists that 'non passione ma vertù' was his motive in writing them, and that he does not intend in any way to 'derogate' from the *Vita Nuova* but rather to enhance it by the *Convivio*. The *Vita Nuova* was entirely reasonable and suitable to Dante's age at the time in its fervour and passion, but the poetry that followed was rightly temperate and virile. The *Vita Nuova* belongs to his 'adolescence' in his scheme of the four ages of man, expounded in *Conv.* IV. xxiii–xxviii, and even to 'puerizia' (I. iv. 2), not of years but in intellectual maturity. Dante was at least twenty-seven, if not twenty-nine, when he wrote the *Vita Nuova*, and his maturity was at least by two years belated, if the general rule, not the individual 'complexion' is adduced (*Conv.* IV. xxiv. 7). Dante's idea of 'enhancing' the *Vita Nuova* was presumably to show how it had laid the foundations for his subsequent progress. At one moment in this development he tried to hold the balance between the competing ladies, in the sonnet 'Due donne in cima de la mente mia' (Contini 33). The conflict between 'Bellezza' and 'Virtù' is resolved by the verdict of 'Amor': 'beauty can be loved for delight and virtue for the sake of action'. If in *Par.* iv. 1–6 Dante declared that one, a man, a lamb or a hound, could remain suspended between two equally distant objects of desire or fear, he soon found that he might hold the balance between two ladies, but not between the two kinds of poetry which they represented and inspired, and after a long struggle (*Conv*. II. ii. 3 and xv. 9) Beatrice had to cede the 'rocca de la mia mente' ('rocca' is the equivalent of 'cima' in the sonnet). The 'new thought', 'ch'era *virtuosissimo* sì come *vertù* celestiale' (ibid. 5), could also claim 'bellezza', as the last line of 'Voi che 'ntendendo' says. Dante says that he was, as it were, looking for silver, consolation in Boethius and Cicero, and found gold, 'non forse sanza divino imperio' (*Conv*. II. xii. 5), the exercise of reason, proper to maturity. He draws a firm line between the sensitive and the rational parts of the soul, (*Conv*. II. vii. 3–4): to depart from reason and remain immersed in passion and sensation, is 'to live as a beast not a man'. This is surely a great reversal of *Vita Nuova* ii. 9 on the 'nobilissima vertù' of Love's sovereignty, which was 'never without the faithful counsel of Reason', and of *VN* xxxviii. *Conv*. II has much to say on the 'nobility' of Dante's new love.

Now the second stanza of 'Voi che 'ntendendo', describing the 'molta battaglia' between the two ladies or two thoughts, and speaking of Beatrice in heaven, recasts, as we have seen, the last sonnet of the *Vita Nuova*, 'Oltre la spera', but it does not mention the 'mirabile visione' that ensued, unless her 'gracious revelation that she was in heaven' (*Conv*. II. vii. 6), goes beyond 'Oltre la spera' and implies the further vision. Anyhow in *Conv*. II. viii. 13 Dante mentions dreams, which are no part of the experience of 'Oltre la spera', as providing in their 'divinations', 'continuous experience of our immortality', and this must surely mean the 'mirabile visione'. But there is no word of the promise of a greater poem in Beatrice's honour, and, moreover, Dante had no need of this proof of immortality, unusual as Nardi has shown,[18] and superfluous as the previous paragraphs indicate. The promise to Beatrice has been fulfilled for her rival, and this I take to be the basis of Beatrice's reproofs in the Earthly Paradise. But it must be admitted that Dante introduces his discussion by saying that he does not intend to speak further of Beatrice 'in his book'. In what book, then, did he propose to return to her? A later book of the *Convivio* itself? Certainly not the *De Vulgari Eloquentia*, though in *Convivio* he speaks of this as yet to come (I. v. 10). In it he speaks of himself

as the poet of 'rectitudo' (II. ii. 9) though he also quotes two of
the *canzoni* of the *Vita Nuova*. I cannot think that he had the
Comedy in mind, or even a *canzone*, but rather something like
what he contemplates as suitable to old age, the return to God
and the blessing of life's journey (*Conv.* IV. xxviii. 1 and 11),
illustrated by the strange allegory of Marzia and Catone (ibid.
13–19; cf. *Purg.* i. 78–90). Not anyhow a poem of sensuous love,
from which he speaks of himself in the roughly contemporary
sonnet to Cino da Pistoia (Contini 52) as liberated:

> Io me credea del tutto esser partito
> da queste nostre rime, messer Cino;

he puts only a 'tired finger' to his poetic pen, and urges Cino to
cultivate 'vertu' and to follow Dante's 'different path' ('altro
cammino'; very different from the 'altro viaggio' of *Inf.* i. 91)—
perhaps not so much the *Convivio* as already the *Monarchy*, where
there is no Beatrice at all.

Furthermore, it must be granted to the upholders of the continuity of Dante's path from the *Vita Nuova* via the *Convivio* to the
Comedy, that in *Conv.* II. ii. 1, Dante says of Beatrice that 'she
lives in heaven with the angels and on earth with my soul', as a
treasured, not eclipsed, memory. Yet when he takes his leave of
her, he changes the present tense to past (*Conv.* II. viii. 16; 'là
dove quella gloriosa donna vive de la quale *fu* l'anima mia
innamorata'). This perfect tense refers to the argument of
Conv. II. viii. 4–7 from planetary influences; those of Venus, to
whose angelic motors the *canzone* is addressed. As Beatrice is
now in heaven above the planets, she is beyond their influence,
which must be transferred to a soul in the body on earth. Love
for Beatrice must inevitably vanish, and Dante briskly dismisses
the question as an easy one. But he has explained only his new
love for a different woman likewise of flesh and blood, in the way
that *Epistle* iii (as we shall see) makes more explicit, not for 'the
most noble and beautiful daughter of the emperor of the
universe', Philosophy, presumably in heaven above the influence of Venus (*Conv.* II. xii. 9 and xv. 12); and the whole
Comedy contradicts the argument, notably *Purg.* xxxiii. 91–9, in
the dialogue between Beatrice and Dante. He protests that he
cannot remember any estrangement whatsoever from Beatrice,
and feels no remorse, but she reminds him with a smile that he

has just drunk the water of Lethe; this proves the fault in the misdirection of his will, and Lethe is not lightly administered without repentance and confession (*Purg.* xxx. 142–5). Providentially, with his return to Beatrice from 'elsewhere', his estrangement supplied much of the matter of the poem which describes how Grace rescued him from it, and the poetic art acquired in the interval could all be put at the service of Beatrice. The argument in *Conv.* II. viii. 4–7 may perhaps explain why Beatrice should say, *Purg.* xxx. 124–6, that 'as soon as she . . . died, Dante removed himself from me and gave himself to others', and Dante in his confession (*Purg.* xxxi. 36) repeats 'tosto', 'as soon as your face was concealed from me'. The *Vita Nuova* asserts that Dante fell away from Beatrice only in the second year after her death and then only for a few days, *VN* xxxix. 2—he thus observed the rule of Andreas Capellanus that mourning for the beloved may or should last for two years.[19] The *Vita Nuova* seemed to have transcended Beatrice's death, but Dante's fall from grace began with her death, as stellar influences decreed.

The *Comedy* does not solve the problem of stellar influence,[20] but it modifies it, as it does also the relation of the rational to the lower souls.

Dante's much discussed account in the *Convivio* of his transition to philosophical poetry, at first disguised as love poetry, then explicit in 'Le dolci rime d'amor', the subject of *Convivio* IV, is by no means perspicuous, and is perhaps disingenuous, or at least ingenious, in trying not to derogate from Beatrice and the *Vita Nuova* while in fact operating a reversal. But *Epistle* iii, in answer to a sonnet of Cino da Pistoia, accompanying the sonnet 'Io sono stato con Amore insieme' (Contini 50A), is much more explicit about the sensuous nature of Dante's love for Beatrice, a passion not unique and unrepeatable, but likely to recur, in a fickle will not set on 'virtù', without that 'stability of mind' that Dante claims (*Conv.* III. i. 12). Ovid is quoted as an authority to back the syllogism about love as a passion of the sensitive soul, an 'accident in substance'. Dante here adopts the attitude to love of Guido Cavalcanti in his famous and pessimistic analysis of love as destructive of reason in the canzone 'Donna me prega'. Philosophy is the remedy, and Dante recommends Cino to read the treatise, attributed to Seneca, *de remediis fortui-*

torum (accidents in substance!). He speaks with assurance, but
he was to suffer a more violent fall into love than Cino's, as
Epistle iv and its *canzone* 'Amor da che convien' testify. The
dates of Dante's correspondences with Cino are uncertain, but
there is much in the imagery that is close to the *Convivio* (e.g. on
finding gold, Cino's 'Cercando di trovar minera in oro',
Dante's 'Segno fa voi trovar ogni tesoro', 7 minera, Conv. II. xii.
5; Dante's 'Io sono stato', 3 affrena . . . sprona, *Conv.* IV. xxvi.
8–9 in praise of Aeneas' abandonment of Dido and descent into
the Underworld).

In the philosophical *canzoni*, allegorical or direct, Dante does
not claim to have produced a novelty, such as had not been
written before. Though he later in exile returned both to the
allegorical mode in *Tre Donne* and the direct treatment of
liberality in 'Doglia mi reca', about 1296 he entered a new
phase of technical experiment after the model of Arnaud Daniel
in the poems to the Donna Pietra. In one of them, 'Amor, tu
vedi ben', the 'congedo' proclaims that in it he has the ardour
and boldness to attempt an unheard of novelty; 'a thing never
conceived before at any time':

> la novità che per tua forma luce
> che non fu mai pensata in alcun tempo,

(The novelty such as was never before conceived at any time is
resplendent in your form.)

and, some ten years later, reviewing his poetic progress he
defends the *canzone* from the charge of excessive repetition of
rhymes because it can claim thereby to have achieved 'a novelty
unattempted yet' in technical virtuosity: 'novum aliquid atque
intentatum artis'; and he compares the achievement to the
attainment of knighthood, the day when the aspirant 'wins his
spurs', disdaining to let his vigil pass by without some special
'prerogative', some claim to supreme excellence. The commentators on the *canzone* and the *DVE* see no connection with the
promise at the end of the *Vita Nuova*. But I see it as its fulfilment,
and for another woman; and it accounts for the special animosity that Beatrice shows in the last of her rebukes in the
Earthly Paradise, *Purg.* xxxiii. 74: 'fatto di pietra e, impetrato,
tinto' (if the text and its punctuation are uncertain, the meaning is clear and the repetition emphatic). Here too, curiously,

the commentators do not refer to the Pietra poems. This is natural, even inevitable, in an interpretation of Beatrice in the Earthly Paradise as alternating between symbol of the Church and Florentine girl: as the Church in her chariot in *Purg.* xxix, and as exhibiting its vicissitudes in *Purg.* xxxii, but in flesh and blood, 'carne', in *Purg.* xxx. 127 and xxxi. 48–50. But the final scene in *Purg.* xxxii is a transposition of the last stanza of the Pietra poem 'Così nel mio parlar voglio esser aspro', and so leads on naturally to Beatrice's 'fatto di pietra' in the next canto. The lady Pietra can hardly be separated from the 'Pargoletta', since she is called 'pargoletta' in the last line of 'Io son venuto' (Contini 43, 'se in pargoletta fia per core un marmo'; cf. 'giovane' in 'Amore, che movi', 25 and 57), and the 'pargoletta' of *Rime* 34 and 36 seems to be the same as the 'giovinetta' of *Rime* 35, where her hardness of heart is stressed. 'Pargoletta' is mentioned in *Purg.* xxxi. 59, where Beatrice, after denouncing Dante to the bystanders, turns directly on him with her 'sword' (*Purg.* xxx. 57), and is classed along with 'altra vanità (or novità) con sì breve uso'. Petrocchi's reading of 'novità', defended in his Introductory volume (p. 221), is preferable, and welcome to me, though not in the sense of 'giovanile esperienza' (on *Purg.* xxxi. 60), but rather of the poetic novelty of which Dante had boasted. Admittedly '*nuovo* augelletto' in the following line means 'young', but the 'pargoletta' of the *ballata* (Contini 34), possesses 'bellezze . . . al mondo nove', i.e. original, and, when she says that she is 'bella e nova' (line 1), it is the beauty and novelty of the poem that is meant; 'young' would be mere repetition of 'pargoletta'.

But we should expect the Lady Philosophy to be Beatrice's special target, if the inspirers of Dante's poetry, rather than the odd women whom he may have loved, Violetta, Lisetta, etc., are in question. Beatrice indeed denounces in *Purg.* xxxiii. 85–7.

> quella *scuola*
> c'hai seguitata, e veggi sua dottrina
> come può seguitar la mia parola;

(cf. *Par.* xxix. 70 where she returns to 'le vostre scole' on earth, with their varying opinions, 'filosofando', 86). But, in my view, this has been prepared by the dream of the Siren in *Purg.* xix; and in *Purg.* xxxi. 45 she punctually warns Dante against fall-

ing again for the sirens. For me (see n. 11b) this dream anticipates (like the dream in *Purg.* xxvii of Lia and Rachel) what will
be explicit in the Earthly Paradise, and shows Beatrice rebuking
Virgil, because he is awake and Dante's guardian, and exhibiting the filthiness of the Siren. Now Virgil, like Dante, had been
enchanted by Casella's singing of Dante's philosophical (as
Convivio III would have it) *canzone* 'Amor, che ne la mente mi
ragiona' in *Purg.* ii. 112, and rebuked there by Cato for negligence and sloth (120–3). It is absurd to accuse Virgil, known as
Parthenias in Naples (Donatus, *Life of Virgil*, 11), of lustfulness,
and not to recognize that his interpretation of the dream (*Purg.*
xix. 58–60) is erroneous. The change of the Siren from hideous
to attractive dramatizes Dante's difficulty at first with philosophy and then delight; and Dante knew from Cicero, *De
Finibus*, v. 49, that what the sirens promised Ulysses was not the
satisfaction of lust, but knowledge, which indeed he pursues in
Inf. xxvi. The siren comes from Boethius, *De Consol. Phil.* i,
prose 1, 11; the philosopher Boethius' siren was poetry, but
Dante's is philosophy since he is a poet by vocation, but
tempted to be a philosopher (cf. on vocation, *Par.* viii. 143 ff.).

   But, it will be said, how can Beatrice denounce philosophy,
when, as the commentators say, she has absorbed into herself as
theology the symbolism of the 'donna gentile', philosophy? She
is indeed in the *Vita Nuova* and the *Comedy* not merely a Florentine girl, of the Portinari family, but transformed into a Muse,
the guardian angel of his best poetry, but she is not theology,
revelation, the Church, any more than Virgil represents reason,
as is usually said; to guide and be guided through Hell is a gift
of grace, a revelation, and Virgil's second utterance, after
introducing himself, is a prophecy, which is not the sphere of
reason. But the symbol of the 'donna gentile' is said to be divided
in the *Comedy* into two, Virgil as philosophy and Beatrice as
theology.

   Furthermore, the philosophizing in the *Comedy*, of which
there is much, is in its developed passages devoted to correcting
errors which drew Dante to value philosophy above poetry,
even for himself, as his fear in *Monarchy* I. i. 3 of the accusation
of burying his talent shows (and yet most critics date the
Monarchy and *Comedy* in such a way as to make Dante have this
fear when already embarked on the *Comedy*!). Yet there are

those who will not believe what Dante says of himself and his errors, preferring 'the perpetual concordance' of his views and the total self-consistency of his philosophy.[21]

To take first the lessons which Beatrice inculcates, immediately after her rebukes and her instructions about the future poem (*Purg.* xxxii. 105; xxxiii. 55 and 76), in *Paradiso*, on the spots in the moon and on vows. The argument about the spots in the moon[22] is directed against a quantitative explanation such as *Conv.* II. xiii. 9 (Averroes); III. vii. 2; IV. xxi. 10–11; and substitutes a 'formal principle' (*Par.* ii. 71, 147). The argument is at first general, but it culminates in being applied to the immortal soul, the subject of discussion in the *Convivio*. Beatrice also emphasizes, against the tendency of the *Convivio*, the weakness of reason without sensation (ibid. 54–7; cf. *Inf.* ii. 15; *Par.* iv. 41 'sensato'; *Par.* x. 54 for 'sensibile'). The creation of the soul is the subject of Statius' long exposition in *Purg.* xxv, and there (as in *Par.* iii. 4) Dante confesses that he had been in error, 'che più savio di te fé già errante' (line 63), while the reference immediately following (line 65) to the 'possible intellect' points to Averroes, who is quoted in *Mon.* I. iii. 9. The 'possible intellect' figures also in *Conv.* IV. xxi. 5, a very ambiguous passage. This, however, is a much disputed and exceedingly complex problem. Guido Vernani[23] none the less had pretty good reason to accuse Dante of heretical Averroism in the *Monarchy*; and in the *Convivio* Dante seems much influenced by Neoplatonist philosophy such as he found in the *Liber de Causis*, known as the 'Philosophia Aristotelis', really Proclus. This question must be left to scholars such as Bruno Nardi[24] (if there are any such); I can record only a layman's impression, which I am glad to find supported and developed by Kenelm Foster.

On the relevance of vows, in *Par.* iv, to Dante himself, I feel more secure, even if the commentators are silent, perhaps because Dante says that his doubt about the violence which took Piccarda from her cloister 'has less poison', being 'unable to lead him away from Beatrice, elsewhere'. The more poisonous doctrine was Plato's, of stellar influences as necessitating changes, tending to deny free will, implied in the argument of *Conv.* II. viii. 4–6. For Dante force was not in question, but the new doubt that arises at the end of *Par.* iv and is answered in

Par. v, touches Dante more closely: how to give satisfaction for unfulfilled vows; substitution is allowed but its weight must be notably greater than the original promise. There is indeed no hint of Dante's personal involvement, unless it is concealed in the metaphor of *Par.* v. 82–3:

> non fate com' agnel che lascia il latte
> de la sua madre . . .

Dante had in the Earthly Paradise compared himself to an errant child before its severe mother (*Purg.* xxx. 44–5, 79; xxxi. 64; *Par.* i. 102), and milk is a figure for inspiration (*Par.* xxiii. 56–7), applied by Dante to himself in the *Eclogue* i. 58–9 with reference to the *Comedy*. The theme of vows extends over three cantos and seems inexplicable unless it deeply concerned Dante himself, and if we look for a vow in his works, where is it but at the end of the *Vita Nuova*?[25] After drinking of Lethe in *Purg.* xxxi. 102, he could not mention it, as Beatrice indicates in *Purg.* xxxiii. 96 (cf. what Folco, the poet, says of his 'colpa', *Par.* ix. 103). But as Constanza had remained a nun at heart, so had Dante remained Beatrice's devotee, though from free will and moral liberty he had 'estranged' himself from her.

If such a hypothesis as this makes better sense of Beatrice's rebukes and gives more meaning to her references to 'vita nuova', to 'pargoletta', 'novità', 'pietra', and relevance to such topics as the spots in the moon and vows, otherwise mere padding and pedantry, the question arises how and when Dante returned to Beatrice, to his promise, and to the poem that fulfilled it well over half as much again, 'come 'l quattro nel sei', *Par.* V. 58–60, as the then contemplated *canzone*. What set off in him that 'profound revision' (Nardi) of his philosophy, the return to sensation and passion instead of pure reason? He says that in order to rejoin Beatrice he had to go through Hell (*Purg.* xxx. 136–8) before he could be welcomed by her with her rebukes, and if we look for other evidence for this, there are two documents, *Epistle* iv, and the 'Canzone Montanina', 'Amor, da che convien' (Contini 53).

The 'Canzone Montanina' is much disputed. Years ago I tried to show (see 11a) its importance and to argue that the lady could be only Beatrice, but I have been persuaded by Foster and Boyde that this identification is not plausible; not persuaded, however, that my dating to 1311, when we *know* that Dante was in the Casentino, is likewise to be rejected. We must accept that Dante suddenly fell in love with a girl whom he saw there, thus suffering what he had warned Cino da Pistoia against, and had thought himself safe from ('his ship far out to sea'—like Ulysses!), and so overwhelmingly that he ends the poem with a message to Florence, that even if he were free to return he could not do so. The *Epistle* goes further: this new passion has put an end to all his philosophical and political activity, on behalf of his Emperor Henry VII, as my date requires. I had thought that only the authority of Beatrice, as we see it in the *Comedy*, could have brought about this extraordinary reversal of the direction that Dante had followed since about 1294. But I now find that the more literal interpretation fits my general argument all the better. A vision of Beatrice, as I took it to be, would not have entailed that return to the animal and vegetable 'souls' as the foundation of personality and vocation away from the one-sided emphasis on the rational soul in the *Convivio*. It might even have accentuated Dante's rather neoplatonist, even somewhat mani-chean, spirituality in the *Convivio*. As it was, he was thrown back by the new passion to what he had experienced in the most painful moments of the old, and thus to the style of the 'dolo-rous' poems about his love for Beatrice that he had excluded from the *Vita Nuova*, the *canzoni* 'E' m' incresce di me sì dura-mente' and 'Lo doloroso amor che me conduce' (Contini 20 and 21). Perhaps Dante's experience was like Cino's, who had defended himself against the charge of fickleness in love, in his reply to Dante (Contini 52A), by saying that he had always loved the same woman, Selvaggia, and other women, after her death, only because they resembled her (a theme, as Foster and Boyde remark, found also in Cavalcanti and Petrarch). If so, Dante could say that he had never been estranged from Beatrice for another woman (though certainly estranged from her by what he treated as women in his poetry, while insisting that they were not). Indeed he says of the chief rival, the 'Donna gentile' in *Vita Nuova* xxxvi. 1, that he was often reminded by her of his most noble lady, since her complexion was of the same pallor. I would also still argue that many images from 'Amor, da che convien' are re-used for Beatrice in the Earthly Paradise, and put the date at shortly after *Epistle* vii (17 April 1311).

The 'Canzone Montanina' and the *Epistle* form a cry of desperation and resentment at the shattering of all Dante's aims and activities, from within himself. If the date is about May 1311, external circumstances were no less shattering, as *Epistle* vii makes clear. He had to watch the whole enterprise of Henry VII in Italy crumbling into ruin. He still calls it the 'faustissimus cursus divi Henrici', but his anxiety, almost despair, is just below the surface. By not attacking Florence, Henry was letting his only chance of success slip from him. The grandiose 'tragic' language cannot conceal Dante's well-founded fears; this was to descend into a hell. His utopian dream dissolved and ended when the foiled circuitous wanderer died two years later at Buonconvento, leaving Italy worse confounded and Dante without hope of ever returning from exile after the unforgivable insults to Florence of *Epistle* vi. Cino da Pistoia, and others, wrote laments for Henry's death, but not Dante, because he was engaged on the *Comedy*, the fulfilment of his vow. If his love for Beatrice was an entirely sublimated 'heavenly' love, he had insisted in his sonnet, 'Io sono stato', that it was sensuous (carnal is Foster and Boyde's word), and this it is in the *Comedy*, at least as a basis for idealization and transformation, not into the Church or revelation (since these existed already), but as the inspiration of his best poetry. In the *Convivio* he had tried to exhibit the merits of his philosophical *canzoni*, as superior to the *Vita Nuova*; in the *Comedy* he makes Beatrice dismiss them as 'altra novità con sì breve uso', and rightly. As Contini says of the doctrinal and in technique highly wrought canzone, 'Amor, che movi', 'Dante's poetry naturally rises precisely where it is less philosophical and subtle' (Contini 37, p. 123), and I suggest that Dante himself says so in his own person in the sonnet, 'Parole mie' (Contini 31): all the poems for 'quella donna in cui errai' from 'Voi che 'ntendendo' onwards are bereft of Love, 'ché non v'è Amore'. They must go from her to 'donna di valore' and humbly promise to do her honour. If the sonnet 'O dolci rime' (Contini 32), is a palinode, it was only a temporary fluctuation, part of the 'molta battaglia' needed to reverse that of *Conv.* II. ii. 3, before Dante conceived the *Comedy*, and began it

> pria che 'l Guasco l'alto Arrigo inganni,

before Clement V's perfidy shattered the last of Dante's hopes, in the harmonious collaboration of Church and Empire. Again Dante emphasizes that the experiences between *Vita Nuova* and *Comedy* can now be used for the *Comedy*, in which at last his true 'nobility' will be evident; *Par.* xxix: 'qui si parrà la tua nobilitate', not the nobility which he had awarded himself for his 'Pietra' poem 'Amor, tu vedi ben', but an equivalent (or more!) to his ancestor Cacciaguida's knighthood given by an emperor for services as a crusader, *Par.* xv. 139–41. Beatrice declares Dante to be 'the most hopeful son of the Church *Militant*', privileged to pass from Egypt to Jerusalem before his knightly service is completed, *Par.* xxv. 52–7 (cf. Justinian's words at *Par.* v. 117: 'prima che la *milizia* s'abbandoni'). That service is the writing of the promised poem, which she and her guidance of him to Jerusalem require of him, *Purg.* xxxiii. 55. Thus the family honour is maintained, indeed enhanced, *Par.* xvi. 1–9; xvii. 92–3, where 'the things incredible to those who shall witness them' refer to Dante's future fame.

NOTES

1. Karl Witte, *Dante-Forschungen* (1869), i. 141–82 = *Essays on Dante*, ed. Mabel Lawrence and Philip Wicksteed (London, 1898), 3. 61–96.
2. Étienne Gilson, *Dante et Béatrice* (Paris, 1974), 1. 'De la *Vita Nuova* à la *Divine Comédie*', pp. 9–22; 2. 'La Mirabil Visione', pp. 103–17. Antonio Pagliaro, *Ulisse* (Messina–Florence, 1967), ii. 798–803.
3. Charles S. Singleton, *An Essay on the 'Vita Nuova'* (Cambridge, Mass., 1949). Domenico de Robertis, *Il libro della 'Vita Nuova'* (Florence, 1961). Vittore Branca, in 'Dante nella critica d'oggi', *Cultura e scuola*, 13–14, ed. Umberto Bosco (Florence, 1965), 'La "Vita Nuova"', pp. 690–7; 'Poetica del rinnovamento e tradizione agiografica nella "Vita Nuova"' *Letture classensi* 2 (Longo, Ravenna, 1968?), 31–66, also in *Aggiornamenti di critica dantesca*, ed. S. Pasquazi (Florence, 1972), pp. 41–51.
4. *Enciclopedia dantesca*, ed. Umberto Bosco, v (Rome, 1976), s.v. 'Vita Nuova', 1086–96, Mario Pazzaglia; iv (1973), s.v. 'nuovo', 98–100, Antonietta Bufano.
5. J. A. Scott, 'Notes on Religion and the *Vita Nuova*', *Italian Studies* xx (1965), 17–25.
6. *Encicl. dant.* v (1976), s.v. 'Visione mistica', 1071–3, Vincent Truijen; s.v. 'Visione', 1071–2, Riccardo Ambrosini.
7. Virgil, *Aenid* iii. 97–8. Apollo's prophecy at Delos repeats Poseidon's in *Iliad* xx. 307–8, for which compare the Homeric Hymn to Aphrodite

v. 196–7, a 'prophecy' *post eventum* at the court of kings who claimed descent from Aeneas. For this see now Johannes van Eck, *The Homeric Hymn to Aphrodite* (1978).

8. The theory of the revised edition of the *Vita Nuova* to make it a prologue to the *Comedy* (for bibliography see Branca in *Letture classensi*, 2. 35 n. 7), despite Pietrobono's and Nardi's arguments, may now be considered unacceptable, cf. Mario Marti, 'Vita e Morte della presunta doppia redazione della *Vita Nuova*', *Rivista di cultura classica e medievale* (1965), pp. 657 ff.

If the *Vita Nuova* was reshaped to introduce the *Comedy*, it should not be contradicted, as it is, by *Purg.* xxx. 124–5, where Beatrice dates Dante's falling away from her death 'Sì *tosto* come . . . mutai vita', not after the first anniversary, *VN* xxxv–xxxix.

As for the date of the *Vita Nuova*, the second anniversary is not mentioned, which suggests a date before 8 June 1292. The chronological data of *Convivio* II. ii. 1 and xii. 7 can be reconciled if the two circuits of Venus 'in that circle of hers, which makes her appear as morning and evening star' are the circuits of her epicycle, which he emphasizes with a lengthy, otherwise otiose, explanation at II. iii. 16–18 and v. 16–18. This means 1 year $2\frac{1}{2}$ months, rather than 584×2 days, 3 years $2\frac{1}{2}$ months; namely August 1291, not 1293, for the first appearance of the 'Donna Gentile'. The thirty months, 'a short time', of intensive philosophical study brings us to February 1294, for the composition of 'Voi che 'ntendendo', and *Par.* viii, 31–9 reports the recitation of this *canzone* to Carlo Martello when he visited Florence in March 1294. The period of the epicycle has seemed to the commentators too heliocentric, but Jacopo, Dante's son, in his *Dottrinale* says 'Venus . . . il suo epiciclo gira in sette mesi e nove di.' Dante had to express his date in terms of Venus because her influence determined the dissolution of his love for Beatrice (*Conv.* II. viii. 4–6; cf. the acrobatics of *VN* xxix to express the date of her death in terms of nines).

9. *Encicl. dant.* v, s.v. 'visione mistica', as in n. 6. But see Giorgio Padoan, *Dante e Roma* (Florence, 1965), pp. 283–314 ('La Mirabile Visione di Dante e l'epistola a Cangrande'), though he does not discuss *VN* xlii, and accepts the *Epistle* as genuine (p. 292).

10. Bruno Nardi, *Dante e la cultura medievale* (Bari, 1942), ix. 258–334; (1949), xi. 336–416 ('Dante Profeta').

11. I have tried to defend these unorthodox theses in detail elsewhere: a. 'Dante's Canzone Montanina', *Modern Language Review*, 55 (1960), 359–70; b. 'Beatrice's Chariot in Dante's Earthly Paradise', *Deutsches Dante-Jahrbuch*, 39 (1961), 137–72; c. 'Cacciaguida's Prophecy in Paradiso 17', *Traditio*, 19 (1963), 267–94; d. 'The "Veltres" in the Chanson de Roland and Dante's Veltro', *Deutsches Dante-Jahrbuch*, 41/2 (1964), 158–72; e. 'Il Canto XIX; the Dream of the Siren', *Lectura Dantis Internazionale*, ed. Vittorio Vettori (1965), *Purgatorio*, pp. 217–49; f. 'The Symbol of the Gryphon in *Purgatorio* xxix, 108', *Centenary Essays on Dante*, Oxford Dante Society (1965), pp. 103–31;

g. 'The Date of the Comedy and the "Argomento barberiniano"',
Dante Studies, 86 (1968), 1–16; h. 'Un cinquecento diece e cinque',
Purgatorio 33, 43', *Deutsches Dant.-Jahrbuch*, 51/2 (1976/7), 84–98.

I cannot believe that Dante ventured on prediction after events had
so quickly and drastically refuted the confident prophecy of *Epistle*
vi. 17.

12. Cf. Kenelm Foster and Patrick Boyde, *Dante's Lyric Poetry* (Oxford,
1967), ii. 332: 'in the *D.C.* where Dante the creative poet is incessantly
dogged by Dante the observer of the poetic activity'.

13. Charles S. Singleton, *Paradiso* (Princeton, N.J., 1975), 2. 584.

14. Richard of St. Victor, *PL* 177. 426: 'canticum est vita; canticum
novum vita nova . . . nova vita iustitia . . . qui bene vivit bene cantat',
quoted by Branca, *Letture Classensi* 2. 34 (see n. 3).

15. Salvatore Santangelo, *Saggi danteschi* (Padua, 1959), pp. 21–91, 'La
composizione della "Vita Nuova"', p. 75.

16. Mario Marti, *Poeti del dolce stil nuovo* (Florence, 1969).

17. Edmond Faral, *Les Arts poétiques du XIIᵉ et du XIIIᵉ siècle* (Paris, 1923
and 1962); see also Patrick Boyde, *Dante's Style in his Lyric Poetry*
(Cambridge, 1971).

18. Bruno Nardi, *Dante e la cultura medievale* (Bari, 1949), ix. 284–308
('L'immortalità dell 'anima').

19. Andreas Capellanus, *Trattato d'Amore*, ed. Salvatore Battaglia (Rome,
1947), p. 356: II. viii, Regula amoris 7: 'biennalis viduitas pro
amante defuncto superstiti praescribitur amanti' (cf. p. 328: II. vii,
Iudicium amoris 14).

20. Manfredi Porena, *Paradiso* (Bologna, 1955), pp. 71–2, n. on canto 8,
'Dubbi e difficultà sulla teoria degl' influssi'. On the earlier period see
Foster and Boyde, *Dante's Lyric Poetry* (n. 12), Index, ii. 374, col. 2, s.v.
astral influences, and add pp. 322, 321, 324, 326. Purg. xviii. 40–74
corrects the error, 'where erotic stimuli at least are concerned'.

21. The reverence for 'Theologus Dantes, nullius dogmatis expers'
(Giovanni del Virgilio in Boccaccio, *Vita di Dante*) of such scholars as
Zingarelli, Busnelli, and Cosmo no longer prevails; see Kenelm Foster
in *Enciclopedia dantesca* v (1976), s.v. 'Teologia'. But some hagiography
continues, as Giorgio Padoan complains in 'Il Limbo dantesco', *Il
pio Enea, l'empio Ulisse* (Ravenna, 1977), pp. 103–24. He also notes
that to understand how Dante interpreted the Aenid 'è un lavoro
ancora tutto a fare'.

22. Bruno Nardi, *Saggi di filosofia dantesca* (Florence, 1930 and 1967), pp.
3–39, 'La dottrina delle macchie lunari'.

23. Guido Vernani da Rimini, *De Reprobatione Monarchiae*, ed. Nevio
Matteini, in *Il più antico oppositore politico di Dante: Guido Vernani da
Rimini* (Padua, 1958).

24. Bruno Nardi, 'L'origine dell 'anima umana secondo Dante' (1931–2),
in *Studi de filosofia medievale* (Rome, 1960); 'Sull' origine dell' anima
umana', in *Dante e la cultura medievale* (Bari, 1942 and 1949), viii.
260–83; 'Filosofia e teologia ai tempi di Dante', in *Saggi e note di*

critica dantesca (Milan, 1966), i. 3–109, esp. 75–9 for examples of revision of earlier views in the *Comedy*.

25. The words in *VN* xlii. 1–2, 'proposal' and 'hope' are described as a 'solemn vow' by Alessandro d'Ancona in his edition of the *Vita Nuova* (Pisa, 1872).

7

Dante's Theory and Practice of Poetry[1]

CECIL GRAYSON

When Dante, at the age of about forty, wrote his major work of poetic theory, entitled *De Vulgari Eloquentia*, he was in exile from Florence, where he had established over some twenty years a leading reputation as a poet. He had begun in early youth in the style of Guittone d'Arezzo, but he soon broke away, together with certain Florentine contemporaries and under the influence of the Bolognese Guinizelli, from the rhetorical mannerisms and dialectical contortions of Guittone, to concentrate his attention exclusively and in a particular way on the theme of love.[2] Dante then created what he himself calls the 'dolce stil novo' (sweet new style), of which he gives a much discussed definition in a conversation with the poet Buonagiunta da Lucca in *Purgatorio*, xxiv. 49–63:

> 'Ma dì s' i' veggio qui colui che fore
> trasse le nove rime, cominciando
> *"Donne ch'avete intelletto d'amore".*'
>   E io a lui: 'I' mi son un che, quando
> Amor mi spira, noto, e a quel modo
> ch'e' ditta dentro vo significando'.
>   'O frate, issa vegg' io' diss' elli 'il nodo
> che 'l Notaro e Guittone e me ritenne
> di qua dal dolce stil novo ch'i' odo.
>   Io veggio ben come le vostre penne
> di retro al dittator sen vanno strette,
> che de le nostre certo non avvenne;
>   e qual più a gradire oltre si mette,
> non vede più da l'uno a l'altro stilo';
> e, quasi contentato, si tacette.[3]

A full consideration of this passage is not possible here, but certain points may be underlined: first, that Dante distinguished himself, not from contemporaries, but from earlier generations of poets, Giacomo da Lentini (il Notaro), Guittone, and

Buonaguinta; second, that this distinction lies in strict adherence to the inspiration of love; third, that his new style began
with a particular *canzone* which figures in his *Vita Nuova*. Indeed
the entire conversation takes us back specifically to this early
work, and it is there we must look for a more precise interpretation of its meaning and especially of the apparently Romantic
canon of inspiration expressed by Dante in his reply to Buonagiunta. The *Vita Nuova*, composed about 1292, consists of a prose
account in forty-two chapters of the story of his love for Beatrice
from the age of nine until some time after her death, set around
a selection of his poems, thirty-one in all between *canzoni*,
sonnets, and *ballate*. Besides being a kind of amorous autobiography the *Vita Nuova* is also a poetic autobiography, binding
in strict relation the progress of his Muse with that of his love.
In this sense it represents Dante's view of his own poetic
evolution from the sonnet that brought him the friendship of
Guido Cavalcanti, through lyrics still savouring of Provençal
and Guittonian style and attitudes, and marked by preoccupa-
tion with the tragic nature and vicissitudes of love, to a serene
and simpler celebration of love that ennobles the mind and
transcends even death itself. The turning-point in his outlook on
love and poetry is described in chapter xviii, which is the prelude to the *canzone* 'Donne ch'avete intelletto d'amore'.
Suddenly, it would seem, love ceased to exist outside Dante in
material manifestations like the salutation Beatrice had denied
him, and became instead part of himself, no longer uncertain
of its object but identified with a new poetry of praise. It is this
assurance and this identity which determine the 'sweet new style'.
Dante then tells us how he came to write his famous *canzone*:

Avvenne poi che passando per uno cammino lungo lo quale sen
gia uno rivo chiaro molto, a me giunse tanta volontade di dire, che io
cominciai a pensare lo modo ch'io tenesse; e pensai che parlare di lei
non si convenia che io facesse, se io non parlasse a donne in seconda
persona, e non ad ogni donna, ma solamente a coloro che sono
gentili e che non sono pure femmine. Allora dico che la mia lingua
parlò quasi come per se stessa mossa, e disse: *Donne ch'avete intelletto
d'amore*. Queste parole io ripuosi ne la mente con grande letizia, pensando di prenderle per mio cominciamento; onde poi, ritornato a la
sopradetta cittade, pensando alquanti die, cominciai una canzone
con questo cominciamento . . . (*VN* xix).[4]

Dante's *canzone* celebrates Beatrice as a creature of divine origin, whose mission on earth is to purify and ennoble through love those who look upon her (and especially the poet himself), and whose return is desired by heaven. What in Guinizelli's *canzone* 'Al cor gentil ripara sempre amore' had been an elaborate apology to God (he had mistaken his lady for a divine messenger), here is transformed into the central substance of a new love poetry. The process of its creation as described by Dante is not, however, such as to support any Romantic interpretation of the inspiration of love mentioned by Dante in his reply to Buonaguinta. The inspiration he writes of in *Vita Nuova* moves from a generic impulse to write something on this theme of praise, through reflection on how he shall do so, to the spontaneous formulation of an opening line of address; and only after several days and further thought does he compose the poem. The dictates of love referred to by Buonagiunta are emotional, but they are also intellectual, and as Dante then came to realize, they were the only ones justifiable for vernacular poetry. Chapter xxv of *Vita Nuova* makes this major point abundantly clear: it is historically wrong to write vernacular poetry except about love. In the sonnet of the preceding chapter Dante had represented Love as a being, speaking and smiling. He now digresses in order to explain this personification and to make his first important programmatic declaration of poetic theory:

A cotale cosa dichiarare, secondo che è buono a presente, prima è da intendere che anticamente non erano dicitori d'amore in lingua volgare, anzi erano dicitori d'amore certi poete in lingua latina . . . E non è molto numero d'anni passati, che appariro prima questi poete volgari; ché dire per rima in volgare tanto è quanto dire per versi in latino, secondo alcuna proporzione. E segno che sia picciolo tempo, è che se volemo cercare in lingua d'*oco* e in quella di *sì*, noi non troviamo cose dette anzi lo presente tempo per cento e cinquanta anni. E la cagione per che alquanti grossi ebbero fama di sapere dire, è che quasi fuoro li primi che dissero in lingua di *sì*. E lo primo che cominciò a dire sì come poeta volgare, si mosse però che volle fare intendere le sue parole a donna, a la quale era malagevole d'intendere li versi latini. E questo è contra coloro che rimano sopra altra matera che amorosa, con ciò sia cosa che cotale modo di parlare fosse dal principio trovato per dire d'amore. Onde, con ciò sia cosa che a li poete sia conceduta maggiore licenza di parlare che a li prosaici dittatori, e questi dicitori per rima non siano altro che poete volgari, degno e ragionevole è che a loro sia maggiore licenza largita di parlare che a li altri parlatori volgari: onde, se alcuna figura o colore rettorico è conceduto a li poete, conceduto è a li rimatori (*VN* xxv).[5]

Dante goes on to exemplify the use of personification by Virgil, Lucan, Horace, and Ovid, who used this figure with proper justification, unlike some vernacular poets he knows. Apart from this polemical aside, it is notable that Dante here looks back over the tradition of Romance vernacular poetry and sees it as the continuator, if in a restricted field, of Latin verse. Indeed, he goes further and claims the identity of poetic activity whether it be in Latin or vernacular: the modern 'dicitori' are specifically called 'poete volgari'. Love poetry in vernacular has for Dante a practical, historical origin, but its function and its means of expression are not different: it is on a par with, and may take its measure from ancient Latin poetry. These are the first seeds of a poetic theory of imitation of Latin poetry which Dante will elaborate later in his *De Vulgari Eloquentia*. Yet at this stage there are no very evident traces of such imitation in the *Vita Nuova* poems themselves beyond the parallel of personification already mentioned. It is therefore impossible to speak in any usual sense of 'classicism' in this work, which in its poetry is firmly set in the Romance tradition, while owing something in its prose to Cicero, Boethius and medieval hagiography.[6] We shall understand more clearly what kind of imitation Dante had in mind in his early writings when we come to examine his *Convivio* and *De Vulgari Eloquentia*.

The composition of *Vita Nuova*, however, marked the climax, not the beginning of the kind of poetry referred to as the 'dolce stil novo'. Very soon after it was completed, he left the narrow confines of its poetic theory and practice—several years in fact before the imagined conversation with Buonagiunta of 1300 in Purgatory, which looks back to a particular moment of his poetic career already past. To that same moment there refers also the encounter, again in Purgatory, with Guido Guinizelli, whom he reveres as

> .... padre
> mio e de li altri miei miglior che mai
> rime d'amore usar dolci e leggiadre;[7]

the Guinizelli whose pregnant equation of love and the gentle heart Dante had resolved into his own poetry of praise in *Vita Nuova*. Yet Guinizelli modestly diverts Dante's eulogy of his fame to another figure in the same circle of Purgatory, that of the Provençal poet Arnaut Daniel, who stands for another, slightly later moment of Dante's poetic development quite different from the poems for Beatrice. Nor is this the only diversion from the 'dolce stil novo' in the years after her death. The final chapter of *Vita Nuova* clearly promised some work in further, fuller praise of Beatrice after a 'mirabile visione', something the like of which had never been said of any woman; and for this purpose Dante professed to be studying with all his might.[8] The promise was not kept until fifteen or more years later and in a very different form in the *Comedy*. It is inconceivable that when recording that promise he could have had anything in mind resembling that later fulfilment, which was impossible without the intervening expansion of his own conception and experience of poetry. To this experience we now turn.

Whatever his intention in 1292, and whether or not this promise was the motive, Dante devoted himself for a period to philosophical studies, and wrote certain love poems which he later interpreted in his *Convivio* allegorically. If these were still outwardly love poems, however interpreted, and in a similar style to the *canzoni* of *Vita Nuova*, they were not for Beatrice. Nor were the so-called 'rime petrose' (stone poems) of 1296, which in their linguistic and metrical brilliance imitated from Arnaut Daniel, and in their violent protests of unrequited love, are the reverse of the earlier 'sweet new style'. The limits of his poetic experience widen still further with the exchange, also in these years, of crude, realistic, slanging sonnets with his relative by marriage Forese Donati.[9] This is for Dante a period not only of much technical experiment in verse but of evident violence and involvement in affairs, which soon lead him away from philosophy and into the arena of the growing political conflict within and outside Florence. In the years 1292 to about 1298 Beatrice seems to be eclipsed from his poetry: contemporary issues and problems of a philosophical, moral, and personal nature find expression in verse that is merely in part, and even then in appearance only, based on the poetic theory of *Vita*

Nuova. Outside such theory, for instance, fall the so-called doctrinal *canzoni* (on topics such as nobility, courtesy, avarice), which are usually ascribed to the decade before Dante's exile.[10]

It is not surprising that Dante's muse is virtually silent between 1298 and 1302, or that this silence should be broken with the great canzone 'Tre donne intorno al cor mi son venute', lamenting the decay of justice.[11] As soon as the profound upheaval of his life permitted, we find him striving to repair the damages of his experience, and to draw together in a new theoretical formulation the scattered elements of his past, to sum up, as it were, and also to explain to himself as well as to others what he had tried to do, and where he stood poetically. Simultaneously or in rapid succession he began and subsequently left unfinished two important works, *Convivio* and *De vulgari eloquentia*, written between 1304 and 1307. *Convivio* is explicitly a work of self-justification and rehabilitation with Florence and with his critics. By a prose commentary in Italian on fourteen *canzoni* he intends to elucidate their true meaning and so spread a banquet of learning before a wide audience; for, although literally they appear to be love poems, they in effect express love of philosophy, whom Dante says he meant by the compassionate 'donna gentile' who comforted him for a short time after Beatrice's death in *Vita Nuova*.[12] I do not propose to discuss the credibility of this identification. One thing is absolutely clear: *Convivio* is a justification of his having embraced philosophy to the detriment of Beatrice, and a defence of a very different conception of poetry from that practised and to some extent explained in Beatrice's book, *Vita Nuova*. Although, as we have seen, Dante there discussed the use of personification and referred to other rhetorical devices, he made no mention of allegory or of a possible different interpretation of the poems included in the work. There are some explanations in the prose of *Vita Nuova* of the structure and intention of the lyrics, but they are simple, often superfluous, and have nothing to do with allegory. The literal sense of *Vita Nuova* is by no means easy for the modern reader to grasp and appreciate, yet there is nothing in it to suggest that the work is intended to convey a different message. Hence the difficulty in accepting Dante's later statement about the role of the 'donna gentile'.

The theory behind the *canzoni* of *Convivio*, on the other hand, explicitly postulates a poetry which exists on at least two levels: the literal, whereby they appear superficially to be love poems (of 'passione'), and the allegorical, whereby they are shown in fact to be poems about philosophy (of 'vertù') needing and being the occasion for displaying considerable knowledge. Poetry, says Dante, is 'una bella menzogna' (a beautiful lie) which conceals 'una veritade ascosa' (a hidden truth). He possibly got this formula from Horace, but he could have found it in a long traditional dispute from Augustine to Thomas about the truth or falsehood of poetry. Yet there are no explicit allusions in *Convivio* to that past controversy, which was soon to flare up again around Albertino Mussato, and to provoke the defence of poetry by Petrarch and Boccaccio. Dante's love poetry included in *Vita Nuova* had needed no other defence than the historical and rhetorical tradition he outlined in chapter xxv. Sufficient defence of this new poetry is that, like that of antiquity, its outward beauty is an attractive fiction that conveys to those who can understand an inner 'sentenza' or truth. Its beauty is one thing, its goodness another. The only echo in *Convivio* of the ancient controversy lies in the reference, which he does not develop, to the difference between poets' and theologians' allegory; that is, that whereas poets start from a literal truth that is invented or imagined (and its opponents belittled this as a falsehood, and so of little account or even positively dangerous), theologians move from the scriptural text which is historically true in itself.[13] Even though Dante might appear to imply by his exposition of the four possible senses that the moral and analogical, applicable to the scriptures, also apply to his poetry, he does not pursue them in the remainder of his commentary; only the first two senses, the literal and allegorical, are explained, while the other two seem to be the inert remains of a traditional exegetical framework. At the time of writing *Convivio* Dante evidently saw no problems in using such a scheme. Yet these same four senses recur in a very similar form in the letter to Can Grande della Scala, commonly attributed to Dante, concerning the interpretation of the *Comedy*, which we shall consider later, since it is probable that there they were intended to have different weight and more far-reaching implications.

The allegorical conception of poetry in *Convivio*, however, needs qualification. Firstly, we do not know for certain that when Dante wrote these *canzoni* originally, he intended them to have such a double sense. Most scholars attribute them to the early 1290s, ten years before the *Convivio* commentary was written. Whether or not he did so conceive them, they become in this work like so many pegs on which to hang a demonstration of wide moral and philosophical knowledge in Italian prose, and it is this, far more than the poetry, which seems to occupy his attention. Indeed, in Book IV, the *canzone* 'Le dolci rime d'amor ch'io solia' is in no sense an allegorical canzone, but a disquisition in verse on nobility, which is then amplified at considerable length in the last and longest book of the unfinished work. Whenever he wrote this *canzone* (my own view is that it belongs to his early exile and not before), it in no way fits the initial pattern of *Convivio*, which promised to open up the true sense of certain love poems and show them to be expressions of love of philosophy. This seems to indicate clearly that it is the moral, scientific and political content that urges him to write, together with the explicit conviction that this Italian prose will permit him to show far more clearly than in poetry the beauty and powers of the vernacular.[14] In this context poetic considerations, and with them the allegorical virtues of poetry theorized about at the beginning of Book II, recede into the background, and the suspicion arises that these were in some way a mere excuse and a point of departure for quite unpoetic goals. *Vita Nuova* had been written at the climax of a particular poetic experience which he there summed up to pass almost at once to others quite different and even totally opposite; and yet prose and verse in *Vita Nuova* were intimately bound up together in a unity of style and content. By contrast *Convivio* looks like an afterthought, a deliberate superimposition on a poetic experience long past, of more urgent considerations which he had not yet found the means to express in poetry. There is something artificial and forced about this marriage of poetry and prose, and consequently about the entire concept of poetry as allegory which is its ostensible basis.

In the second place, something should be said of the nature of the allegory Dante expounds. The form and content of the poems are similar in general to those of his earlier love *canzoni* and sonnets: the beauty of the lady, her eyes, her effects on him, and so on, are described in the verse and then interpreted in the prose in terms of the virtues of philosophy and Dante's own experience and difficulties in pursuing its study. Yet a great part of the explanation is taken up, not with strictly allegorical interpretation of the poems, but with erudite commentary and digression about topics arising from this, as, for example, the long explanation of the heavens equated with the parts of the trivium and quadrivium arising from the mention of the heaven of Venus in the first line of the first *canzone*.[15] All this adds still further to the impression of a late superstructure standing on a very narrow base not designed originally to carry it. The object of these observations is to clarify the nature and extent of Dante's allegorical conception of poetry at that time, and to show that it was relatively undeveloped and of limited import- ance except as a means to an end. We do not know why he abandoned the *Convivio* unfinished (before completing the fourth of the projected fourteen books), but the work seems to contain the seeds of its own disintegration, especially in Book IV. To leave the 'dolci rime' for plain statement in verse was to recognize what is abundantly evident from the prose, that the bounds of amorous poetry, however allegorically interpreted, were impossibly narrow and indeed a failure for any other purpose than that for which he had originally used it. If he wanted to say more in poetry as opposed to prose, he would have to find another more capacious form, not in itself necessarily allegorical.[16]

There is reason to suppose that *De Vulgari Eloquentia* was begun after *Convivio* and possibly abandoned not long after that work had also been left unfinished. It reflects Dante's confidence in his poetic achievement and in his ability to teach others how to select and handle the 'vulgare illustre' of Italy. For this supreme instrument he believes only the supreme form of the *canzone* and the most excellent style are appropriate. By way of illustration Dante quotes himself as *the* poet of 'vertù', that is of the *canzoni* of *Convivio*, and his friend Cino da Pistoia as *the* poet of love. This does not exclude the citation also of Dante's love poetry, nor does it imply any superiority of or necessity for allegory, which is at no point mentioned or discussed. His definition of poetry as 'fictio rhetorica musicaque poita' might suggest that he is reformulating the idea of the 'beautiful lie', but recent examination of the history of the term 'fictio' has shown it might but did not inevitably mean for Dante a false or at least different device for concealing another truth.[17] Besides, such a restricted interpretation of 'fictio' simply would not fit the range of poetry quoted by him in *De Vulgari Eloquentia*. The term is therefore most probably used by Dante merely to indicate in the most general way the imaginative substance of the poet's creation to which he gives material expression through the medium of rhetoric and music, that is through established artistic elaboration of language and numerical, rhythmical disposition into verse. 'Fictio' is simply what the poet makes within him as opposed to what is created or exists outside him. Dante says little of the process involved, but it is clear that he had a high conception of the poetic activity, at least at the superior level of what he calls the 'tragic style', and that he equated, as he had already done in *Vita Nuova*, the vernacular and classical poets. The definition of poetry already quoted applies to both. The difference between them is that the great poets have composed in a language and with an art controlled by rules, whilst the moderns have written and still write 'casu magis quam arte', that is, as it were, by rule of thumb. The whole object of *De Vulgari Eloquentia* is to remedy this situation; and Dante's fundamental originality lies in recognizing the possibility of a regularized vernacular literary language and an organized art of vernacular expression for all purposes.

Dante goes on to declare that the closer we imitate the classical writers, the more correctly will we write vernacular poetry, not only by studying their theoretical works such as the *Ars Poetica* of Horace (frequently referred to in *De Vulgari Eloquentia*), but by learning from their example the most noble constructions and expressions.[18] Yet Dante was not intending the kind of imitation later preached and practised by humanists. When he meets Virgil at the beginning of *Inferno*, he greets him with the words:

> Tu se' lo mio maestro e 'l mio autore,
> tu se' solo colui da cu' io tolsi
> lo bello stilo che m'ha fatto onore.[19]

This 'bello stilo' cannot be other than that of his *canzoni* of

Convivio. We have the clear confirmation in *De Vulgari Eloquentia* in the passage where Dante classifies tragedy as the highest style, comedy as the lower, elegy as the most humble. These were not for him specific genres; still less, in the case of the first two, dramatic forms. They were distinct qualities of subject and appropriate expression. So he writes: 'Si tragice canende videntur, tunc assumendum est vulgare illustre, et per consequens cantionem oportet ligare. Si vero comice, tunc quandoque mediocre, quandoque humile vulgare sumatur; et huius discretionem in quarto huius reservamus ostendere. Si autem elegiace, solum humile oportet nos sumere' (II. iv. 6).[20] Dante never got as far as Book IV. Yet when we further recall that he makes Virgil refer in *Inferno* xx, 113, to 'l'alta mia tragedìa', meaning his *Aeneid*, we begin to see more clearly how Dante can have claimed to imitate Virgil's style in his own *canzoni*, and to appreciate how and why Dante came to call his own great poem a comedy. He inherited from medieval rhetorical tradition the distinction of the three styles, high, medium, and low, and their identification with tragedy, comedy, and elegy.[21] These long-established associations are highly significant for understanding Dante's view of classical poetry and of its relation as a model to vernacular poets. In *De Vulgari Eloquentia* we learn this specifically only with regard to the tragic style, which we use 'quando cum gravitate sententie tam superbia carminum quam constructionis elatio et excellentia vocabulorum concordat' (II. iv. 7).[22] The remainder of the unfinished Book II deals in detail with these attributes of vernacular poetry. Little is said of inspiration, much of the need for hard work, sound doctrine and what he calls 'discretio', good taste and discernment. No room for Romantic spontaneity here either. The poet drinks from Helicon: from then on 'hoc opus et labor est'; it needs vigorous intelligence and long apprenticeship to art and learning. But poets who have all these qualities, he writes, 'hii sunt quos poeta Eneidorum sexto dei dilectos et ab ardente virtute sublimatos ad ethera deorumque filios vocat, quanquam figurate loquatur' (II. iv. 10).[23] Echoing Virgil Dante is conscious of being one of these select few, of resembling the ancient poets, not because there is close material similarity between his *canzoni* and their epics, but in the pursuit of a high artistic ideal of poetic expression, a perfect marriage between grave content and noble form, as in the 'bello stilo' of his lyric and doctrinal verse that had brought him fame.

Like *Vita Nuova* and *Convivio*, *De Vulgari Eloquentia* looks back on and sums up poetic experience already past, this time extracting not a sentimental or philosophical lesson, but the essence of an aristocratic ideal of language and art, the technique of word selection, verse construction, and composition suited to the three noblest subjects: Salus, Venus, Virtus (Arms, Love, Virtue). Although in its basic principles this work may be said to be prophetic for Italian language and literature, for Dante it had no future. As with *Vita Nuova* and *Convivio*, reflection and theory follow after practice, they do not dictate it. We are here at the extreme end of a conventional traditional love poetry from Provence down to Dante, from which almost everything possible has been extracted. Only the intensely personal note of Petrarch, who is the true heir to the linguistic and artistic aristocracy of *De Vulgari Eloquentia*, remains to complete the process. As with *Vita Nuova* and *Convivio*, so with *De Vulgari Eloquentia* fresh practice supervenes to absorb, transcend and even contradict the theory formulated or in the very process of formulation. We do not know exactly when Dante began the poem he calls his 'comedìa' in contrast to Virgil's 'tragedìa'. It certainly follows, possibly interrupts *De Vulgari Eloquentia*, and it certainly precedes, in its beginning, 1313.[24] But, whenever within the limits of 1307–13 he began, this vast narrative personal poem far exceeds the boundaries of Dante's previous practice and poetics as we know them. Admittedly he never wrote the part of *De Vulgari Eloquentia* about comedy, but it is highly improbable that so wide a mixture of styles and language could there have occurred to him. The general statement we have noted belies this. There the comic style would mingle the medium and the humble, whereas it can be maintained that in his major poem there is also the sublime, in those passages which we might describe in Dante's own terminology as 'tragic'.[25] In effect the *Comedy* cuts vertically through the essentially horizontal stylistic-linguistic stratification of *De Vulgari Eloquentia*, and contravenes by its mixture in one composition of grave, grotesque, and sordid, the classical Horatian principle of decorum. It is true that we may find here and there in Dante's past, seeds of the vigour and realism, crudeness and sublimity that go into his poem: the particular experiences of the pre-exile decade, the exchange of sonnets with Forese, the 'rime petrose', the doctrinal and allegorical *canzoni*, even perhaps the controversial sonnet sequence based on the *Roman de la rose*, known as the *Fiore* (though I am not wholly convinced by the arguments advanced for the attribution to Dante).[26] In any event these are brief and isolated moments, stylistically coherent and compact in themselves. They foreshadow neither the extent nor the amalgam of the *Comedy*, only perhaps some of its elements. From having at different times played on different strings of the poetic lyre, with preference for that of the 'bello stilo', Dante now sounds them all at once, accommodating his style to the vastness and variety of his subject, exploring and wilfully expanding that vernacular which he had striven not long before to contract and refine as the most sublime poetic instrument of Italy. The classical ideals of *De Vulgari Eloquentia* seem to have been thrown to the winds. In their place is a new view and a new use of the ancient poets. In his 'tragic' *canzoni* Dante had imitated Virgil in a particular way, learning from him a general lesson of grave and harmonious balance in poetic expression. As Dante enters Hell, this 'bello stilo' is behind him; before him lies a journey like that of Aeneas, through a realm full of Virgilian reminiscences, though scarcely less rich in Ovidian echoes.[27] This sort of classicism in the *Comedy*—borrowing, imitating freely, vying with the classical poets, using their mythology, invocations, similes, and comparisons—is obviously quite different from the kind of imitation he had in mind in *De Vulgari Eloquentia* or had ever practised before in his own verse. If the result proves to us the power of Dante's genius to bring together in one vast poetic synthesis the pagan and Christian worlds, assimilating ancient art and learning to medieval philosophy and theology, while infinitely extending the capacities of a medium he had once believed inferior to Latin and appropriate only to poetry of love, it created for subsequent generations serious problems of aesthetic appreciation which lie at the basis of a long tradition of fragmentation of the poetry of the *Comedy* from the fifteenth century down to Croce. The very variety and range of vision and style of the poem, which we regard as its strength, was for centuries an obstacle to its acceptance and recognition, being the very antithesis of what Dante himself had earlier striven for, and the opposite of the classical tendencies which dominated European literature down to the eighteenth century.

We do not know, and may never know precisely what profound experience inspired the *Comedy* and determined this fundamental change in direction of his poetic art from an aristocratic ideal to a democratic necessity to communicate to all men a personal vision of a universal significance. From the impersonal, esoteric, allegorical love poet in the tragic style he becomes the poet–prophet of the *Comedy*, intensely personal, omniscient, masterful, and confident that his is a creation to which both heaven and earth have lent their hand. He has the enthusiasm and spiritual vitality of the biblical prophets, sharing their reforming zeal and their pregnant, enigmatic, and figurative language. His medium is a powerful narrative, dense with realistic pictorial detail, for which medieval vision literature offers only pale precedents. Dante's journey through Hell, Purgatory, and Paradise is not a vision like many of those imaginary voyages of the Middle Ages. It is not a fiction constructed to convey something else; not a this for that; not a 'beautiful lie' concealing a 'hidden truth'; not, like his allegorical *canzoni*, a poetic invention in one set of terms which hides a different meaning. In a sense it is a true fiction, an account of something which Dante would persuade us to believe actually happened to him, and it is in itself totally and literally true and meaningful. It is evident that we are faced here with a quite different concept of poetry from that of *Convivio*. There, when explaining the four senses, Dante had observed on the distinction between poets' and theologians' allegory; and he was right not to try to make them all apply to his *canzoni*, as they are properly applicable only to the Scriptures, whose literal sense, being the word of God, is true and not an invention like that of poets. The scriptures can bear such different senses because God alone has the power to confer eternal significance on the words and things of this world. Dante did not presume so much in *Convivio*. His poetics there follow a traditional concept of poetic invention sustained and justified by hidden truth, and within this tradition he is at pains to uphold the right of his amorous canzoni to the respect of the learned because of their underlying moral and scientific content. In the *Comedy* on the other hand, the need for that kind of justification disappears because poetry as fable, as a 'lie', has given place to the idea of poetry as the direct expression of the truth.

How then should we take the letter to Can Grande della Scala, which is accepted by the majority of scholars as an authentic work of Dante? In the letter the poem is said to have several senses, and specifically the four we have already encountered. The example cited by way of illustration is the same as in *Convivio*, the biblical 'Israel ex Aegypto', but there is no mention here of the distinction between theologians' and poets' allegory—a silence which might be taken to imply the author's belief in the truth of his poem on a par with the Scriptures.[28] Yet the letter clarifies only two of the four senses, the literal and allegorical, which are said respectively to be: 'status animarum post mortem simpliciter sumptus' ('the state of souls after death, pure and simple'), and 'homo prout merendo et demerendo per arbitrii libertatem iustitie premiandi et puniendi obnoxius est' ('man according as by his merits or demerits in the exercise of his free will, he is deserving of reward or punishment by justice').[29] These statements raise some difficulties. In the first place the definition of the subject of the poem seems far too simple, and the allegorical sense is hardly distinguishable from the literal. Furthermore a fundamental problem arises when we try to compare the poem with the biblical example cited, for it is difficult to parallel a historical event in this world which prefigures the next, with the description of a voyage in the next world itself.[30] The *Comedy* already represents the other world, and would therefore seem to embrace all within its literal sense. In short it is not easy to discover another, otherworldly interpretation in something which of its nature already appears to contain the whole truth. For this reason, whatever past and present commentators and interpreters may say, it is a hopeless task to attempt to distinguish, throughout the whole poem, clear-cut different levels of meaning on the basis of the four senses. This is not to deny that there is allegory in the *Comedy*, but it is sporadic rather than fundamental and consistent. On occasions Dante calls our attention to the meaning hidden behind his verse (cf. *Purg.* viii. 20), and there are certainly episodes and descriptions with obvious allegorical significance (e.g. the procession in the Earthly Paradise). But the meaning and power of the poem lie in the open and direct nature of its vast and complex narrative, in the vigour and drama of the representation of men and things.

If we are left with a sense of dissatisfaction by the letter to Can Grande, must we conclude that it cannot be by Dante? I do not think so. Indeed the history of his poetic career, as I have tried to show, leads us to suppose that poetic creation would for Dante automatically be followed by critical reflection upon it. As we saw with *Vita Nuova, Convivio,* and *De Vulgari Eloquentia,* Dante paused at various stages in his career to look back on his production and formulate his poetics on preceding experience. There could be nothing more natural, therefore, in such a series than some attempt at self-commentary also for the *Comedy.* Nor should we necessarily be surprised at what may appear the inadequacy of such an attempt, if it is in fact represented by the letter to Can Grande, as Dante made use of the only critical-exegetical method available to him, the traditional 'accessus ad auctores' and the scheme of the four senses. If this instrument turns out to be incapable of explaining the poem critically to our satisfaction, so much the worse for that traditional type of exegesis. We should also beware of falling into the trap of believing that Dante composed his poem starting from the poetics enunciated in the letter. Such a manner of proceding would be entirely contrary to the whole of his experience, throughout which the moment of critical reflection always comes after the poetry, and never precedes and dictates it. If we look at the letter in this light, it should acquire the purely relative importance it deserves, and cease to be the strait jacket some scholars have wished to make of it.

Any reader of the *Comedy* must be aware, and take due account, of Dante's often repeated conviction that he is fulfilling a divine mission, having been chosen like Aeneas and St. Paul to reveal to men a special vision of God's justice. In the letter to Can Grande the expression of the ineffable in *Paradiso* is compared with the language of Ezekiel and Daniel and with that of the mystics Richard of St. Victor and Bernard, and Plato is cited to illustrate the use of metaphorical language to express things perceived by the intellect which normal speech cannot formulate.[31] In other words the author of the letter seems to claim for poetry, as Dante himself also does in his poem, the power to express, on a par with theology and philosophy, the eternal truths the intellect perceives. Such a concept of poetry and its role is very different from that which informs *Convivio*: put into effect in the *Comedy* it produces a poetry far more varied than the limited range and functions of his allegorical *canzoni*. Already in *Convivio* Dante glimpsed the possibility of poetry achieving, albeit indirectly, the expression of philosophical truth. In the *Comedy*, however, he faces directly and without intermediary fictions the expression in poetry of the deepest intellectual and spiritual experiences. Here beauty and goodness ('bellezza' and 'bontà') are one in the splendour of the poetry of the literal sense.

Beneath this literal meaning readers will continue to find deeper layers of truth, for the *Comedy* has in common with few other great works of art the quality of an inexhaustible fount of wisdom and inspiration. It is in no sense my intention to undervalue this quality. My purpose has been rather to concentrate attention on the poetic innovation of the *Comedy* in relation to Dante's earlier theory and practice; to which I now return in conclusion. It has often been said that the poem draws together all Dante's knowledge and experience in a final autobiographical and at the same time universally valid statement, for which *Vita Nuova* and *Convivio* were the essential prelude and preparation; and that, in a wider context, the *Comedy* represents a kind of medieval *summa*—the last great encyclopedia of the Middle Ages. On the plane of his poetic evolution this ultimate achievement is neither a logical nor a predictable development; although, as he formulated in *De Vulgari Eloquentia* the ideal of a refined, aristocratic poetry within narrowly prescribed limits, he was already reaching out in the prose of *Convivio* to extend its bounds and spread its message to a wider audience. The eclectic solution of the style of the *Comedy* contradicts and at the same time absorbs that theory and practice. Allegorical love poetry and doctrinal *canzoni* are then abandoned for a wider, all-embracing concept of poetry capable of expressing directly within the same composition philosophy and theology, science, invective, prophecy, emotional and spiritual experience from the lowest depths of squalor to the vision of God Himself.

To Renaissance critics Dante not only thereby transgressed stylistic and linguistic decorum, he tried incorrectly and unjustifiably to be more than a poet. Although classical prejudices of form have largely disappeared, and more modern times have accepted and appreciate the multiformity of language and style as the necessary clothing of the *Comedy*, the extension of the range of poetry into the realms of thought and science, the expression through poetry of aesthetically speaking non-lyrical subjects has seemed to many a major problem of Dante scholarship, involving fundamentally the poetic unity of the *Comedy*. We cannot, however, expect Dante to have anticipated Croce's aesthetic, nor his work to conform to ideas of poetry outside his own age and experience. None the less, even in relation to his own age and experience, his *Comedy* is a remarkable departure. Dante called it his 'comedìa', but he would not have demurred, as we certainly do not, at the addition by a sixteenth-century editor of the epithet 'divina'; for before Dante had finished, he referred to the *Comedy* as his 'poema sacro', not merely because its subject concerned divine things, but because he felt himself as a poet endowed with sacred inspiration. It was this powerful conviction and his all-embracing vision of heaven and earth, of man and eternity, that broke down all his earlier theories of poetry, and dictated in practice a kind of artistic freedom which no rules and prescriptions could then contain, nor have ever since succeeded in classifying.

NOTES

1. This general survey of Dante's evolution as a poet originated as a public lecture prepared and delivered in various universities for the seventh-centenary celebrations of Dante's birth in 1965. An Italian version of it was published in my *Cinque saggi su Dante* (Bologna, 1972), under the title: 'Poetica e poesia di Dante'. The text has been revised and partly rewritten for the present occasion, and a few essential notes added.

2. For reasons of brevity I compound in one sentence Dante's youthful experience and the complex problems of his relations with his Florentine contemporaries, in particular his debt to Guido Cavalcanti (cf. G. Contini, 'Cavalcanti in Dante', in his *Varianti e altra linguistica* (Turin, 1970), pp. 433–45, and most recently, M. Ciccuto, 'I sonetti di G. Cavalcanti a Dante', *Atti della Accademia Naz. dei Lincei*, Rendiconti, Classe di sc. morali, storiche e filologiche, xxxii. 5–6 (1977), 399–433).

3. 'But tell me, do I see here the person who brought out the new rhymes beginning "Ladies who have understanding of love"?' And I to him: 'I am one who takes note when Love inspires me, and give utterance according to his dictates within me'. 'O brother, I now see', he said, 'the knot which kept the Notary and Guittone and me on this side of the sweet new style I hear. I see well how your pens follow closely the dictates of Love, which was certainly not so with ours; and whoever seeks to go beyond, finds no other difference between the one and the other style'. Then, satisfied, he fell silent.

4. 'It happened that as I was walking along a road beside which ran a clear stream, I was overcome by so strong a desire to write poetry that I began to think how I should express myself; and I thought that it was unsuitable to speak of her (i.e. of Beatrice) except by addressing ladies in the second person, and not ladies in general, but only those of noble mind and not simply women. Then my tongue spoke as if of its own accord and said: "Ladies who have understanding of love". I stored these words in my mind with great satisfaction, intending to take them as my opening line; so when I had returned to the city and meditated on the matter for some days, I began a canzone with that opening line.'

5. 'In order to explain this matter as far as is here necessary, it is essential to understand that in olden days there were no love rhymsters in the vulgar tongue, but there were certain poets in Latin who wrote love verses . . . And it is not many years since these first vernacular poets first appeared; (I call them poets too) since composing verses in vernacular is, to a certain extent, the same as writing verses in Latin. The evidence that it is not so long ago lies in the fact that if we look in Provencal and Italian, we will not find such compositions more than 150 years back from now. And the reason why some famous men had a reputation for writing is because they were more or less the first to write in Italian. The first to compose as a vernacular poet did so because he wanted to make himself understood by woman, who found it difficult to understand Latin verse. And this is an argument against those who rhyme about subjects other than love, for this manner of composition was invented from the start for love poetry. So, as greater licence is allowed to poets than to prose writers, and as these rhymsters are none other than poets in the vernacular, it is right that they should have greater licence than other vernacular writers: and so, if any figure or rhetorical device is permitted to (Latin) poets, it is also permitted to vernacular poets.'

6. Cf. D. De Robertis, *Il libro della 'Vita Nuova'* (Florence, 1961); V. Branca, 'Poetica del rinnovamento e tradizione agiografica nella *Vita Nuova*', in *Studi in onore di I. Siciliano*, i (Florence, 1966), 123–48.

7. 'Father to me and my betters who ever dealt in sweet and graceful poems of love.'

8. Cf. in this volume the contribution of C. G. Hardie.

9. For the 'petrose' (so called because addressed to a 'madonna Petra' whose name symbolizes her hardness of heart), and the 'tenzone' with Forese Donati, see G. Contini's edn. of Dante's *Rime*, pp. 43–6.

10. One of these ('Le dolci rime d' amor') is commented on in *Convivio*, IV. Others in the group are: 'Poscia ch' amor' and 'Doglia mi reca' (ed. Contini, pp. 30, 49; cf. also K. Foster and P. Boyde, *Dante's Lyric Poetry* (Oxford, 1967), pp. 70, 83.

11. 'Tre donne' (ed. Contini, 47) is an allegorical *canzone* of a rather different kind from the love poems written for philosophy. The three ladies who appear to the poet in disarray represent three aspects of Justice. The poem's conclusion indicates that it was written when Dante still hoped to return to Florence (i.e. before 1304).

12. *VN* xxxv–xxxix; *Conv.* II. ii ff.; II. xii.

13. *Conv.* II. i. 3–4.

14. *Conv.* I. x. 12–13.

15. *Conv.* II. xiii–xiv.

16. On the tension between prose and verse in *Convivio*, see 'Dante e la prosa volgare', in *Cinque saggi*, cit., pp. 46ff.

17. *De Vulg. Eloqu.* II. iv. 2. On 'fictio' see G. Paparelli, *Ideologia e poesia di Dante* (Florence, 1975), pp. 53–138.

18. *De Vulg Eloqu.* II. iv. 3–4; vi. 7.

19. 'You are my master and my author; you alone are the one from whom I took the fine style which has brought me honour' (*Inf.* i. 85–7).

20. 'If composition is to be in the tragic style, the illustrious vernacular should be used and consequently the form of the canzone. If in the comic style, then the medium should be mingled with the humble vernacular.'

21. See *Enciclopedia dantesca*, v (Rome, 1976), s.v. 'stili, dottrina degli'.

22. 'When with the gravity of the subject there accord sublimity of verse form, nobility of construction and excellence of words used.'

23. 'These are those whom the poet in *Aeneid* vi calls the dear to God, raised to the heavens by their ardent virtue, and sons of the gods, though he is here speaking figuratively.'

24. See *Enciclopedia dantesca*, ii (1970), s.v. 'Commedia', 2. Comparizione.

25. This movement into the higher register of style, not foreseen in *De Vulgari Eloquentia* (cf. n. 20 above), is however given some prominence, on the authority of Horace, in the Epistle to Can Grande, 10.

26. See G. Contini's article on the *Fiore* in *Enciclopedia dantesca*, ii. cf. also C. Paolazzi, in *Lettere italiane*, xxviii. 2 (1976), 137–59.

27. Cf. A. Robson, 'Medieval Allegories on Ovid and the *Divina Commedia*' in *Centenary Essays on Dante* (Oxford, 1965), pp. 1–38.

28. Cf. G. Padoan, *Il pio Enea, l'empio Ulisse* (Ravenna, 1977).

29. I quote text and English translation from Toynbee's Oxford edition, where the letter is no. X (no. XIII in that of the Società Dantesca).

30. For a recent, and persuasive, attempt to establish such a parallel see L. Ricci Battaglia, 'Polisemanticità e struttura della *Commedia*', *Giorn. stor. d. Lett. Ital.*, clii, fasc. 478 (1975), 161–98.

31. See J. Mazzeo, *Structure and thought in the 'Paradiso'* (Ithaca, N.Y., 1958).

8

The Dantean Stamp

VALERIO LUCCHESI

The purpose of this essay is to bring into focus certain aspects of Dante's language and versification which I believe to be especially important in characterizing his poetic style and for tracing its evolution in the *Comedy*. Some of these aspects have been studied in detail—sometime in great detail—by other scholars in publications that appeared before or after January 1977 (the date when I gave the lecture reproduced in this essay).[1] I believe that to present the results of my independent study will not be totally useless, and that it will help at least to identify and stress the essential points. Other features, about which too little has been written so far, have been brought into stronger relief; but this is far from saying that I have treated them exhaustively. Only with regard to one aspect (the relationship between sense and rhythm) have I embarked on a more detailed and systematic investigation.

Dante's versification—or rather some of its traits—forms the first half of this study. As the unit of analysis will be the verse rather than the line, it will not be out of place to remind the reader of certain features of Dante's *terzina*. This all-purpose vehicle of the poet's imagination is a grammatical, as well as a metrical unit; normally each *terzina* coincides with a whole sentence or, as happens in the great majority of cases, with a whole period. Thus the poem unfolds as a sequence of periods, each having perhaps a different syntactic and rhythmic structure, but approximately the same length. Shorter periods are exceptional, whereas longer ones recur at fairly frequent intervals. But on the whole the norm prevails by an overwhelming margin, and the single-sentence, or rather the single-period *terzina* forms the fabric of the whole poem. And yet within its narrow boundaries it offers an astonishing variety of grammatical and rhythmic combinations. My purpose is to identify and describe some of the most frequent and characteristic patterns which can be encountered at the metric as well as the syntactic level. Perhaps I should add at the outset that, whereas the relationship between syntax and metre has been extensively studied, the attention given to the rhythmic patterns of the *terzina* has been insufficient and indirect. It is therefore to this particular subject that I should like to address myself in the first place.

By rhythmic pattern of the *terzina* I mean the form in which the various reading pauses are distributed across the metric space. By reading pauses I do not mean exclusively those that are dictated by the punctuation established in the text; nor those that mark the end of a clause (the criterion chosen by P. Boyde in his study of the links between grammar and metre in Dante's lyric poetry). My definition covers all the pauses required for the meaningful and rhythmic delivery of the poet's words, and therefore includes those that mark a definite change in intonation. As they can only be established through the sense and rhythm of the whole *terzina*, they are grammatically unpredictable. Besides occurring at the end of a clause (as they often do), they can coincide with the boundary of a phrase, of a complement or an adjunct. Only meaning and context can guide us in deciding for instance whether a relative clause, or a nominal phrase introduced by *di*, should be separated from their antecedents by an audible pause, or whether they should be recited as a continuous sentence. Let us compare for instance the two lines:

'*Amor che ne la mente mi ragiona*' (*Purg.* ii. 112)

and

l'amor che move il sole e l'altre stelle. (*Par.* xxxiii. 145)

The reader who is familiar with the *canzone* from which the first line is taken, and wants to reproduce its original rhythm, will insert a strong pause after 'Amor'.[2] But the second line does not warrant a similar break because the relative clause which it contains has, as can be seen from the passage, a periphrastic, i.e. a non-parenthetic, value:

> ma già volgeva il mio disio e 'l *velle*,
> sì come rota ch'igualmente è mossa,
> l'amor che move il sole e l'altre stelle.

An analogous difference can be observed between the two
'possessive' constructions contained in the following passages:

(a)   Così vid' i' adunar *la bella scola*
        di quel segnor de l'altissimo canto
        che sovra li altri com' aquila vola.

                                        (*Inf.* iv. 94–6)

(b)   Così prendemmo via giù per *lo scarco*
        di quelle pietre, che spesso moviensi
        sotto i miei piedi per lo novo carco.

                                        (*Inf.* xii. 28–30)

In (a) one is justified in allowing a pause at the end of the first
line because, in spite of its logical links with 'la bella scola',
'di quel segnor' merges with the following words in a well-
balanced, self-contained phrase. In (b) the first line is firmly
fastened to the second and 'lo scarco/di quelle pietre' represents
a classical example of *enjambement*. No proper pause should
therefore be made or heard at the juncture of the two lines. Not
even the conjunction *e* can, by itself (i.e. without the context),
suggest whether or not it should be preceded by a pause. In
Purg. xxiv. 23–4,

        '. . . dal Torso fu, e purga per digiuno
        l'anguille di Bolsena e la vernaccia',

the final line contains two co-ordinated objects so intimately
connected by sense and rhythm that no pause seems necessary
between them. But in the third line of our next example the two
gerunds must be separated by means of a suitable pause,
because they express two distinct actions and because the
second is closely connected with its object:

        E quel nasetto che stretto a consiglio
        par con colui c'ha sì benigno aspetto,
        morì fuggendo e disfiorando il giglio.

                                        (*Purg.* vii. 103–5)

Our exemplification could easily be extended to show how
the scansion of a line or a *terzina* can be influenced by other
factors such as word order. One line alone will be sufficient to
make the point:

        me degno a ciò né io né altri 'l crede.

                                        (*Inf.* ii. 33)

Given the proleptic position of the object ('me degno a ciò') and its proximity to the subject ('né io né altri'), a suitably strong pause and an intonational difference between them are required in order to avoid confusion. In all probability such a pause would not have been necessary had the constituents of the sentence been arranged in their 'normal' order (subject, verb, object).

Of course not all pauses are as uncontroversial as the ones we have chosen so far. In many cases it may be hard to say whether a line should allow a break, and how strong that break should be. It may for instance, take a long time and considerable hesitation before deciding what to do with *Inf.* xiii. 106–9:

> . . . 'Qui le strascineremo, e per la mesta
> selva saranno i nostri corpi appesi,
> ciascuno al prun de l'ombra sua molesta'.

In order to detach the phrase 'de l'ombra sua molesta' from the rest of the line and give it adequate relief, it would seem necessary to raise the pitch of the voice over 'prun' and follow it with a slight pause. But is such a pause sufficiently strong to be counted as a break and lead us to reckon the line as a 'mid-stopped' one? What is the difference between this pause and an ordinary caesura? It must be confessed that the answer to these questions can be difficult, and that agreement on the status of many pauses may be hard to reach. When faced with similar cases, where no expressive or logical consideration seems sufficiently strong to relieve our perplexities, we shall, on the whole, adhere to the following principle: (a) allow the pause if it occurs at the end of the line; (b) disallow it if it falls in the middle of the line. We will, in other words, subscribe to the view that run-on lines and mid-stopped lines are exceptional, and that the recognition of their status is subject to more stringent terms than those which apply in the case of their opposite. This leads us to the problem of pause distribution in the *terzina*, a problem which is just as important as the definition of the pause itself, and closely related to it.

At the root of the *terzina*, as at the root of any other verse, lies the convention that the end of each line signals automatically an audible pause in the voice and a change in intonation. It is, however, for the poet to decide whether, and to what extent, the pauses required for the meaningful delivery of his words should coincide with those suggested by the metre. In practice he may do one or other of the following three things:

(1) Observe the signals and arrange a pause at the end of each line. Each metrical pause will then coincide with a grammatical pause (or a sense pause), and vice versa. The resulting *terzina* consisting, so to speak, of three self-contained units, can be described as having a 'closed' structure.

(2) Do the same, but add further internal pauses to one or more of the three lines.

(3) Disregard the signals and abolish[3] the pause between the first (or second) line and the next. This is, of course, the technique described as *enjambement*. The line whose end is overrun by the grammatical unit, can be described as 'open-ended' and the structure of the resulting *terzina* as 'open'.

What now is Dante's practice in the *Divine Comedy*, and what are the most frequent rhythmic patterns which can be encountered in the poem? Before attempting these questions, it should be pointed out that the answers are not based on an examination of the entire peom, but only of thirty-one *canti* (or 1,450 *terzine*) selected in equal proportions, and at regular intervals, from the three *cantiche*.[4] I regard this sample (over 30 per cent of the whole text) as adequate for our purposes and capable of providing reliable answers for the whole poem and for its different parts.

As might perhaps be expected, the most frequent single occurrence is represented by the 'closed' *terzina* described in (i) above, of which we will give immediately an example and a model:

1. Nel mezzo del cammin di nostra vita   —————— ,
   mi ritrovai per una selva oscura,   —————— ,
   ché la diritta via era smarrita.   —————— .
                    (*Inf.* i. 1–3)

Here, as shown by the symbolic commas of the model, all the pauses required, or authorized, by sense and grammar, coincide with the metrical ones: i.e. they fall at the end of the line with no pause in the middle. This type of *terzina* (obviously the most orthodox and simplest of all) appears in our sample 240 times, i.e. in more than 16 per cent of all cases. But significantly

enough, it is more frequent at the beginning than it is in later
parts of the poem.[5]

A decline in frequency can also be observed in the two groups
of 'closed' patterns which share the common denominator outlined in (ii) above: 2A, in which the 'closed' *terzina* contains
further internal pauses in the first and/or in the second line;
and 2B, in which the pause occurs in the third line. The importance of the distinction between 2A and 2B will be illustrated
later. In the meantime, here are the various examples and
models belonging to group 2A:

2A 1 : Ed elli a me: 'Questo misero modo   —— , —— ,
        tegnon l'anime triste di coloro   ———— ,
        che visser sanza 'nfamia e sanza lodo . . .'[6]   ———— .
                      (*Inf.* iii. 34–6)

   2 : 'Da che tu vuo' saver cotanto a dentro,   ———— ,
        dirotti brievemente', mi rispuose,   —— , —— ,
        'perch' i' non temo di venir qua entro . . .'   ———— .
                      (*Inf.* ii. 85–7)

   3 : Questi sciaurati, che mai non fur vivi,   —— , —— ,
        erano ignudi e stimolati molto   —— , —— ,
        da mosconi e da vespe ch'eran ivi.   ———— .
                      (*Inf.* iii. 64–6)

The most frequent of the three types is 2A 1, of which I have
counted 127 cases; the least frequent 2A 2, with eighty-two
cases. Altogether this group (which accounts for 21.1 per cent
of the total sample) shows a declining rate of incidence as we
progress from *Inferno* (where it represents over 24 per cent of
all cases) to *Purgatorio* (22 per cent) and *Paradiso* (only 16 per
cent).

By comparison 2B is a smaller group, especially when projected against the aggregate of the previous two groups (from
both of which it differs with respect to the third line). Its most
frequent type (with the internal pause confined to the third line
itself) occurs altogether in ninety-two *terzine*:

2B 1 : 'Quando sarò dinanzi al segnor mio,   ———— ,
        di te mi loderò sovente a lui'   ———— ,
        Tacette allora, e poi comincia' io: —— , —— .
                      (*Inf.* ii. 73–5).

Considerably less frequent are the other patterns showing, *in addition* to a mid-stopped third line, a pause in the first or second lines, or even in both.

2: 'Per che, se del venire io m'abbandono,   ——— , ——— ,
    temo che la venuta non sia folle.   ——————— ,
    Se' savio; intendi me' ch'i' non ragiono.'   ——— , ——— .
                    (*Inf.* ii. 34–6)

3: vid' io lo Minotauro far cotale;   ——————— ,
    e quello accorto gridò: 'Corri al varco;   ——— , ——— ,
    mentre ch'e' 'infuria, è buon che tu ti cale'. ——— , ——— .
                    (*Inf.* xii. 25–7)

4: Quel s'attuffò, e tornò sù convolto;   ——— , ——— ,
    ma i demon che del ponte avean coperchio,   ——— , ——— ,
    gridar: 'Qui non ha loco il Santo Volto!'   ——— , ——— .
                    (*Inf.* xxi. 46–8)

Altogether the three patterns (of which 2B 2 and 2B 4 are the most frequent) recur in 116 *terzine*, bringing to 208 the total number of examples found in category 2B. Bearing in mind that categories 1 and 2A contain 546 *terzine*, there is no doubt that Dante shows considerably more reluctance to break the third line of his verse than the first or second. As we shall see later, this cannot be a purely fortuitous or mechanical result. For the time being I should like to point out that this tendency seems to increase as the poet progresses in his work and his handling of the verse becomes proportionately skilful and experienced.

We must now turn to the third category of *terzine*: those where Dante is no longer restricted by what we could call the rule of the terminal pause. Although it would be naïve to assign any intrinsic value to a formal feature, or mistake as a source of poetic beauty what could only be its most outward and accidental shell, there is no doubt that by cultivating the technique of *enjambement* Dante has transcended the limits of the 'closed' verse and created the conditions for a more difficult and exciting experience. I feel, therefore, justified in subjecting the 'open' *terzina* to a careful analysis.

In dealing with category 3, the distinction between class A and class B which we have drawn within the previous category of patterns will be maintained. But as it is often correlated with the position of the *enjambement* in the *terzina*, and largely dependant upon it, this distinction will not form the basis of our classification. Instead I shall divide the examples according to whether the reading 'phrase' overruns the first line (3.1), or the second (3.2), or both (3.3).

Cat. 3.1: The cases in which the *enjambement* is confined to the first line constitute the largest of the three groups. As might be expected, the most common type (133 *terzine*) is characterized by an unbroken third line, and belongs therefore to class A:

3.1A 1: Io vidi una di lor trarresi avante   —— , ——
        per abbracciarmi, con sì grande affetto,   —— , —— ,
        che mosse me a far lo somigliante.   —————— .
                   (*Purg.* ii. 76–8)

The model is self-explanatory: it contains four pauses (including the final one) and four phrases, two 'long' and two 'short'. Of the 'long' phrases, one straddles the first two lines, the other coincides exactly with line three. It is a rhythmically well-balanced verse, capable of providing a suitable build-up, and sufficient space for the culmination in the third line.

The other two most frequent types in group 3.1A are exemplified respectively by *Inf.* xxiv. 82–4, and *Par.* xix. 4–6:

3.1A 2: e vidivi entro terribile stipa   ——————
        di serpenti, e di sì diversa mena   —— , —— ,
        che la memoria il sangue ancor mi scipa.   —————— .

    3: parea ciascuna rubinetto in cui   —— , ——
        raggio di sole ardesse sì acceso,   —————— ,
        che ne' miei occhi rifrangesse lui.   —————— .

Both models belong to class A, but unlike the previous one they are characterized by a tripartite structure: three pauses and three phrases, one of which is longer than a whole line. At times such a length can be uncomfortable; and unless the grammatical structure is sufficiently solid, the reader may be tempted, against the sense of the phrase and the obvious wish of the poet, to restore the abolished pause, or to introduce a new one. But this is not a frequent occurrence, at least not as frequent as it is in other patterns, where the phrase originating in the middle of the second line is stretched to the very end of the *terzina*.

Such patterns belong to a different group and will be

illustrated later. Meantime, let us consider the fourth and last pattern of Cat. 3.1A, a very rare type consisting of only two phrases, the first of which stretches from the beginning of the verse to the end of the second line. The difficulties just mentioned in connection with the excessive length of some phrases become more prominent in these *terzine*, as can be seen from the following example:

3.1A 4:   Virgilio mi venìa da quella banda
                de la cornice onde cader si puote,
                perché da nulla sponda s'inghirlanda;
                        (*Purg.* xiii. 79–81)

I shall not insist on the features of this *terzina*, especially as the reader may object to my raising to the rank of model what could merely be the result of neglect or infelicity. But it is worth noticing that this pattern has its equivalent in Cat. 3.2A, where its image is reproduced, as it were, in a mirror with the long phrase encompassing the last two lines.

With the exception of this last one, all the patterns described in Cat. 3.1A have their counterpart in Cat. 3.1B where they reappear with the same structure but with an additional pause in the middle of the third line:

3.1B 1:   'Ma tu chi se', che nostre condizioni
                vai dimandando, e porti li occhi sciolti,
                sì com' io credo, e spirando ragioni?'
                        (*Purg.* xiii. 130–2)

        2:   Ma quel padre verace, che s'accorse
                del timido voler che non s'apriva,
                parlando, di parlare ardir mi porse.
                        (*Purg.* xviii. 7–9)

        3:   Qual pare a riguardar la Carisenda
                sotto 'l chinato, quando un nuvol vada
                sovr' essa sì, ched ella incontro penda:
                        (*Inf.* xxxi. 136–8)

Not much needs to be said about these cases. The pause in the third line does not confer incisiveness on the last phrase, nor does it solve the problem of balancing a previous phrase when this happens to be too long and kept together only loosely by sense and grammar. What is important, however, is the question

of comparative frequency. Against 282 examples in category
3.1A there are only 100 in category 3.1B: a further proof that
the perfect coincidence of the final phrase with the third line of
the verse is a prevailing feature of Dante's versification.

   Cat. 3.2: If, however, the *enjambement* affects the second line
(as it does in all types belonging to Cat. 3.2), the conditions for
preserving this coincidence are removed, because now the final
phrase will either lie in part outside the third line, or be too
short to take up its entire length. In other words the poet,
having overrun the terminal pause in line two, can only choose
between type A (stretching the phrase to the very end of line
three) or type B (stopping it before its end). Faced with such a
choice, it is the latter rather than the former course that Dante
clearly prefers. Of the 168 *terzine* with an unstopped second
line, 113 (about two-thirds) show an internal pause in line
three. Thus in the context of Cat. 3.2 the relative strength of
classes A and B is roughly the opposite of what it was in Cat.
3.1. In arranging and describing in order of frequency the
patterns of Cat. 3.2 we shall, therefore, begin this time from
those that belong to class B:

3.2B 1 :   Per letiziar là sù fulgor s'acquista,   ———— , ———— ,
      sì come riso qui; ma giù s'abbuia   ———— , ————
      l'ombra di fuor, come la mente è trista.   ———— , ———— .
              (*Par.* ix. 70–2)

   2 :   Tu dici che di Silvïo il parente,   ———————— ,
      corruttibile ancora, ad immortale   ———— , ————
      secolo andò, e fu sensibilmente.   ———— , ———— .
              (*Inf.* ii. 13–15)

   3 :   Li occhi rivolsi al suon di questo motto,   ———————— ,
      e vidile guardar per maraviglia   ————————
      pur me, pur me, e 'l lume ch'era rotto.   ———— , ———— .
              (*Purg.* v. 7–9)

   4 :   ché la mia vista, venendo sincera,   ———— , ———— ,
      e più e più intrava per lo raggio   ————————
      de l'alta luce che da sé è vera.   ———— , ———— .
             (*Par.* xxxiii. 52–4)

3.2B1 and 3.2B 2 are approximately equal in their frequency
(forty-four and forty-one cases respectively). There are

eighteen examples of 3.2B 3 and only ten of 3.2B 4. It should perhaps be pointed out that the two least common types contain one 'very long' phrase which encompasses the whole of the second line and a segment of the third.

We can now turn our attention to the patterns of class 3.2A. These, as will be remembered, are characterized by the fact that the third line does not show any pause and the final phrase is therefore 'very long' (i.e. longer than a whole line):

3.2A 1 :   Né lascerò di dir perch' altri m'oda;   ————— ,
              e buon sarà costui, s'ancor s'ammenta   ——— , ———
              di ciò che vero spirto mi disnoda.   ————— .
                        (*Purg.* xiv. 55–7)

     2 :   Tu argomenti: 'Se 'l buon voler dura,   ——— , ——— ,
              la vïolenza altrui per qual ragione   ——— , ———
              di meritar mi scema la misura?'   ————— .
                      (*Par.* iv. 19–21)

The first model recurs in our sample thirty-four times, the second, sixteen. Taking into account two other minor types,[7] the total number of *terzine* in class 3.2A is fifty-five which, as we pointed out, represents only 32.7 per cent of all examples contained in the whole of Cat. 3.2.

Cat. 3.3: This category includes, as I have already said, all the *terzine* where Dante allows the phrase to overrun the 'natural' pause in both the first and second lines. The ultimate form of the verse, however, varies considerably according to the length of the overrunning phrases. On the one hand, when both of them stretch from the middle of one line to the middle of the next, the structure of the *terzina* will consist of four segments (two short and two long) arranged in the following pattern and exemplified in *Purg.* xiv. 58–60:

3.3B 1 :   Io veggio tuo nepote che diventa   ——— , ———
              cacciator di quei lupi in su la riva   ——— , ———
              del fiero fiume, e tutti li sgomenta.   ——— , ——— .

At the other end of the spectrum one will find another type of *terzina* containing two phrases separated from each other by a pause. This falls around the middle of the second line and divides the verse into two symmetrical parts like the two halves of a shell:

3.3A 1 :   Io mi rivolsi 'n dietro allora tutto   _____
         a' miei poeti, e vidi che con riso   ____ , ____
         udito avëan l'ultimo costrutto;   _____ .
                        (*Purg.* xxviii. 145–7)

Halfway between these two extreme varieties lie another two types, both characterized by a 'very long' phrase and by a tripartite structure:

3.3A 2 :   Ciò ch'io vedeva mi sembiava un riso   ____ , ____
         de l'universo; per che mia ebbrezza   ____ , ____
         intrava per l'udire e per lo viso.   _____ .
                        (*Par.* xxvii. 4–6)

3.3B 2 :   cotai si fecer quelle facce lorde   _____
         de lo demonio Cerbero, che 'ntrona   ____ , ____
         l'anime sì, ch'esser vorrebber sorde.   ____ , ____ .
                        (*Inf.* vi. 31–3)

The frequency of these four types is proportional to the number of pauses (or phrases) which they contain: the more the pauses, the higher the incidence. Thus the most common pattern is 3.3B 1 (with four phrases) which appear in fifty-five *terzine*, the least common 3.3A 1 (two phrases) which appears only in twenty-four. 3.3A 2 and 3.3B 2 occur respectively thirty-five and thirty-one times.

As to the relative frequency of classes A and B within this group, the situation is not too dissimilar from that which we have already observed inside group 3.2: the two types which show a broken third line outnumber those which do not (eighty-eight against fifty-nine). This is not surprising if one bears in mind that in both groups the second line is an open-ended one, and the options possible to the poet in regard to line three are identical in both cases. One point, however, ought to be stressed in this connection; where the phrase is extended to the end of the *terzina*, its classification may become particularly difficult. This is due to the fact that the pause at the end of the second line may be too weak to be counted, yet too strong to be ignored. For this reason a number of examples which in the course of this work had been originally assigned to 3.3A 1 and 3.3A 2 have, after further consideration (and in compliance with the principle outlined on p. 169), been reclassified under 3.1. This shows that phrases of more than one line can be a useful

instrument for enriching the rhythmic texture of the poem; but
also, especially in the critical end-of-verse position, one that
needs handling with extreme precision. In fact the only examples which were assigned immediately and without any mis-
giving to 3.3A. 2 are those that, like the following one, belong to
an unfinished verse:[8]

> Per ch'i' mi mossi col viso, e vedea
> di retro da Maria, da quella costa
> onde m'era colui che mi movea,
> > un'altra storia ne la roccia imposta;
>
> > > (*Purg.* x. 49-52)

We can now draw our conclusions. Leaving aside those cases
in which the *enjambement* affects the second line and therefore
leaves no choice to the poet, there is no doubt that Dante shows
a marked tendency to round off the verse with an unbroken
third line. A quick calculation will show that in those contexts
where the poet is free to break any of the three lines of the
terzina, he will—on average—do so, on one occasion in every
two, if he is dealing with lines one or two; but only once every
four times if he is dealing with line three. This practice cannot
be wholly independent from the fact that the third line represents the metrical, and often the logical and syntactic climax of
the *terzina*. Everything said by the poet at that point acquires
the tone of a memorable conclusion; and a single undivided
phrase appears, if not as the only one, as its most natural form
of expression. No wonder perhaps that Dante's inclination to
preserve the compactness of the third line should, as we have
already noted, become stronger as he progresses from the
narration of the incidents and the broken dialogues of *Inferno*,
to the calm descriptions of *Purgatorio* and the rapturous,
triumphant tones of *Paradiso*. The over-all percentage of mid-
stopped third lines, which in the first *cantica* is 33 per cent (or
one in three), falls to 27 per cent in the second, and to 19 per
cent (one in five) in the third.

The second conclusion concerns the relationship between
'closed' and 'open' verses. The over-all totals would seem to
suggest that the two groups are, roughly speaking, numerically
equivalent. Against a total of 753 *terzine* in categories 1 and 2,
697 are found in category 3: too small a difference to be con-

sidered as something more than the result of accidental circumstances. This, and the fact that all types will be found to coexist in the poem from the very beginning, must, however, not obscure the question of their relative frequency at different stages in Dante's stylistic career. I have already provided detailed figures for the falling rate of incidence of categories 1 and 2, but it will now be useful to recapitulate and compare these figures with those concerning the open models described in category 3:

	Inferno			Purgatorio			Paradiso			TOTAL
CAT. 1		100			72			68		250
CAT. 2A	119			109			77			305
CAT. 2B	100			70			38			208
Total Cat. 2		219			179			115		513
TOTAL CAT. 1 & 2			319			251			183	753
CAT. 3.1A	58			102			122			282
CAT. 3.2A	13			14			28			55
CAT. 3.3A	7			15			37			59
Total Class A		78			131			187		395
CAT. 3.1B	37			35			28			100
CAT. 3.2B	37			43			33			113
CAT. 3.3B	17			28			43			88
Total Class B		91			106			104		301
TOTAL CAT. 3			169			237			291	697
TOTAL			488			488			474	1450

The figures show a gradual abandonment of the 'closed' models for models of the 'open' type. In *Inferno* the 'closed' models (319) are nearly twice as numerous as the 'open' ones (169). In *Purgatorio* the two types tend to balance each other. In *Paradiso* the initial ratio is largely reversed, and the number of *terzine* belonging to category 3 (291) is substantially higher than the aggregate of categories 1, 2A, and 2B (183). The numerical decline of the 'closed' models affects both categories 1 and 2, but it is particularly noticeable in class 2B, where the proportion of *terzine* with a mid-stopped third line falls from about 20 per cent of the total in *Inferno* to about 8 per cent in *Paradiso*. By contrast one notices a dramatic increase in all sections of category 3A, whose aggregate incidence rises from about 16 per cent in the first *cantica* to 40 per cent in the last. This is a clear sign that in the course of his stylistic journey Dante felt a gradual need to abandon the metrical moulds in which most of the poem had up to then been conceived and cast, for others more unusual and sophisticated. It is significant in this respect that the models whose frequency shows the highest rate of increase are those that allow the poet to expand the last phrase even beyond the usual limits, or to overrun both the first and second lines. It is difficult to say to what extent this is the result of new expressive needs and to what extent the result of a natural and almost mechanical evolution of the poet's technique. Whatever the exact balance between these two factors, there is ample evidence and justification for calling the *Paradiso* the *cantica* of the open rhythms.

So far we have dealt with the rhythmic patterns created by the words—the acoustic shadows, as it were, of the underlying grammatical patterns. Although it could be shown that there is a correlation between the number of pauses found in the *terzina* and its syntactic profile, the two measurements can be at variance with each other. Verses with a complex syntactic structure can conform to a prosodic model which is comparatively simple, and vice versa:

> Ben sai come ne l'aere si raccoglie
> quell' umido vapor che in acqua riede,
> tosto che sale dove 'l freddo il coglie.
>
> (*Purg.* v. 109–11)

This is not the most complex of all Dante's *terzine*, but with its concatenation of four dependent clauses (plus the main one) it is certainly much more complex than the straightforward statement of the poet's own perdition at the very beginning of the poem:

> Nel mezzo del cammin di nostra vita
> mi ritrovai per una selva oscura,
> ché la diritta via era smarrita.
>
> (*Inf.* i. 1–3)

Yet both verses conform to the same rhythmic model and can be classified under the same group (Cat. 1). On the other hand the following *terzina*, which in terms of syntactic complexity lies intermediate between the two, belongs, from the rhythmic point of view to a very different and more 'sophisticated' model (3.1 A 3):

> E Cirïatto, a cui di bocca uscia
> d'ogne parte una sanna come a porco,
> li fé sentir come l'una sdruscia.
>
> (*Inf.* xxii. 55–7)

It is impossible for me to say how many of Dante's verses conform, syntactically, to one or other of the three types which have
just been discussed; or for that matter to any of the numerous
other types to be found in the poem. All we can do in the context of this essay is to stress once again the immense variety of
the constructions used by Dante and identify some of the more
frequent or characteristic ones, bearing in mind that variety
itself is a characteristic feature of the poem in this, as well as in
other respects.

At the extreme end of the syntactic spectrum one finds the
plain paratactic technique exemplified by the following *terzina*:

> Questo passammo come terra dura;
> per sette porte intrai con questi savi:
> giugnemmo in prato di fresca verdura.
>
> (*Inf.* iv. 109–11)

At a slightly higher level lies this description of the second step
leading up to the Gate of Purgatory:

> Era il secondo tinto più che perso,
> d'una petrina ruvida e arsiccia,
> crepata per lo lungo e per traverso.
>
> (*Purg.* ix. 97–9)

From here we ascend, through a scale of increasing complexity,
to the form already exemplified in *Purg.* V. 109–11:

> Ben sai come ne l'aere . . . etc.

In spite of its higher number of subordinate clauses, this form
shares with the paratactic ones a very important feature: all the
constituent elements are ordered in what we might call the
normal sequence, i.e. the sequence which we would use in
ordinary speech (after making allowances for certain historical
differences). So in spite of their dissimilarities we might say that
they belong to the same mode of expression.

The other category of verses is represented by sentences or
periods in which the normal word order or clause order is dis-

torted in order to suit the metre or the rhyme. The degree of
deviance varies, and some form of measurement will have to be
used in order to arrive at an adequate classification, but a clear
departure from the norm is always present.

> Da questa tema a ciò che tu ti solve,
> dirotti perch' io venni e quel ch'io 'ntesi
> nel primo punto che di te mi dolve.
>
> (*Inf.* ii. 49–51)

The way in which the final clause anticipates the main clause
and the proleptic position of 'da questa tema' are of course the
result of Dante's choice of the rhymes 'solve' and 'dolve' which
are rare or difficult; so rhyme and grammar are very closely
bound together. But whatever causes or accompanies them,
constructions of this type bear, more clearly than others, the
genuine stamp of Dante's art. They are an eloquent proof of his
victory over the recalcitrant medium ('la materia . . . sorda') and
a frequent source of beauty. Proust once wrote: 'une forme
grammaticale elle même peut être belle . . .'

Aesthetics apart, let us now try to identify some of the
syntactic structures which one comes across more frequently in
Dante. A *stilema*, a stylistic feature, can of course consist of a
phrase as much as of a sentence or period: and one would be
tempted to start from the bottom of the scale stressing resemb-
lances such as these:

(a) Io fui da Montefeltro, io son Bonconte; (*Purg.* v. 88)

(b) Cesare fui e son Iustinïano, (*Par.* vi. 10)

(c) Uomini fummo, e or siam fatti sterpi: (*Inf.* xiii. 37)

(d) '. . . che fu già vite e ora è fatta pruno'. (*Par.* xxiv. 111)

And one could now move up and compare:

> 'Flegïàs, Flegïàs tu gridi a vòto',
> disse lo mio segnore, 'a questa volta . . .'
>
> (*Inf.* viii. 19–21)

with

> 'Volgi, Beatrice, volgi li occhi santi',
> era la sua canzone, 'al tuo fedele . . .'
>
> (*Purg.* xxxi. 133–4)

But as we are trying to identify some of the most common and general features of Dante's syntax, we must operate at a more abstract level and discuss examples like these:

> Allor con li occhi vergognosi e bassi,
> temendo no 'l mio dir li fosse grave,
> infino al fiume del parlar mi trassi.
>
> (*Inf.* iii. 79–81)

> L'animo mio, per disdegnoso gusto,
> credendo col morir fuggir disdegno,
> ingiusto fece me contra me giusto.
>
> (*Inf.* xiii. 70–2)

The common feature here is that the main clause is placed entirely in the third line and coincides with it. Such a colloca-tion is comparatively rare: it only occurs in 6 per cent of all verses. Normally the main clause is situated, or at least initiated, in the first or second line of the *terzina*—the third line being thus left completely outside its range or only allowed to accommodate a segment of it. Sometimes this segment is represented by a nominal or adverbial phrase stretching across the entire length of the line:

> Tratto m'avea nel fiume infin la gola,
> e tirandosi me dietro sen giva
> sovresso l'acqua lieve come scola.
>
> (*Purg.* xxxi. 94–6)

About 8 per cent of all verses are characterized by this syntactic structure. In another 7 per cent of cases the clause ending in the middle of the third line is rounded off by a relative clause:

> '. . . Merrenti a gli occhi suoi; ma nel giocondo
> lume ch'è dentro aguzzeranno i tuoi
> le tre di là, che miran più profondo'.
>
> (*Purg.* xxxi. 109–11)

Far more frequently, especially in the earlier parts of the poem, the third line of the *terzina* is occupied by an independent sentence or a coordinate clause introduced by *e, ma, e poi, però, o*. The binding force of these conjunctions varies according to sense and is usually, but not invariably, reflected in the punctu-ation (comma, no comma, semicolon) at the end of the preceding line. This type of *terzina* becomes less frequent as we progress towards the end of the poem;[9] but on average it occurs in about 19 per cent of the sample which I have analysed.

However, the most frequent structure which appears in the final line is a dependent clause introduced by a relative pronoun or adverb or by a subordinating conjunction: *che, il quale, cui, quel che, ciò che, colui che, ove, onde, quando, prima che, poscia che, come così, come se, quanto, più che, non altrimenti che, quasi, sì come, tale, tanto, quale, sì che, avvegnaché, ben che, perché, però, per cui, se, qualunque, chi?, come?,* etc. Relative, consecutive, comparative, causal, temporal, and other dependent clauses account for nearly one-third of all final lines. If one adds to them the gerundive and infinitive constructions which appear in the same position one reaches 40 per cent of the total: a figure which is statistically significant and represents a constant feature of Dante's poetic syntax. But the importance of this practice is not so much quantitative as qualitative: it plays an important part in our subconscious definition of what we call the Dantean *tone*. The use of certain pronouns and conjunctions to introduce the final statement often reinforces the climactic quality of the third line and clinches the verse. This is particularly true of *sì che* and *che*. Of 136 lines opened by *sì che* that I have counted in the poem, eighty-eight (i.e. about two-thirds) are third lines: not just consecutive, therefore, but also conclusive (and often memorable: *sì che 'l piè fermo sempre era 'l più basso; sì che tre ne facea così dolenti; sì che 'l Giudeo di voi tra voi non rida*). The equivalent role of *che* (often used as a conjunction as well as a pronoun)[10] is already apparent from the outset ('Nel mezzo del cammin di nostra vita/ mi ritrovai per una selva oscura,/ *ché la diritta via era smarrita*). I should like to add that some of the most celebrated circumlocutions of the poem are relative clauses which form the culminating line of the verse: 'lo dolce piano/ *che da Vercelli a Marcabò dichina*'; 'come gente . . ./ *che va col cuore e col corpo dimora*'; 'la infinita via/ *che tiene una sustanza in tre persone*'.

Equally characteristic, although less frequent, is Dante's use of a comparative clause in the third line. This is part of a well-defined structure which encompasses the whole *terzina* and reappears at regular intervals. It forms what I call the *comparatio brevis*, the short comparison, as opposed to the *comparatio prolixa*, or long comparison, which I shall illustrate later. Like the latter it consists of two parts: the *comparandum* which is the object of the poet's alleged vision and for which he is seeking an adequate illustration within the range of the reader's experience, and a *comparator*, the object with which the reader is familiar. The short comparison occupies one whole *terzina* and takes two basic forms:

> (1)   E come 'l volger del ciel de la luna
> cuopre e discuopre i liti sanza posa,
> così fa di Fiorenza la Fortuna:
>
> (*Par.* xvi. 82–4)

Here the *comparatio* is articulated in two parts: the first coincides with the initial lines of the *terzina*, the second (i.e. the *comparandum*, Florence's fortune) with the final one. But this structure is not as frequent as its opposite, in which, as in the following example, the *comparandum* precedes the other part of the simile:

> (2)   Ed ecco intorno, di chiarezza pari,
> nascere un lustro sopra quel che v'era,
> per guisa d'orizzonte che rischiari.
>
> (*Par.* xiv. 67–9)

I said, earlier on, that not all Dante's *terzine* are formed by a single sentence or a single period. At regular and not infrequent intervals one comes across periods which run into the following verse or encompass two or more full *terzine*. This is, for instance, an example of what I call 4+2, that is, of a sentence which is carried into the following *terzina* but which does not progress beyond the first line:

> Ma perché Malebolge inver' la porta
> del bassissimo pozzo tutta pende,
> lo sito di ciascuna valle porta
>   che l'una costa surge e l'altra scende:
> noi pur venimmo al fine in su la punta
> onde l'ultima pietra si scoscende.
>
> (*Inf.* xxiv. 37–42)

In addition to the 4+2 structure we also find the 3×2 construction, that is, a period that encompasses two whole verses. This structure can be observed in a high proportion of Dante's long similes, where it appears more than 100 times. In its most typical form, the simile consists of two symmetric parts, with the *comparator*, introduced by *quale* or *come*, neatly housed in the first verse, and the *comparandum*, introduced by *tale* or *così*, in the second:

> Come 'l ramarro sotto la gran fersa
> dei dì canicular, cangiando sepe,
> folgore par se la via attraversa,
>   sì pareva, venendo verso l'epe
> de li altri due, un serpentello acceso,
> livido e nero come gran di pepe;
>
> (*Inf.* xxv. 79–84)

This type of construction is not just more elaborate than the single tercet simile; it is often more powerful and arresting. The sense of wonder and expectation which the poet achieves through its use is also much higher than in those similes where the *comparandum* has no syntactic link with the previous *terzina* and is allowed to follow on in the form of a comment or after-thought. No wonder that Dante's use of this construction should be less frequent than the integrated two verse similes.

The longer the *comparator*, the higher the suspense and solemnity of the object which it precedes and announces. This rule, which Dante must have absorbed from classical models, explains why many of his three verse similes (the most readily identifiable of his 3 × 3 periods) coincide with the most memorable moments of his journey; as in this famous simile where Dante describes his own emotions after Beatrice's chastisement:

> Sì come neve tra le vive travi
> per lo dosso d'Italia si congela,
> soffiata e stretta da li venti schiavi,
>   poi, liquefatta, in sé stessa trapela,
> pur che la terra che perde ombra spiri,
> sì che par foco fonder la candela;
>   così fui sanza lagrime e sospiri
> anzi 'l cantar di quei che notan sempre
> dietro a le note de li etterni giri;
>
> (*Purg.* xxx. 85–93)

But periods formed by three verses are not confined to similes. The famous description of sunset—'Era già l'ora che volge il disio . . .'—belongs to a whole series of 3×3 constructions in which the temporal clause, stretching over six lines, either follows or precedes the main clause. We have, for instance, the beginning of Canto xxx of *Purgatorio*:

> Quando il settentrïon del primo cielo,
> che né occaso mai seppe né orto
> né d'altra nebbia che di colpa velo,
>   e che faceva lì ciascuno accorto
> di suo dover, come 'l più basso face
> qual temon gira per venire a porto,
>   fermo s'affisse: la gente verace,
> venuta prima tra 'l grifone ed esso,
> al carro volse sé come a sua pace;

This, and the even longer periods which one could produce, are an eloquent demonstration of Dante's technical ability and a further proof of his familiarity with classical models. They are often used to impart variety, to raise the tone of the narration, or to confer solemnity, eloquence, or pathos on the speeches of his protagonists. A typical example is offered again by Canto xxx of *Purgatorio*, where the encounter with Beatrice is narrated in long, slow waves of music. Translated into the language of grammar this means that there are three periods of the type 3×3; two of the type 3×4 (of which there are only thirty-six in the whole poem) and four periods of the type 3×2. The single verse sentences only number twenty-four, a comparatively low figure. A similar observation could be made for *Paradiso* xxiii which describes the triumph of Christ. On the other hand it could be said that the expressive role of a long period can be emphasized by its contextual isolation, just as a single mountain of moderate height appears higher if it rises up from a flat plain. For example, Dante's invective against the Simoniacs contains two constructions of the type 3×2, and thus stands out in the almost uninterrupted sequence of single verse sentences that form canto xix. Similarly in canto v of *Inferno*, the attention is suddenly awakened by the two-verse simile of the doves ('Quali colombe dal disio chiamate . . .' etc.) followed immediately by Francesca's eloquent address to Dante ('O animal grazïoso e benigno . . .', introducing another long period with a complex conditional sentence 'se fosse amico . . . noi pregheremmo . . .').

But one must not overstate a case, especially where Dante's style is concerned. There are in the *Comedy*, some long, or very long periods that bear no relation to the tone of the subject. In fact their length would seem to be in inverse proportion to it. The picturesque simile of the Venetian arsenal in the circle of the Baraters is a four-verse simile, and so is the comic description of the various sounds and signals, which according to Dante, can never match the originality of the sound of the marching devils. But these are special cases which have to be seen in the light of the poet's tendency to ornamentation, or as examples of sheer virtuosity. They are, from this point of view, very similar to the genuine examples of alliteration that Dante uses in the *Comedy*: that is, intermittent and often gratuitous decorations, whose purpose is to add interest, variety, and complexity to the poem: something that Dante shares with other medieval artists and craftsmen, with the architects of Notre-Dame as well as the great miniaturists of his age. But it is now time to move on and to take a quick look at another aspect of Dante's poetry, that is, the linguistic one.

We shall begin with the use of periphrasis. Periphrasis is the earliest and the last of Dante's rhetorical figures. In the first sonnet of the *Vita Nuova* he calls the night 'il tempo che onne stella n'è lucente'; and the last sonnet opens with the line 'Oltre la spera che più larga gira' (beyond, in other words, the ninth heaven). The opening line of the *Comedy*—'Nel mezzo del cammin di nostra vita'—should be regarded, strictly speaking, as a traditional metaphor, although it qualifies as a periphrasis as well. But there is no doubt that *Paradiso* ends with one of those sacred circumlocutions with which he always refers to God throughout the poem: 'l'amor che move il sole e l'altre stelle'. In all its various forms (astronomical, theological, geographical or otherwise) periphrasis is used by Dante throughout the whole of the *Comedy*, and remains a constant source of poetry. Perhaps we should remind ourselves that the celebrated passage 'Era già l'ora che volge il disio . . .' is only an expanded periphrasis. Dante's refusal to mention the name of God has the same stimulating effect on his imagination as does the tyranny of rhyme. It brings out the best in him. The inventiveness and virtuosity which Dante displays in his perennial quest for Divine periphrases are inexhaustible. God is:

(a) colui che tutto move   (*Par.* i. 1)

(b) colui che tutto vede   (*Par.* xxi. 50)

(c)   magno volume

du' non si mostra mai bianco né bruno (*Par.* xv. 50)

(d)   . . . lo seme

del qual ti fascian ventiquattro piante. (*Par.* xii. 95–6)

And so on in circumlocutions of ever-increasing lyricism.

Whereas periphrasis was a very early companion of Dante's poetry, metaphor was a later acquisition; and the stages of his poetic career can be better measured through the use of metaphorical language than by any other single element of style. Not that there were no metaphors in his poems of the 'dolce stil nuovo' period, but they had a gentle, self-effacing quality about them, and came so close to ordinary language as to be almost indistinguishable from it: 'gli assalti d'Amore', 'le donne vestute d'umiltà', Beatrice seen as the 'luce d'amore'. The personification and dramatization of Love, sighs, and other categories of 'spiriti' seem to exhaust the poet's capacity for more concrete imagery. Only in his *Risposta a ignoto rimatore* (which is probably later than is commonly supposed) and in isolated images here and there (for instance, in the *canzone* 'Donna pietosa') do we have premonitions of a different style. But it is not until after Dante's encounter with the poetry of Arnaut Daniel that we can see the rise of that bold metaphorical language that will triumph in the *Comedy* and will earn for the poet the name of *metaforicissimo*.

By metaphorical language we mean not only metaphors *strictu sensu*, but all tropes that are based on transference and resemblance of meaning, including similes; and not only similes, but also that vast area of words, locutions, and constructions that cover the extreme fringe of the metaphorical realm and border upon the norm. I propose to survey briefly the various levels of this stylistic dimension, starting with a few words about the respective status of simile and metaphor in the *Comedy*. To say that simile is an explicit metaphor or that metaphor is a compressed or disguised simile, is to point out their fundamental identity; at the poetic level, however, the two figures are, or can be, very different. Metaphor is a potentially more effective figure than the simile because it is an integral part of the poet's vision, and is submitted to us without warning. Let us take an example. When Dante compares the expiating souls of Purgatory to a flock of sheep in the celebrated simile—'Quando le pecorelle escon dal chiuso'—we admire its precision and aptness. But when Dante says that Forese let the other souls overtake them, and refers to them as 'la santa greggia' ('sì lasciò trapassar la santa greggia') the image strikes, in its brevity, a deeper and more suggestive chord.

Yet the 400 similes one finds in the poem are, as they deserve to be, a source of perpetual fascination and the recurrent object of critical attention. Their uniqueness has been identified with their inevitability. Not only do we accept that things are what Dante says they are, but it does not even occur to us that they could be in any other way. This naturalness however can be pushed too far and become tautological. When Dante says, after breaking the twig in the suicides' wood, that he felt like a man seized by terror ('stetti come l'uom che teme'), he is obviously comparing himself with himself: and indeed it would be better to leave out from any future anthology of Dante's similes this and other comparisons of the same type. We must remember, however, that these weaker comparisons represent a very distinctive feature of Dante's style; not only because of their archaic flavour, but also because they tend to coincide with the end of the *terzina*, and thus become more memorable than their emptiness would otherwise justify.

Below the level of the simile one enters the central zone of Dante's imagery: that of metaphor proper. It is here that the return of the sixth hour of the day is likened to the return from her service, of a handmaid; that 'to approach the study of theology' becomes 'drizzare il collo al pan degli angeli' (to lift up one's neck for the bread of angels); 'to proceed as speedily as possible' is 'to urge one's boat along with sail and oar'; 'to have a certain opinion confirmed the hard way through bitter experience rather than by hearsay' is 'to have the opinion nailed in the middle of one's head with stronger nails than men's words', 'to condemn the sin of laziness' is 'to sink one's teeth into the sin of laziness'.

These last two metaphors exemplify very well the underlying tendency of a considerable part of Dante's imagery; not only is it concrete and vigorous, but it reveals a stream of violence flowing beneath it. A cornice running along a mountain is said to 'squeeze a mountain'; to impede an intention is 'to slash an intention'; to say something true is 'to strike at the truth with one's bow' (and this latter is only one of many images taken from the language of archery and horse-riding).

This is something which is connected with, but goes in a sense beyond, the well known ability with which Dante chooses his words to match the violence of Hell: the 'rime aspre e chiocce', the 'graffi' and 'raffi' of the demons in the circle of the Barattieri, the 'scaglie', 'spranghe', and 'stregghia' of the circle of the Forgers. There is positive relish in the way Dante chooses his verbs to describe the operations of Divine Justice against the sinners: 'martellare', 'pungere', 'sommergere', 'spronare', 'mungere', and that terrible verb 'frugare', which we do not know whether to define as a sinister euphemism or a term taken from the language of the executioner.

In spite of its different atmosphere, similar expressions reappear in *Purgatorio*. There we are told that the second cornice 'sferza la colpa dell' invidia' (although we are reassured that the thongs of the whip are only inspired by love); and the extreme emaciation of Forese's face is described with that marvellous, but cruel word: 'trapunta'. Nor is Dante willing to mitigate the words with which he describes the punishment of his old friend:

> ov'el sentia la piaga
> de la giustizia che sì li pilucca.
>
> (*Purg.* xxiv. 38–9)

Nor does the habit of the 'rime aspre' seem to be completely forgotten in *Purgatorio*: see the tercet 'lacca'/'biacca'/'fiacca' in the Vale of the Princes, and 'toppa'/'troppa'/'disgroppa' in the mouth of the 'cortese portinaio'. This vigorous, and sometimes over-vigorous language, is, in a sense, further proof of Dante's passionate love of the concrete. At the same time it reminds us that even the greatest artists can become the victims of their own style: Michelangelo does, and so does Shakespeare; Dante is no exception. There is a *manierismo dantesco* as much as there is a *manierismo michelangiolesco*.

We now descend into the last and most elusive layer of Dante's metaphorical language which I call the counter-metaphor or sub-metaphor. The prevailing technique here consists in replacing a metaphor of current usage with another one, different, but very similar to the first. Let us take the lines:

> Lettor, tu vedi ben com' io innalzo
> la mia matera, e però con più arte
> non ti maravigliar s'io la rincalzo.
>
> (*Purg.* ix. 70–2)

'To sustain or support one's poetic theme with more art' would hardly be a metaphor, because 'sustain' has long since lost its original, literal meaning (i.e. to hold up from underneath). In fact *sostenere* is replaced by Dante with the verb *rincalzare*, whose meaning is that of *sostenere*; but unlike *sostenere* has a primarily literal, that is, physical, association: it is in actual fact a verb used by builders for reinforcing walls and foundations etc. The result is that the expression 'rincalzare la materia con più arte' is presented as an almost physical operation; we say here that the metaphor has been revitalized. Another example: the dividing line between life and death has produced the crystallized metaphor *essere sull'orlo della morte*, and no one would say *sull'orlo della vita*, as does Dante, if, by that, he meant 'to be dying'. But strictly speaking, there is no reason why the expression *essere sull'orlo della vita* should not mean the same thing if we imagine life as a road ending over a precipice. This is obviously the image underlying 'attende,/pria che si penta, l'orlo della vita' (*Purg.* xi. 128), which turns the current expression on its head and runs against the expectation of the reader (at least of the modern reader). In the same way Shakespeare talks of the floor of Heaven inlaid with shining stars, thus reversing the metaphor of the heavenly vault. Yet another example: Dante uses the expression 'solvere un nodo' in the sense of expiating a sin.[11] The phrase, as Tommaseo vaguely points out, is probably connected with *vincolo di colpa* and *vincolo d'obbligo*. These are figurative expressions which have produced other metaphors such as, for instance, *sciogliere o assolvere da una colpa*. But Dante's mind takes a different course: if, as the basic image suggests, sin is a bond or a knot, to free oneself from it is simply to untie the knot. Nothing could be more logical, and nothing could be more subtly and poetically, removed from the paths of ordinary speech.

The extreme border of the metaphorical territory is occupied by another category of locutions: 'del ponte avean coperchio', 'ammirazione (*meraviglia*) traean di me', 'nessun tuo passo caggia', 'tanto che l'acqua nulla ne 'nghiottiva', etc. All these expressions do not seem to conform with ordinary linguistic usage (neither ancient nor modern). And yet they do not sound completely wrong: do we not use the expression *avere copertura* in the military and financial sense? do we not say *prender coraggio*; do we not say that *le spalle cadono un po'*, and that the waves *inghiottono una barca*? What is happening here is that Dante pushes the words just that little bit further than one expects, and without creating a metaphor proper, gives us a tiny spark of that *meraviglia* that seventeenth-century poets claimed to be the ultimate effect of metaphorical usage. The way in which the historical dictionaries (Crusca, Battaglia, Tommaseo–Bellini) have reacted to these sub-metaphors is an excellent proof of their ambiguous status. The same example may be entered in one dictionary and given a special place because of its special meaning; entered, but taken for granted in another (without realizing that it deviates from the norm); and ignored by a third, presumably on the assumption that it is a metaphor which nobody should or could imitate.

This series of minor, but incessant infringements and displacements of the linguistic norm accounts for a good part of the *tension* which we experience and associate with Dante's poetry, even before the great images arrive.

A word of warning is necessary however at this point. Several features of Dante's language, which at first sight could be taken as bearing his individual stamp, were in fact features of the contemporary language. The choice of the verb *sfogliare* which so aptly describes the punishment inflicted upon the gluttons of Purgatory, shows all the marks of the master's hand. With its ambiguous meaning of 'removing the leaves or petals of a plant' and 'peeling' (for instance in the case of peeling onions), it conveys, at one and the same time, the realistic description of the torment and the pity felt for the sinners by Dante himself. It is, in fact, a word to be found in many of the early vernacular poets, who use it in the sense of 'to waste'. Again, when Dante uses *imaginare* in the sense of 'to reproduce an image on marble', one is struck by the novelty and beauty of the word (words of

course can be beautiful in themselves), and perhaps one might
credit the poet with having invented it. But it is a word one
could still hear in Tuscany some 200 years ago (Tommaseo
remarks: 'bel senso che ora non vive più nell' uso'), and Dante
must have taken it from contemporary usage. *Mordere* in the
line 'una medesma lingua pria mi morse', said of Virgil's re-
proaches to Dante, could be taken then and there for yet
another metaphor. In fact it is used in the sense of *rimproverare*
and *criticare* by all the authors of the *Trecento*, and Boccaccio is
full of it. Even certain grammatical features of the *Comedy* which
the sensitive reader might regard as adding to its beauty, or
useful for its stylistic characterization, may have their counterpart in the contemporary language. I am thinking, for example,
of Dante's intermittent omission of the article before the
possessive pronoun ('nostro peccato fu ermafrodito'—so much
more exciting for the modern reader than '*il* nostro peccato fu
ermafrodito'). But this is an oscillation which can be found even
in the account books of the Florentine merchants of the time, and
it is therefore less significant than we thought.[12] Unfortunately,
what we know about Dante's contemporary language is not
enough, not enough anyway to draw the line between current
usage and poetic usage in the *Comedy*. We know for instance,
that in the lines 'La turba che rimase lì, selvaggia/parea del
loco', *selvaggia* does not mean 'wild', but 'inexperienced'. The
word reappears with the same meaning in Cino (who uses it for
punning on the name of his beloved) and in the *Ragionamenti* of
Andrea da Barberino when he recommends that a new bride
should *show* herself suitably *selvaggia*. But we do not know
whether and to what extent Dante goes beyond the accepted
usage of the time when he attaches a preposition to this adjective and treats it exactly like *esperto*: 'selvaggio del loco' and
'esperti d'esto loco'. Is this another arbitrary extension of a
construction, another poetic and stylistic licence? Or simply the
reflection of usage?

The problem, important as it may be to us as critics, philolo-
gists and scholars, is of no great concern to us as readers. If a
certain feature of Dante's language strikes us for its expressive
quality, it does not matter where it comes from. And if we discover that it comes from the language of the time rather than
from the poet himself, we shall have to readjust the balance of

our praise, and give less to the poet and more to the century: 'Quel secolo', as Manzoni says with tongue in cheek 'in cui tutti parlavano bene'. It cannot be denied that time has conferred on Dante's language a patina of antiquity which adds, without being essential, to its beauty and our pleasure.

With this qualification in mind, we can resume and bring to an end our survey of Dante's style. Having dealt with the metaphorical aspect of the language, we can now deal with its elliptical quality. This is important because it accounts to a considerable extent for that *brevity* which we sometimes see to be the stylistic essence of the *Comedy*. When Dante says that 'nostro peccato fu ermafrodito', or 'non sia di qua vostra reddita', he short-circuits the grammar. And when, talking of the 'Piche misere', he uses the expression 'sentiro/lo colpo tal, che disperar perdono', he compresses two separate moments or aspects of their story: the realization that the song of the rival Muses was better than theirs, and, together with it, the sudden terror of their impending fate. Similarly, when asking the hypocrites, weighed down by their cloaks of golden lead, in what exactly their punishment consists, the sense of his question is: 'What punishment is inflicted upon you by the cloak that glitters so much?' But the form of the question is: 'che pena è in voi che sì sfavilla?' ('what punishment is it that glitters so much upon you?'). The fact that these examples can be described and classified through the aid of tropes, does not alter the final effect which they produce on the reader, nor disguise their genuine paternity. The same power and desire to contract produces those abbreviated accounts of classical and biblical events which strike us for their obscure and epic forcefulness, as in:

> '. . . e de li Ebrei ch'al ber si mostrar molli,
> per che no i volle Gedeon compagni,
> quando inver' Madïan discese i colli'.
>
> (*Purg.* xxiv. 124–6)

The last stylistic feature I should like to illustrate is Dante's choice of adjectives and nouns. Earlier on I called attention to the expression 'la santa greggia' as a metaphor. I now propose to look at it from another angle—as an example of the boldness with which Dante brings together two words which are not normally associated with one another. 'La santa greggia' shows a contrast which will reappear in 'la mandra fortunata', 'la régge sacra', 'li egregi Romani', 'la fiamma antica', 'i bramosi fantolini', 'il cortese portinaio', and many others. Even when the attribute is more predictable or compatible with its object, something, either in the meaning or in the form of the combination, will lift it above the level of bread-and-butter associations: 'la costa superba' of *Purgatorio*, 'le care piante' of Virgil, 'l'orazion picciola' of Ulysses, 'lo sparvier grifagno', are some of the examples which come to mind. Some times the effect is achieved through alliteration ('foco furo', 'sparvier selvaggio', 'giusto giudizio', 'dogliosi danni', 'pelaghi cupi'); but whatever the reason, these are the simplest and sometimes the most beautiful units of Dante's poetry. It is also interesting to note here that most of the adjectival constructions of the *Comedy* contain one attribute only: examples such as 'sconcia e fastidiosa pena', 'tempesta impetuosa e agra', 'la maladetta e sventurata fossa', are much rarer. (The rate, I should guess, is about one double adjective for every five single ones). After what we have said about the basic quality of Dante's style—its brevity, energy, and tension—this is not surprising. Double adjectives dilute the force of the attribution and take up metric space; especially when (as in the 'maladetta e sventurata fossa') they are quasi-synonymous and polysyllabic. A most illuminating comparison could be made between the practice of Dante and that of Petrarch in this respect, but I shall not go into this. I can only say that lines such as 'un signor valoroso accorto e saggio', or 'il lungo e dolce ragionar con lei', could never belong to the *Comedy*, any more than 'i gelati guazzi' and 'il primo intoppo' could belong to the poetry of Petrarch. Great poets have their own unmistakable style as do great painters and sculptors; and as a square inch of marble or canvas is sufficient to reveal the hand of the master, so is a line, or even half a line, of poetry.

NOTES

1. A comprehensive bibliography of recent stylistic works on the *Comedy* is contained in the following essay of this collection. In order to avoid unnecessary repetition the reader is referred to pp. 231 ff. of this volume.
2. The pause is clearly required by the parenthetic nature of the relative clause:

> Amor che ne la mente mi ragiona
> de la mia donna disïosamente,
> move . . .

3. 'Abolish' is in fact too strong a word. The interval between two lines can become *almost* imperceptible, but can never be totally effaced.

4. In particular: *Inf*. iii, vi, ix, xii, xv, xviii, xxi, xxiv, xxvii, xxxi, xxxii.
   Purg. ii, vi, x, xiv, xviii, xxii, xxvi, xxviii, xxx, xxxii.
   Par. i, iv, vii, ix, xv, xix, xxiii, xxvii, xxx, xxxiii.

5. One hundred examples belong to *Inferno*, seventy-two to *Purgatorio*, and sixty-eight to *Paradiso*. The frequency of occurrence in the three *cantiche* is about 20, 15, and 14 per cent respectively.

6. For the sake of simplicity a single comma has been used for all mid-stopped lines irrespective of whether they contain only one pause or more. For the same reason, no attempt has been made to distinguish from the others, those pauses that may occur at the end of a sentence and are therefore marked in the text by a colon, a semi-colon, or a full stop.

7. In addition to 1 and 2, group 3.2A includes two types which are extremely rare (five examples in all) and which we have already mentioned in connection with 3.1A 4. Like 3.1A 4, these two types contain an exceptionally long phrase which embraces two whole lines. Their models are given below:

   3.2A 3: _____,   3.2A 4: _____ , _____ ,
            _____   _____
            _____.   _____.

8. Ten of the thirty-four examples belonging to type 3.3A 2 share this characteristic.

9. Its incidence can be treated as a rough indicator of the paratactic level of Dante's syntax at different stages of composition: very high in *Inferno* (nearly 25 per cent of all verses), and very low in *Paradiso* (11 per cent). By contrast one notices a corresponding increase in the number of third lines that bring to a close a syntactic unit begun earlier in the verse: 16 per cent in *Inferno*, 22 per cent in *Purgatorio*, and nearly 29 per cent in *Paradiso*. These figures are obviously correlated with the changing distribution of the rhythmic patterns already illustrated.

10. 35 per cent of all subordinate clauses are relative clauses; and nearly two-thirds of all relative clauses are introduced by *che*. Since, as well as a pronoun, *che* is used as a conjunction in the sense of *so that, because, when, than,* etc., about 40 per cent of all third lines containing a dependent clause begin with *che*. This amounts to nearly 14 per cent of all third lines in the poem.

11. '. . . e d'iracundia van solvendo il nodo' (*Purg*. xvi. 24).

12. It will remain in Florentine usage until at least as late as the beginning of the seventeenth century.

9

The stylistic analysis of the *Divine Comedy* in modern literary scholarship

DAVID ROBEY

Dante scholarship, because of its predominant interest in historical interpretation and explanation, has often been accused of neglecting the specifically poetic qualities of the *Divine Comedy*.[1] A vast stream of academic effort has been concerned with elucidating the historical content of the poem (its original meaning and references), and with relating this to the life, culture, and society of the author; in contrast relatively little explanation has been offered of the poem's effect on the reader as a work of art. The purpose of the pages that follow is to survey the contribution made by this less common type of academic study to our understanding of the *Comedy*. What passes in Italy under the name of 'aesthetic' criticism, however, will not be included in my discussion.

'Aesthetic' criticism of the *Comedy* began, it is well known, with Croce's *La poesia di Dante* of 1921.[2] Croce's polemic against contemporary Dante scholarship rested on his view that the proper object of literary study is the aesthetic quality or *poesia* of the individual work, not such external factors as the historical circumstances and personal experience of the author.[3] *Poesia*, for Croce, was the simultaneous intuition and expression of states of 'lyrical' feeling, which can usually be perceived and comprehended in a work without reference to the work's genesis or to information about the author as a man. The critic's task is simply to say where *poesia* is present, and to offer a brief formulation of its character. Thus, in *La poesia di Dante*, Croce distinguishes between those parts of the *Comedy* which are, in his belief, poetic, and those parts which are not. For the second he uses the term *struttura*, including under it such major elements of the poem as its moral system, Dante's conception of the two guides, his description of the geography of the three worlds and of his journey through them. The function of these, according to Croce, is essentially practical: they serve to link together the brief moments of 'lyric' poetry, which constitute the aesthetically significant element in the work.

In Italy, if not elsewhere, an important strand of Dante criticism has been devoted to the discussion of Croce's *struttura/poesia* distinction and of his characterization of the *Comedy*'s poetry. Quantitatively this type of criticism may not have been very remarkable in relation to the greater part of Italian work on Dante, which remained faithful to the historical approach.[4] Yet its influence on Italian academic life has clearly been considerable; as late as the centenary celebrations of 1965 surveys of the state of Dante studies devoted much of their space to the *struttura/poesia* debate.[5] But while this means that in one way a good deal of work on Dante has indeed been concerned with the *Comedy*'s specifically poetic features, the results of this work have been severely limited by the idealist aesthetics, the conception of poetry as a purely mental phenomenon, on which it rests. Since, for Croce and his followers, the words on the page served merely to stimulate the reader to reproduce in his mind the intuition in the mind of the poet, the requirement that the critic should formulate the character of a text's *poesia* led only to an impressionistic description of the effect created on the reader, not to a study of the means by which the effect is communicated.[6] 'Aesthetic' criticism is synthetic and subjective, not analytical and (to the extent that this is possible in literary study) objective. It can stimulate the reader to find new aesthetic experiences in the *Comedy*, or to formulate more clearly experiences he has already enjoyed. But it does not substantiate or develop its argument by systematic examination of the specific forms of expression to which such experiences are due. One can see how Crocean critics, for all their concern with the aesthetic, may still be accused, like scholarship of the historical kind, of limiting their attention to content.[7]

The main subject of this essay will be those studies that have attempted to explain the *Comedy*'s poetic quality through the exact analysis of its forms of expression, rather than through the approximative description of its content. Such studies are normally termed 'stylistic', though the word stylistics can cover a number of approaches to literature, not all of which are exact and analytical. While 'aesthetic' criticism introduces vertical divisions, as it were, separating whole passages felt to be poetic from other passages that are not, the kind of exact and analytical stylistics I shall consider operates by separating horizontally the various levels of expression in a text (rhythm, lexis, syntax, poetic figures, etc.) and attempting to identify the characteristics of each. It can also be called structural stylistics, in that its object of study is the relationships or structures in a text— relationships within the text, between its components; and extratextual relationships, between these components and others that might have taken their place. This kind of analysis is therefore more rigorous, logical, and objective than most sorts of literary criticism, let alone the Crocean sort. But as we shall see its capacity to use exact methods is circumscribed in some important ways, and there can evidently be no question of its explaining everything about the poetic quality of a text.

There is no single book that attempts a systematic and comprehensive description of the *Comedy*'s style—nothing, that is, remotely comparable to Patrick Boyde's study of Dante's lyric poetry.[8] Malagoli's *Linguaggio e poesia nella Divina Commedia* (1949) formulates in a stimulating way certain aspects of the poem, but is far from systematic. According to Malagoli, Dante's style is characterized by: a preference for substantival constructions, deriving from a fascination with 'things', and frequently taking the form of the attribution of active qualities to an abstract noun; a preference for material and spatial terms over vague and logical ones, and for the precise individuation of objects in their external aspects (*frontalità*); and a preference for alogical and elliptical constructions, especially the irregular arrangement of objects and images in strings of elements unrelated to one another. The weakness of Malagoli's formulations lies in the indeterminate character of his categories, his non-systematic approach, and a consequent tendency to overstate his case. A firmer distinction between the levels of the text and a closer attention to the relationship between Dante's and other writers' usage would have lent a much greater degree of exactness to his argument.

The most fruitful general discussion of Dante's style is in Auerbach's *Mimesis* (1946) and his *Literary Language and its Public in Late Latin Antiquity and the Middle Ages* (1958), neither of which devotes more than a few pages to the *Comedy*. *Mimesis*, a history of the 'representation of reality in Western literature', is mainly a history of the style in which reality is represented, starting from the classical doctrine of the three levels of style, high, middle and low. In this history the *Comedy* occupies a special place. Its themes 'represent a mixture of sublimity and triviality which, measured by the standards of antiquity, is monstrous' (p. 184);[9] it shows a 'contact with real life which is responsible for all the verbal forms whose directness and rigor . . offended classicistic taste' (p. 189). None the less the 'tone remains that of the elevated style', and Dante 'subdues every turn of expression to the gravity of his tone' (p. 199). Dante, Auerbach concludes in the later book, 'created a sublime poetry on a level with the great models of antiquity' (p. 232), but, evidently, a sublime poetry fundamentally different in character from theirs.

It was not in the nature of Auerbach's work to substantiate this interpretation through a systematic analysis of style, although he offers an excellent starting point for the explanation of the *Comedy*'s poetic effect in linguistic and rhetorical terms. In both books he spoke of the complexity of Dante's syntax; he mentions its 'richness of sentence structure', its 'sustained rolling movement' in the second (p. 229), where he also emphasizes (p. 230) that in Dante's elevated style, as in Homer's, 'rhetoric does not govern but serves'. Apparently he was content to stop at these suggestive formulations, uncertain, no doubt, that systematic analysis was either possible or worthwhile. Yet both his idea of the mixture of styles and the place that he assigns to rhetoric in Dante's poem have been challenged quite forcefully.[10] If his interpretation is to be firmly established, this can only happen on the basis of a more extensive stylistic study of the *Comedy* than any we at present possess.

A more recent discussion of Dante's style, with greater faith in the possibilities of exact analysis, is Pagliaro's chapter on the poetic language of the *Comedy* in his *Ulisse* (1966). Pagliaro starts from the structuralist assumption that in poetry, as opposed to other forms of communication, the forms of expression are 'actualized' (in the sense that they attract attention as much as, if not more than, the content) through deviation from the linguistic norm. Unfortunately, as Pagliaro points out, a major obstacle to the stylistic analysis of the *Comedy* is that we know all too little about the linguistic norms of Dante's time, and it is in any case extremely difficult to measure Dante's usage against what we do know, since so much of his language was created by him for himself. Thus Pagliaro's attempt to define 'scientifically' (p. xvi) the specifically poetic features of the *Comedy* is confined to a very limited set of procedures: the use of rare words, or of current words in an unusual sense; the use of ellipsis, metaphor and rhythm. Pagliaro does succeed in showing how, in respect of these four factors, the poetic quality of the *Comedy* can be explained up to a point in exact linguistic and stylistic terms. The main defect of his explanation is that it gives only a fragmentary idea of the distinctive character of Dante's poetic usage, since all the four factors he discusses are fundamental features of a great many poets' style. The essay is an interesting and promising one, but stops at a very early stage of analysis.[11]

Scholarly contributions to the exact analysis of Dante's style are therefore to be found almost entirely in the form of discussions either of individual aspects or of individual passages of the *Comedy*. What I wish to consider, however, is the progress that has been made towards the systematic and comprehensive explanation of the *Comedy*'s forms of expression, insofar as this can ever be achieved. I shall therefore exclude studies of individual passages from this survey, even though many separate points on stylistic matters may be found, for instance, in the various *lecturae Dantis*. I shall instead discuss one after another the various aspects or levels of the *Comedy* which modern stylistic analysis has worked on, beginning with the poem's rhythm. This is best considered under the separate headings of syllable and stress structure on the one hand (which poetry has in common with prose) and verse structure on the other. At this level forms of expression are relatively easy to describe in exact terms, even if there is a continuing debate concerning the scanning of Dante's hendecasyllable; the main difficulty arises, as we shall see, over the relationship between rhythmical structures and the other levels of the text.

The systematic study of syllable and stress structure in the *Comedy* begins with Garlanda's *Il verso di Dante* (1907), according to which the poem is characterized by an extensive use of alliteration and assonance, notably between the first and last tonic syllables of each line; and by a predominantly iambic rhythm, in contrast to which the occasional shift to a trochaic pattern (notably on the first and seventh syllables of the line) acts as a source of special effect. The poetic significance Garlanda attributed to his findings is rather vague (he speaks (pp. 35, 75) of 'musical unity' and 'harmony'); but while subsequent critics interpreted Dante's rhythm according to rather different principles, the factual observations from which they started remained very much the same. The theme of Frascino's *Suono e pensiero nella poesia dantesca* (1928) is, as the title suggests, the perfect unity in the *Comedy* of sound and sense. Similar rhythmical structures correspond to similar elements of content: the assonance of the 'dark' vowels *o* and *u* evokes the darkness of the *Inferno*, for instance; an iambic rhythm conveys a sense of 'peaceful movement', and anapaestic rhythm (where the stress falls on the fourth and seventh syllables, and sometimes also on the first) is associated with the idea of violence (pp. 41, 73–7). The notion that the poetic value of the *Comedy* is closely tied to its representational qualities is developed in a still more extreme and extensive form in M. Amrein-Widmer's *Rhythmus als Ausdruck inneren Erlebens in Dantes Divina Commedia* (1932), the aim of which is to show how, in Dante's poem, 'inner experience forms and governs the language' (p. 138). Assonancing *is* and *es* emphasize a sense of dazzling, streaming light, for instance; stresses on the fourth and seventh syllables of a line express 'easy, rapid, even intense movement (*Bewegtheit*)' (p. 16), whereas an iambic rhythm expresses movement of a peaceful kind.

The difficulty with these and the many similar conclusions in Amrein-Widmer's work is that the association of sound and sense which she purports to demonstrate may very frequently be doubted, even if it is not to be excluded altogether. Moreover, since a unity of sound and sense can be seen in a great many poets' work, this type of analysis says little about the distinctive qualities of Dante's poem.[12] What it does show, however, is the extent to which the qualities critics perceive in the *Comedy* can depend on the aesthetic assumptions with which they approach it. The representational or expressive aesthetic to which

Amrein-Widmer evidently subscribes leads to one kind of analysis of Dante's rhythm; a more formalist aesthetic leads, as we shall shortly see, to another of a very different sort. But while, in the form in which she puts them, Amrein-Widmer's conclusions may nowadays seem rather naïve, the belief that the unity of sound and sense is an essential quality of Dante's poetry has continued to inspire a number of more recent studies. A. Franz argued in 1958 that shifts of stress from even to odd syllables ('antirhythms') serve to provide emphasis or relief, and also to express emotion, the dominant even rhythm creating in itself an impression of peace. During the centenary celebrations of 1965 A. Oxilia developed this point, suggesting that of the three main stress patterns of the Italian hendecasyllable (with accents on syllables 6 and 10; 4, 8, and 10; 4, 7, and 10), the first two had a quiet and solemn character, whereas the third and least common was in itself, on account of its 'ternary' rhythm, 'suited to signify a certain excitement (*concitazione*)', and was used for this purpose by Dante. In the Oxford Dante Society's *Centenary Essays* of the same year, Alfred Ewert attempted to show the 'marvellous concordance' in Dante's poem between the 'nature of his rhythm . . . and the emotional state of the poet and the emotional content of the line' (p. 86). More extreme instances of what might be called, unsympathetically, the 'representational fallacy' are to be found in Glauco Cambon's *Dante's Craft* (1969), where it is maintained, for instance, that the line 'se non che al viso e di sotto mi venta' (*Inf.* xvii. 117) expresses, with its alliteration and the 'rhythmical impedance' of the stress pattern, the 'rush of thick air' on Dante's face (p. 86).

This type of approach was criticized in 1969 by M. Rossi, with the suggestion that alliteration between two words of the same section of a sentence may serve simply to isolate this section from others; and that between parts of different sentences it may serve to mark the identity of an episode, or a part of an episode (pp. 187 ff.). The same point has been made by Fubini, who proposed in 1972 that assonance may often have a delimitative rather than a psychological function. Baldelli, in his article on the *endecasillabo* in the *Enciclopedia dantesca*, observes that, while rhythmical patterns may possess a representational value—Oxilia's third type, for instance, often being

connected with situations of 'particular prominence', an accent
on the first syllable of the line with 'situations of striking intensity' (pp. 674–5)—this value depends very much on the situation
in which it occurs, and is far from being constant. But a more
polemical treatment of the meaning of phonetic patterns has
developed in the wake of a now famous suggestion of Contini's,
thrown out in the course of the 1965 celebrations, that Dante's
poetic memory 'is not purely verbal, [functioning] through
stimuli derived from related objects, but is organized in
rhythmical figures'; and that these figures, consisting for instance in 'identities of grammatical structure or scheme', indicate a 'preponderance of the signifier over the signified' in the
poem (pp. 83, 86–8). This interpretation is evidently as much
concerned with structures of syntax and vocabulary as with
sound patterns; it clearly played an important part, however, in
two of the most interesting recent studies of Dante's rhythm,
P. M. Bertinetto's *Ritmo e modelli ritmici* of 1973, and the essays
published by Beccaria in 1975 under the title *L'autonomia del
significante*.

Both contributions start from the formalist or structuralist
principle, that forms of expression in poetry may possess a
function independent of their content; as Bertinetto puts it, a
text has a 'rhythmical meaning' different from other levels of
meaning (p. 52). Bertinetto's thesis draws on a computer
analysis of the *Comedy*, which led him to the following principal
conclusions: first, that the even syllables of the line tend to be
stressed far more than the odd ones, thus yielding a predominantly iambic rhythm, which the *Comedy* shares with the sample
of contemporary texts in *terza rima* that Bertinetto also put
through his computer; second, that within this iambic framework the variety of rhythmical patterns is very great, though
not notably more so than in the contemporary sample; third,
that much more than the contemporary sample, the *Comedy* is
characterized by the recurrence at more or less constant intervals of similar rhythmical figures or schemes, usually unrelated,
at least directly, to the content. The first conclusion only con-
firms the conclusions of older studies; the third, on the other
hand, seems a most profitable development of the interpretation
of Contini.

One of the essays ('Figure dantesche') of Beccaria's book also deals with the *Comedy*'s accentual rhythm, and also offers a development of Contini's interpretation. Here, as in his article on *ritmo* in the *Enciclopedia dantesca*, Beccaria argues that the association of certain patterns of stress with certain feelings, images or situations is by no means constant, that the same accentual rhythm can be linked to entirely different types of content. This is not to say that a given image etc. may not be reinforced by a particular rhythm, but that rhythm should also be studied as a self-sufficient element in poetry. For instance the immediate succession of two stresses on the ninth and tenth syllables of a line (which, according to Amrein-Widmer (p. 22), served to express unusual tension) tends to occupy a privileged position at the end of the *terzina*, its function being principally to provide a sense of rhythmical closure, often reinforced by alliteration.

The same approach and the same aesthetic govern Beccaria's essay on 'Alliterazioni dantesche', a sustained attempt to demonstrate how syllable structures are best seen not as possessing, individually, an expressive function, but as contributing in a more general way to the poetic effect of the *Comedy*. Beccaria shows that alliteration in Dante is even more pervasive and complex than previous students had supposed. It is frequently reinforced by the positioning of identical sounds in situations of special relief, for instance together at the end of a line or on either side of a caesura, or, further apart, at the beginning of each hemistich or in the first and last words of a line. Such patterns are also frequently reinforced by assonance, or continued or anticipated in the immediate context; and groups of alliterations are often linked through having in common their mode or point of articulation, all being labials, for instance. But the main burden of Beccaria's argument is that the relationship between these alliterations and the associated content is, as in the case of stress patterns, extremely uneven. This means that, apart from occasional instances of onomatopoeia, their function must be to provide emphasis or relief; or that they merely contribute to the general tendency towards unity which Beccaria, on Roman Jakobson's authority, considers characteristic of all poetry. One may disagree with the second of these conclusions; Dante's use of alliteration may be a distinctive feature of his poetry, and it would be interesting to see Beccaria's study extended by a comparative survey of other poets (on a much earlier count Dante occupied only a middle position among Italian poets in this respect).[13] Nevertheless Beccaria's main point that the effect of alliteration is largely independent of content is a powerful alternative to the earlier view. In a line like 'E caddi come corpo morto cade' (*Inf.* v. 142), one could agree with Franz's view that the alliteration evokes the thud of Dante's body on the ground;[14] but, together with the location at the end of the canto, the regular iambic stress, the fact that each stress begins a new word, and the chiastic structure of the vowel sequence, this is more convincingly seen as providing a purely formal satisfaction to the reader.

It must already be evident that my distinction between syllable and stress structure and verse structure is very artificial, since in the treatment of phonetic patterns reference has more than once been made to the form of the hendecasyllable. Be that as it may, I shall now consider separately those studies that concern Dante's characteristic use of his chosen metrical form, as opposed to the procedures, considered so far, that are at least in part independent of metre. The first important study of this kind is Lisio's *L'arte del periodo nelle opere volgari di Dante Alighieri e del secolo XIII* (1902) which, as its title suggests, is mainly concerned with questions of sentence structure; a good deal of it, however, is devoted to a study of the relationship between sentence structure and metre which still remains largely valid today.[15] Of the 3,422 periods or sentences in the *Comedy*, according to Lisio's count, two-thirds are coterminous with a single *terzina*, 774 (about 22 per cent) cover two *terzine* exactly, and 174 (about 5 per cent) three. Very few, therefore, end in the middle of the *terzina*. Moreover, in the *Comedy*, as in the Italian poetry of Dante's time, there is a very strong tendency towards the use of end-stop lines; *enjambement* (a term not used by Lisio) occurs only in about one-seventh of the lines of the poem, and only on 208 occasions between one *terzina* and the next. Lisio's count thus demonstrates the high degree of regularity and balance in Dante's use of the *terzina*, which must contribute significantly to the overall poetic effect of the work. The relative rarity of *enjambement*, especially between *terzine*, also indicates a possible source, when it does occur, of emphasis, contrast, or surprise.

These conclusions of Lisio's are difficult to contest (though Baldelli, in his article on the *terzina* in the *Enciclopedia dantesca,* suggests he may have exaggerated the conformity of syntax and metre in the *Comedy*); since the war, however, they have been developed in two ways characteristic of different trends in recent criticism. The first is in Fubini's *Metrica e poesia* of 1962. Although he took as his subject the technical issue of metrics, Fubini was in most respects a Crocean critic, and his adherence to the 'aesthetic' approach is evident in the strikingly non-technical character of some of his discussion of Dante's verse structure. This discussion involves a degree of separation of form and content of which Croce would presumably not have approved, but it remains within the Crocean ambit in so far as its object is more to characterize synthetically the impression created by Dante's use of the *terzina,* than to describe this aspect of the poem systematically in exact analytical terms.[16] Dante's chosen rhyme scheme, according to Fubini, is characterized by two tendencies: 'on the one hand to enclose the image firmly between the first and third lines [of the *terzina*] which rhyme with one another, and on the other hand to prolong itself' (p. 207). The first is reinforced by the use of rare words in rhyme position at the end of the *terzina,* creating a strong terminal effect; and by the fact that the 'most intense lines are always the last ones' (p. 217). The second tendency (originating from the fact that the middle rhyme of each *terzina* is the first and the third of the next one) is also reinforced by Dante's extensive use of connectives, which lend the *Comedy* a scholastic style—'scholastic reasoning and the rhythm of the *terzina* are one and the same thing' (p. 201). Thus we have the 'characteristic case of the *terzina* that develops by itself, like a cell multiplying', the 'typical [though hardly so on Lisio's count] period that unfolds across three, four or five *terzine*' (p. 207). Dante, Fubini suggests (p. 201), 'sees the world in *terzine*'.

While there is a great deal that is interesting in Fubini's essay, one might wish that he had expressed himself in a more careful fashion; in the form in which they are put some of his generalizations cannot be allowed to stand. The second development of Lisio's work, on the other hand, exemplifies perfectly the passion for exactness that characterizes much modern literary analysis. In an article of 1976 P. G. Beltrami proposes, in place of Lisio's simple distinction between lines where the final metrical pause coincides with a break in the period and lines in which it does not, a tenfold categorization of types of syntactic connection, the purpose of which is to permit a more precisely graduated definition of the different degrees of unity between one line of the *Comedy* and the next. Much of Beltrami's analysis simply restates in a more exact form Lisio's conclusions about the over-all correspondence between periods and *terzine*—as for instance his point that while almost 30 per cent of the *terzine* have first lines linked syntactically with the last line of the *terzina* before, about half of these links consist in a relationship of coordination or subordination between two clauses, and only 8 per cent (of the 30 per cent) belong to his first six categories, which contain the closest types of syntactic connection. The value one attaches to this kind of formulation evidently depends on the value one attaches to the virtue of exactness; on the other hand a more novel point of Beltrami's raises different sorts of questions. Between the second and the third lines of the *terzina* some 46 per cent of the syntactic connections are those of subordination or co-ordination between different clauses, while between the first and the second lines this type is greatly outweighed by connections between elements of the same clause. The third line tends to begin a new clause, the second to continue a clause begun in the first. One cannot deny that this marked preference on Dante's part for a certain kind of *terzina* structure must contribute in some way, not insignificantly, to the over-all effect of the poem (Beltrami says that it puts the 'centre of gravity' of the *terzina* towards the end). But it is not clear to what extent it reflects a natural tendency of the Italian language, now or in Dante's time; and even if it could be shown to be peculiar to the *Comedy*, there would still be the problem of determining its poetic function in the text.[17]

While Lisio and others have viewed Dante's use of *enjambement* mainly as a source of emphasis or relief, Amrein-Widmer interpreted it, characteristically, in representational terms, as serving to express the 'greatest inner intensity' (p. 71). In this respect she is followed by Tibor Wlassics, who has suggested, in one of a series of studies on Dante's prosody published together in 1972, that *enjambement* in the *Comedy* may express hesitation or irony, as well as merely adding emphasis (pp. 115–33). This slightly modified representational approach also governs Wlassics's treatment of rhyme in the same book (pp. 25–49). For him oxytonic rhymes (*rime tronche*) convey a sense of abrupt speed, proparoxytonic rhymes (*rime sdrucciole*) a sense of surprise (on the other hand, according to E. Pistelli Rinaldi (p. 70) the first 'reproduce sudden action', the second a sensation of swiftness). Two rhymes similar in sound following one upon the other (e.g. -*ale* and -*alle*) suggest, Wlassics maintains, a feeling of confusion or something of the sort—a feeling which must therefore be common in the *Comedy*, if Cipolla's claim is correct that such sequences of similar sounding rhymes are a distinctive feature of Dante's poetry. In another of this series of studies Wlassics emphasizes, as one might expect, the presence of onomatopoeia in the *Comedy*, centring on the rhyme words. But although he qualifies his position by arguing that onomatopoeia can be 'emotive' rather than materially representational ('direct') (p. 59), this essay, like most of his interpretation of Dante's prosody, merely shows how relatively easy it is for a critic to project onto a sound pattern whatever meaning he wishes to see in it.

The articles of Baldelli and Beccaria in the *Enciclopedia dantesca*, respectively on *rima* and *ritmo*, both show a different approach to Dante's rhymes. Parodi had pointed out in 1896 that the rhyming position is frequently occupied by rare words, and 'when the rhyme is not rare and unexpected, the image is' (p. 213). This observation is developed by Baldelli, who states that, of the 14,253 lines in the *Comedy*, little more than 1,000 depend for their rhyme on grammatical inflexions, and very few on suffixes—obviously the two easiest sources of rhymes for an Italian poet. Dante's apparent preference for difficult rhymes is associated by Baldelli in his article on the *endecasillabo* with a 'search for sudden, discordant effects, sometimes violently energetic' (p. 673); while Beccaria in the article on *ritmo* (where he also emphasizes Dante's taste for 'strong scansions' (p. 989), for variety, alternation, tensions, and contrasts in the rhythm of the *terzina*) speaks of the 'singular, bold and vigorous effects' (p. 987) that Dante achieves with his rhymes, often combining contrasting terms in a rhyming set, and thereby lending considerable relief to the meaning of the lines to which they belong. What is interesting and useful about Baldelli's and Beccaria's approach is that, unlike that of Amrein-Widmer and Wlassics, it concentrates on the distinguishing properties of Dante's verse, on stylistic procedures that are to be attributed to the character of the poet as much as, if not more than, to the subject he is describing.

The other elements of Dante's verse structure dealt with by modern stylistic analysis are the use of hiatus, through diaeresis and *dialefe*, and the caesura. Both of these, evidently, raise awkward problems of scansion. In 1924 Casella proposed that the 'exceptional' cases of diaeresis and *dialefe* in the *Comedy* are always aesthetically motivated, in that they always correspond to a 'need for expressive realism' (p. 35). He assumed, that is, that in Dante's verse diphthongs, and a final vowel together with a following initial vowel, regularly (apart from a few constant exceptions) count as a single syllable; and that all deviations from this rule are deliberate and functional, as in the line 'ïo, che al divino da l'umano . . .' (*Par.* xxxi. 37). Casella's interpretation was attacked by Debenedetti, who argued not only that there is no constant association between emotive stress and the use of diaeresis in words such as *io*, but that the supposed cases of diaeresis on which Casella based his thesis were not such at all, being attributable either to mistaken scanning or to corruption of the text. Frascino, in the study already referred to of 1928, adopted a middle position in the matter, suggesting that diaeresis could serve the purpose of *ingentilmento* (as in Bëatrice) or of giving emphasis, as well as occasionally being generated by 'emotive stress' (pp. 118–38); but often it has no aesthetic effect at all, and merely occurs for the sake of the rhythm. This more balanced position is substantially that of Beccaria in his articles on *dialefe* and *dieresi* in the *Enciclopedia dantesca*. Here the rules, such as they are, of Dante's practice are given, with the qualification that this is not absolutely regular. *Dialefe* can be used to mark a pause in thought, and diaeresis can often add effects such as that of 'majesty and patriarchal solemnity' (p. 433) to words. But more than associating these procedures with specific thoughts and feelings, one should attribute them to Dante's 'rhythmical sensibility' (p. 434), and therefore, presumably, assign them a formal rather than a representational function.

Finally, in his encyclopedia article on *cesura*, Beccaria argues against the analysis of Dante's hendecasyllable in terms of the two-part division involving a pause after a stressed sixth or fourth syllable, and the consequent distinction of *endecasillabi a maiore* and *a minore* respectively. Pauses are important in Dante's poetry (often reinforced by *dialefe*), but as part of his technique of contrasts and tensions; they do not occur always, by any means, in regular positions. However, a more recent discussion of Dante's metre has proposed an alternative interpretation in the light of structuralist poetic theory. According to Costanzo Di Girolamo's *Teoria e prassi della versificazione* (1976) Dante's hendecasyllables can and should be scanned according to the *a maiore* and *a minore* distinction, but this does not mean that to the metrical pause after a stressed fourth or sixth syllable there necessarily corresponds a pause in the syntax or sense. In the *Comedy*, Di Girolamo believes, there is as in all poetry a constant tension between metrical structures and the rhythm of normal speech. Yet interesting though it is to see how Dante's verse *can* be made to fit this standard scheme, it remains to be demonstrated that it is necessarily the appropriate one for reading the *Comedy*. And even if it were shown to be so, Di Girolamo's book tells us scarcely anything (but it did not set out to do so) about the distinctive features of Dante's use of metre.

Questions relating to poetic syntax are evidently closely connected with those relating to verse structure; indeed the first systematic study of the syntax of the *Comedy* is Lisio's *L'arte del periodo*, according to which Dante's style is characterized by juxtaposition and fragmentation (*accostamento* and *spezzamento*), a preference for independent constructions 'which could very easily have been made dependent' (p. 185). This is to be seen in the absence of formal transitional elements between periods, in the frequent shifts from subordination to co-ordination within the period, and in the fact that relationships of subordination and co-ordination are rarely protracted over a long stretch of discourse. Lisio's view, impressionistic rather than systematically analytical, was supported by Malagoli, who spoke in a general way of the 'distinct, juxtaposed rhythm of Dante's style'—a 'representational and not logical style', characterized by a 'string of detached images without any relationship to one another'. As an interpretation of Dante's syntax this view evidently conflicts, at least in part, with Fubini's emphasis on

the formal connecting elements in Dante's *terzina*. It was
directly criticized in 1967 by Aldo Scaglione, who pointed out
in an article on 'Periodic Syntax and Flexible Metre in the
Divine Comedy', that while 'Dante's subordinate clauses may
often sound parenthetic', they are in fact 'perfectly integrated
syntactically into the period'. What the 'pauses, silences,
inserts and inversions' to which Lisio drew attention do is to
give a 'heightened sense' of the articulation of the period, not
break it up into fragments. In his *Mimesis* Auerbach had also
spoken of the 'abundance of syntactic connectives' in the
Comedy, of 'periodic articulations and devices of sentence structure which command gigantic masses of thought and concaten-
ations of events'. There are in Dante's poem 'the most varied
temporal, comparative, and graduated hypothetical connections, supported by the greatest possible elasticity of verbal
inflections and verbal order'; though Auerbach also points to
the 'rapid succession of independent episodes or mutually
unrelated scenes' (pp. 178, 182, 199).

The recent emphasis on the organization and unity of
Dante's syntax has received considerable support from the most
extensive example of exact analysis of the *Comedy*'s style, C.
Schwarze's *Untersuchungen zum syntaktischen Stil der italienischen
Dichtungssprache bei Dante* (1970). The aspects of Dante's syntax
with which this deals are the transition to direct speech, co-
ordination, ambiguity, and comparisons; the second of these
evidently relates to the matter of period structure. Schwarze
agrees with Scaglione that syntactic subordination (hypotaxis)
is more prominent in the *Comedy* than Lisio and Malagoli
thought, but points out that co-ordination (parataxis) is an
equally important part of a complex periodic style. Lisio and
Malagoli seem to have assumed that paratactic constructions
were signs of a simple and direct attitude to things, hypotactic
constructions of the opposite. Schwarze's treatment of co-
ordination on the other hand shows its enormous variety and
range in Dante's usage, and its capacity to organize content
into complex and integrated sequences. The syntactic unity of
the sentence in Dante's poem can therefore no longer be
doubted, although Schwarze's investigation certainly does not
exhaust the question of the *Comedy*'s sentence structure. But
Lisio's notions of *accostamento* and *spezzamento* may still retain

their validity at the level of connections between sentences, as Auerbach's description ('mutually unrelated scenes' etc.) would seem to suggest. Here we leave the realm of syntax, and enter the inchoate subject of discourse analysis, where new methods of investigation may well be capable of producing a more exact and systematic account of an important aspect of the *Comedy*'s construction.

An important part of a complex periodic style is the use of syntactic inversion. According to Lisio, this constituted a form of 'violence which the words do to the mind' (p. 164), and occurs when the feelings and imagination of the poet are aroused. Parodi observed in a review of Lisio's book that inversion is in fact so common in the poetic (as opposed to the everyday) language of Dante's time, that to attribute a constant expressive function to it would almost certainly be mistaken. This observation seems to have been ignored by Wlassics who, true to his principles, has suggested in another book of 1975 that inversion, in the form of hyperbaton, may do no more than add emphasis to the terms involved, but can also express an emotive state—such as, for instance, a feeling of effort in the line 'd'un altro vero andare a la radice' (*Par.* xiv. 12). Enough has been said already about the weaknesses of this kind of interpretation. It does, however, confront us, for the first time so far, with a serious conflict between a historical and a 'modern' approach to Dante's text. If we adopt what seems to be Dante's own view, we should see inversion, along with Schwarze, simply as one of the many constituent elements of the elevated style, not as having a specific expressive function. This does not mean that it serves merely as a sort of marker, however. In an interesting study of Dante's relationship to the medieval rhetorical tradition, published in 1967, G. Nencioni has suggested that Dante's practice of inverting the natural order of clauses in a sentence accords with the teaching of medieval as well as classical rhetoricians; but that in Dante's style, unlike that of his immediate predecessors, this becomes an 'organ' which allows him to 'graduate and organize in a subtle hierarchy the moments of the process of demonstration or exposition', lending itself to 'highly articulated developments', creating 'flexible links with the immediately preceding or following text' and 'complex perspectives and rhythmic and tonal orchestrations'.

The same functions of distributing emphasis, organizing perspectives, and contributing to the rhythm as well as the tone of the text might well be attributed also to the inversion of individual words and phrases in the *Comedy*.

Schwarze's treatment of inversion in Dante's style occurs under the heading of ambiguity, where he sets out to show in what ways the difficulties readers may find in interpreting the poem are due to the inversion or breaking up of normal syntactic structures. This can lead either to obscurity (*Strukturverschleierung*), when the extra information provided by normal word order is absent, but the meaning of the sentence or clause is still ultimately accessible; or to complete ambiguity, when the possibility of more than one meaning cannot be excluded. According to Wlassics's second book, instances of the latter effect may be shown to have an expressive function, in that the ambiguity serves to 'give the word its greatest possible range' (p. 11). Thus when it is said that the Harpies 'fanno lamenti in su li alberi strani' (*Inf.* xiii. 15), *strani* can and should be read as qualifying both *lamenti* and *alberi*, and when read in this way adds to the poem's richness of meaning. Wlassics is no doubt within his rights in applying Empsonian criteria to the interpretation of the *Comedy*,[18] but to any reader with a modicum of historical sensibility Schwarze's attitude to the phenomenon is likely to seem more satisfactory: since for Dante difficulty of interpretation seems to have constituted in itself a source of aesthetic attraction, such double meanings as occur are best regarded as obstacles to be overcome, rather than as sources of poetic effect in their own right. It is characteristic of the *Comedy*, as of much poetry in the high style, to require a high degree of effort from its readers; unlike some modernist poetics, however, Dante's assumes that difficulties are there to be resolved, not to be left standing.

Inspired by Contini's interpretation, a number of recent studies have stressed Dante's habit of repeating identical syntectic structures more or less independently of similarities of content—repetitions, as Contini said, 'less of words, semantic connections and images, than of relationships, positions, contacts (*rapporti, giaciture, contatti*) (p. 80). In his encyclopedia article on *ritmo* Beccaria lists a number of reiterated figures that are 'rhythmical and syntactic at the same time' (p. 987); an example, given in *L'autonomia del significante*, is the arrangement of the elements of comparisons 'according to equivalent rhythmical and syntactic matrices' (p. 123). Baldelli also draws attention to such figures in his article on the *terzina*, citing the symmetrical arrangement of the two parts of a simile on each of two contiguous *terzine*, or the distribution of anaphorical constructions across successive *terzine* (pp. 590–1). In an article of 1975 Beltrami has carried this approach further, with the help of the I.B.M. computerized concordance of the *Comedy*.[19] Other 'rhythmical syntagms' that he lists are such sequences as *aere* followed by an adjective, *alta* followed by a two-syllable noun followed by a two-syllable adjective, etc.; the reappearance of the same word in the same position in a number of different lines; the repetition of entire hemistichs in 'substantially free contexts'. Under the same inspiration, G. L. Pierotti has pointed out even more recently that in almost one quarter of the *terzine* of the *Comedy* the third line begins with *che* (as a conjunction or a relative pronoun) or with another relative pronoun, and a great many have the same particles at some other point in the second or third line. Whatever one may think of the significance of these various phenomena—and it is clear that more comparative study needs to be done on their presence in the work of other poets—the prominence of reiterative procedures in the *Comedy*'s syntax is now firmly established.

A number of other aspects of the *Comedy*'s syntax remain to be explored more fully. C. Goffis has pointed, briefly, to the omission of articles as a factor in the elevated style of the *Paradiso*, and emphasized in a general way the extent to which Dante's syntax is modelled on Latin. Malagoli, Nencioni, and Pagliaro have all drawn attention to the element of condensation or concentrated expression in Dante's poetry—the omission, as Pagliaro puts it (p. 619), of the 'connective elements indispensable in normal communication'. This is not the same as the frequent abrupt transition between periods to which reference was made earlier; the example Pagliaro gives is the line 'di sé lasciando orribili dispregi' (*Inf.* viii. 51). But although he shows what the process of condensation has left out in this instance, he offers little more than an impression of the character of this sort of procedure and its importance in Dante's style. On the whole the study of the *Comedy*'s syntax is still a relatively undeveloped field, no doubt in large part on account of the difficulty of relating Dante's usage to that of his contemporaries and immediate predecessors.[20]

Studies of the *Comedy*'s lexis have not progressed far beyond the two articles of Zingarelli and Parodi of 1885 and 1896 respectively, nor perhaps could they. Zingarelli's survey of 'Parole e forme della *Divina Commedia* aliene dal dialetto fiorentino' lists the latinisms, gallicisms, and non-Florentine dialectalisms of the *Comedy*, concluding that Florentine predominates immeasurably over all other linguistic forms, and that French and Provençal words (but only such as had already entered into the written language of Italy) are present in greater number than words from other Italian dialects. Parodi's attention is confined to the rhyme words of Dante's poem, but he extends Zingarelli's discussion by observing that very few rhyme words in the *Comedy* are derived from the non-Tuscan dialects of Italy, and of these only one is not to be found in the existing literary language. Dante belonged to a period of 'dialectal hybridism', but he 'abused of it less than any other, and more than any other contributed to bringing it to an end' (pp. 218–21). Parodi contrasted Dante's theoretical view of vernacular literature, as permitting considerable linguistic licence, with his relatively restricted practice—a point supported much later (1953) by Schiaffini, who argued that while Dante's theory of the comic style (though not, of course, of the tragic style) allowed for an 'autentico poliglottismo', in practice dialectal forms of non-Florentine origin are only used either as a means of linguistic characterization, or because they had already become consecrated through use in the literary language. The position is summed up by Migliorini in his *Storia della lingua italiana*: compared to the 'natural' Florentine usage of his time, the language of the *Comedy* is much richer in doublets; but all the forms used, apart from the florentinisms, have had 'some degree of literary consecration' (p. 181).

The conclusions reported so far may have more linguistic than literary interest, but they form the necessary framework for the assessment of the stylistic effects of Dante's vocabulary. This concerns principally the question of register and that of the degree of deviation, in the *Comedy*, from 'normal' usage, the two evidently being closely connected. For the first, the many studies of the relationship between Dante's stylistic theory and his practice have shown that the numerous more or less colloquial florentinisms in the *Comedy* give it a poetic quality quite different from the high style described in the *De Vulgari Eloquentia*—the quality of contact with real, everyday life to which Auerbach attached so much weight. The range of Dante's style in this respect has also been frequently stressed; much of the *Comedy* is written in the elevated literary language, and much of it in the technical language of scholastic philosophy. But the notion of Dante's *plurilinguismo* put into circulation by Contini has to be qualified, obviously, by Zingarelli's and Parodi's arguments concerning the non-hybrid character of his language.[21] While, as Contini says, Dante is an unceasingly experimental writer, it is important to recognize that his experimentation knows definite limits.

Deviations from 'normal' usage are dealt with specifically by Gmelin and Pagliaro, in their studies of, respectively, latinisms and rare words in the *Comedy* (in the *Paradiso* alone, in Gmelin's case). Dante's latinisms, Gmelin shows, are drawn from patristic and scholastic sources as well as from the classical language. Scholastic terms are used for the representation of metaphysical concepts, while the many 'poetic' latinisms in the *Comedy* serve to increase the solemnity of the language, sometimes to give objects and events a mythical or transcendental character (Migliorini, in his *Storia della lingua italiana* (p. 181), also observes that archaic florentinisms in the *Comedy* may perform the same elevating function). According to Pagliaro's essay (pp. 587–8), the use of rare words is a feature of all poetry, serving to renovate the individual's contact with reality. Rare words in Dante take the form of latinisms and also of neologisms, although the last, as Parodi had pointed out (p. 220), are not all that frequent. Dante's latinisms are, however, often semantic (consisting in the use of an Italian word in its etymological sense) rather than lexical; and in general, more than by the use of rare words as such, his style is characterized by that of more or less common words in an unusual sense (pp. 602 ff.). This second point was dealt with more extensively by Blasucci, in an article of 1957 on the relationship between Dante's *rime petrose* and the *Comedy*. What the two works have in common is a language 'charged with energy'; some of Blasucci's examples are metaphors, but many involve the substitution for a common word of a near synonym used literally but with a more forceful meaning, for instance *torcere* for *volgere* or *girare*. Some of Dante's neo-formations are interpreted in the same light: *disgravare*, for instance, is said to be distinguished by its *valore plastico* from the possible alternatives to it in the standard language. This feature of Dante's style, according to Blasucci, is a consequence not of the demands of the situations described, but of the characteristic disposition of the poet, always inclined to 'extreme solutions' (p. 429).

Studies of this kind are clearly seriously limited, like those of Dante's syntax, by our knowledge of the contemporary language, and by the absence of any remotely comparable literary texts in the period. As Pagliaro observed, in Dante's case it is extremely difficult to distinguish between *langue* and *parole*. One fairly recent study, however, adopts a different approach to the matter of lexis from those considered so far, and is not subject to the same sort of limitations. In an essay on the use of epithets in the *Comedy*, Y. Alaerts makes an interesting distinction between those that are determinative or indispensable, and those that are explicative or ornamental; the second could be removed without substantially altering the sense of the text, the first could not. Taking a more or less random sample of *canti* from all three canticles, she observes first, that the number of epithets increases from the *Inferno* to the *Paradiso*, but the increase is in those of the indispensable kind; second, that passages with a strong emotional content (such as the Ugolino episode) can have a lower than average number of ornamental epithets; third, that compared with both Ariosto and Tasso, Dante employs fewer ornamental epithets, and indeed fewer epithets altogether. These observations indicate in a clear fashion the relative absence of ornamentation in the *Comedy*, and tend to confirm Malagoli's suggestion about Dante's preference for nominal constructions and active forms of expression.

The work considered so far has been concerned with those levels of the *Comedy* that fall within the province of traditional linguistics, and can therefore quite easily be described in exact analytical terms. The conclusions to be drawn from the facts

have been a matter for considerable debate, but the facts themselves have been capable of objective definition, at least in
principle, by means of the categories that linguistics supplies. I
now turn to an aspect of the poem which is normally considered
a part of style, but which is not capable of such definition
because the appropriate categories are in large part lacking:
Dante's imagery, in the sense of his use of simile and metaphor.
This evidently generates complex effects of meaning extremely
difficult to analyse and explain.

Venturi's classification of Dante's similes, now over a hundred
years old, simply divides them up according to the nature of the
second term of the comparison, although it is interesting to the
extent that it shows most of the similes to be drawn from the
world of sense experience. Olivero's *La rappresentazione dell'-
immagine in Dante* (1936) lists some of the different types of
metaphor and simile in the *Comedy* (extended metaphors, expanded similes, personification, etc.), but with reference to a
simplistic view of the function of imagery, as serving merely to
give the reader a clearer and more immediate impression of the
subject. With vastly greater sophistication the same function had
earlier been proposed as a distinguishing feature of the poet's
use of simile in T. S. Eliot's *Dante* (1929). Dante's style is
characterized by 'lucidity' and 'simplicity'; the purpose of his
similes is 'solely to make us see more definitely the scene which
Dante has put before us' (pp. 10–15)—a view which has been
repeated on a number of occasions since, notably by Malagoli
who, on the subject of metaphors (which Eliot however believed
an unimportant feature of the *Comedy*'s style) spoke of the
sensibilismo of Dante's usage, his preference for concrete representation and an exact correspondence between the first and
second terms (pp. 99 ff.).

No doubt much of Dante's use of imagery corresponds to this
description, but another strand of criticism has insisted over the
years, especially in America, on the complexity, rather than the
clarity and simplicity, of his metaphors and similes. This begins
with a somewhat cursory article of 1932 by H. D. Austin on
'Multiple Meanings and Their Bearing on the Understanding
of Dante's Metaphors'. A few years later T. A. Fitzgerald, in
contesting Eliot's view, pointed out that many similes contain
extra details that add nothing to the clarity of the image, and

suggested that these should be taken as evidence that Dante 'was at least as interested in the form of his similes as in their function'. Subsequent criticism has tended, however, to follow Austin in seeing the details of similes as functional, and attempting to identify double or multiple relationships between the two terms of the comparison. Spitzer's analysis (of 1943) of the image of the baptismal fount in Florence cathedral (*Inf.* xix 16–21) was no doubt influential in this respect; according to him the autobiographical statement which Dante attaches to this image should not be viewed as a piece of extraneous information, but as contributing an element of contrast to the scene described—an idea developed in 1964 by J. Applewhite in relation to other 'sustained similes' in the poem. More recently still, however, Pagliaro has insisted on the multiplicity of positive relationships between the two terms of comparison in Dante's similes, on the 'analogies and links that go beyond the specific motive of the reference' (p. 668). In the light of the idea that literary language renovates the reader's contact with reality, he also points to the frequent 'transposition of signs from one sensory sphere to another' through metaphor, an aspect of Dante's imagery discussed at greater length by Glauco Cambon in an article of 1970 on 'Synaesthesia in the *Divine Comedy*'.

The two most substantial book-length studies of Dante's imagery, Y. Batard's *Dante, Minerve et Apollon* (1952) and Irma Brandeis's *The Ladder of Vision* (1960), both offer extensive elucidation of the effects of meaning that individual similes and metaphors create, but neither is particularly concerned with generalizing about the characteristic nature and structure of Dante's use of these devices. Batard is more concerned with tracing their genesis in the author's mind, Brandeis with relating them to the main themes of his work. One can see how Aldo Scaglione could complain in 1967, in an article on 'Imagery and Thematic Patterns in *Paradiso* xxiii', that comparatively little attention had been paid to the question of Dante's imagery. Scaglione himself did not offer a systematic study, but only a suggestive analysis of the famous simile of the moon beginning with the much-quoted 'Quale ne' plenilunïï sereni . . .' (*Par.* xxiii. 25). His argument is that the striking feature of this image is the extent to which the two terms of the comparison do *not* correspond, the second functioning in relation not only to the first, but also to other elements in the narrative context. This idea is taken up in a very recent book on Dante's similes, R. H. Lansing's *From Image to Idea* (1977). In an extensive, but not comprehensive, study of the subject (he lists 83 similes in the index of the book), Lansing attempts to show that the 'power of many similes derives from the network of relationships they establish with their surrounding narrative context' (p. 46), as well as from the more obvious ground of comparison between the two terms. Thus some similes anticipate the subsequent narrative, preparing the reader for what is to come, and others refer back to a preceding episode, 'usually in such a way as to gather together a number of loose thematic threads' (p. 74). Certain classical and biblical allusions enlarge the learned reader's understanding of the narrative by means of the events and situations which they tacitly evoke, while analogies between sets of images impose an element of unity on the poem. Lansing's study offers a good deal of suggestive evidence concerning the peculiar blend of clarity and complexity that seems to characterize Dante's similes. Its weakness lies in its selective character, and in a tendency to overstate its case; not all the relationships Lansing identifies seem as significant as he would have us believe.

With their increasing emphasis on the intrinsic properties of Dante's imagery, these studies show the same progress away from a simple representational aesthetic as was noted in the analysis of the rhythm of the *Comedy*. Such an emphasis is especially evident in three relatively recent essays on Dante's metaphors, the first being Maggini's article on 'Associazioni etimologiche nelle immagini di Dante' (1944–5). Maggini's idea (repeated in an article of 1951 by Batard) is that a number of metaphors in the *Comedy* are derived from the etymological sense of common expressions, for instance 'la punta del disio' (*Par.* xxii. 26) from that of 'un desiderio acuto'. This idea may be intended as an explanation of the genesis rather than the structure of the *Comedy*'s style, but it none the less reveals what may be a distinctive feature of Dante's use of figurative language, even if it is hard to say exactly how such a feature might contribute to the text's poetic effect. The other two essays, on the other hand, are concerned with an aspect of Dante's style much

more evident to the reader. In an article already mentioned on
the subject of lexis, Blasucci argued against Malagoli's use of the
term *sensibilismo* to describe the nature of Dante's metaphors.
Certain 'lively physical metaphors' in the *Comedy* do not serve,
as Malagoli supposed, simply to convey the sensory character of
the subject, but reflect instead a 'habit of violent expressive
creativity' (p. 429). Blasucci's thesis was developed at greater
length by Porcelli in 1968 with regard to the metaphors of the
Paradiso. Porcelli distinguishes between two types of metaphorical expression, according to whether the vehicle corresponds,
or does not correspond, to the demands of 'realistic imitation'.
The second type is particularly prominent in the *Paradiso*, he
argues, and consists in the use of terms characterized by a high
degree of 'energy' and 'concreteness' in contexts far removed
from their 'normal area of employment'—for instance the
images of biting attached to the idea of the love of God (*Par.*
xxvi. 51).

It is not easy to predict the ways in which the exact analysis
of Dante's imagery could profitably be carried further, apart
from restating the obvious need for more systematic work on
his text in this respect. Most of the studies I have considered
are vitiated by the lack of a well developed theory of simile or
metaphor, and this in turn must be due at least in part to the
relative weakness of comparative literary studies. It should be
possible to state in more precise terms what it is that distinguishes Dante's imagery from that of other poets, but apart from
occasional and interesting comparisons with authors such as
Virgil, modern criticism of the *Comedy* has made little attempt
to do this. Tateo's article on *metafora* in the *Enciclopedia dantesca*
proposes a very general classification of the species of metaphor
in the poem (suggesting that Dante's usage is often characterized by an 'exchange between the spiritual and sensible worlds'
(p. 638)), a survey of the different sorts of vehicle employed,
and some comments about their efficacy; but it leaves us,
typically, with only a vague impression of the peculiar nature of
the *Comedy*'s poetic procedures.

As well as metaphor, almost all other poetic or rhetorical
figures employed by Dante (except for simile which was
assigned to Pagliaro) are discussed by Tateo in a series of
articles in the *Enciclopedia dantesca*, the most notable being those

on *anafora, antitesi, chiasmo, metonimia, parallelismo, paronomasia, perifrasi, replicazione, sinecdoche, tautologia, transumptio, variatio.* While these may be open to the same criticism as the article on metaphor, they are by far the most extensive source of factual information about Dante's use of these devices, the enormous importance of which in the *Comedy* they establish, in quantitative terms, beyond all doubt. On the whole, because of the categories made available by the rhetorical tradition, the description of such figures causes little difficulty; disagreement does arise, however, as in the case of rhythmical structures, over the poetic function to be attributed to them. Tateo proposed rather non-committally that they serve the purposes, variously, of elevation (anaphora, paronomasia, periphrasis, synecdoche, *transumptio*), of emphasis (antithesis, chiasmus, parallelism, paronomasia), of variety or decoration (antithesis, chiasmus, periphrasis), or of adding expressive or realistic force to the style (metonymy, paronomasia, synecdoche). Other discussions of the subject have been more controversial.

For Lisio the many figures of repetition—one of the most characteristic features, as Tateo observed, of Dante's style—were mainly instances of negligence on the poet's part (p. 146). Curtius argued in 1947 that two such figures, anaphora and paronomasia, should be taken instead as evidence, along with his use of periphrasis, of Dante's close adherence to the classical and medieval rhetorical tradition; but as A. Vezin pointed out, he gave no attention to the question of their poetic effect in the text. Vezin proposed that periphrasis, in the *Comedy*, always serves to interpret and shape the meaning of the poem, a point made in a slightly different way by Pagliaro, according to whom the meaning, through periphrasis, 'is made perceptible by means of a reference to the concrete'. In the same spirit Wlassics has argued that Dante's repetitions and paronomasia have an expressive or representational function, extending to the whole of the poem Spitzer's famous interpretation of the word-play of the suicides in *Inferno* xiii.[22]

On occasions, no doubt, Dante's poetic figures may well be seen as having the sort of direct and individual relationship to his meaning that Vezin, Pagliaro, and Wlassics propose, and Tateo is also in some cases prepared to accept; that they should constantly have such a function seems, however, very questionable. In the light of Contini's interpretation, the many figures of repetition could plausibly be explained in the way in which Beccaria explains alliteration in the *Comedy*: as contributing to an independent rhythmical quality of the poem, rather than creating a series of particular effects. An equally promising approach to these and other figures is opened up by Auerbach's work, and by a recent article of Bigi's on the character and function of rhetoric in the *Comedy*. Taking issue with Auerbach's idea that the *Comedy* possesses a sublime style in which rhetoric 'does not govern but serves', Bigi argues that it is as much to the extensive use of rhetorical figures as to the type of syntax that this character of sublimity is due. The implication of his argument is, therefore, that Dante's figures contribute in a general way to the tone of the poem, rather than individually to the expression of its content. In the last analysis, no doubt, one's choice between these approaches must depend, as with the study of rhythm, on the aesthetic to which one subscribes. But it is clear that a more extensive comparative study of the use of rhetorical figures in the European literary epic would contribute significantly, in one way or another, to our understanding of the poetic effect of Dante's style.

So far I have considered the contributions that have been made to our understanding of forms of expression, rather than of content, in the *Comedy*—what is normally understood as the subject-matter of the study of style. However the same methods of analysis, consisting in the exact and systematic description of relationships within the text and extratextual relationships, is evidently extendable, at least in principle, to forms of content as well. These can well claim with some right to fall within the province of stylistics, and the structural study of them, in so far as it is possible, must contribute in a major way to our under-standing of literary effect. Such study is, however, a relatively uncultivated field of literary investigation, and, for obvious reasons, far more difficult than that of the level of expression. Not surprisingly, therefore, Dante scholarship has not in this respect advanced very far. The areas in which some little pro-gress has been made are those of narrative structure, narrative point of view, the thematic structure of the canto, and plot structure.

Concerning the first, L. Ricci Battaglia argued in an article of 1976 that the *Comedy* is characterized by a fusion of paratactic and hypotactic narrative structures, but failed to show with any degree of precision the consequences of this very abstract hypothesis for the understanding of individual narrative sequences. More promising work has been done on the second area. An early exponent of *Stilforschung*, Ulrich Leo devoted an article of 1929 to the subject of 'seeing and looking' in the *Comedy*, arguing that the poem is distinguished by its strongly visual character. In this respect he was followed by Malagoli (pp. 7–97), who emphasized what he called Dante's *visività, frontalità, pittoricità, spazialità*, and the *ispirazione dell' esteriorità* operating in his work; Dante tends to 'grasp states of mind through the perception of external objects'. Marzot, in *Il linguaggio biblico nella Divina Commedia* (1956), suggests that Dante shares with the authors of the Bible an inclination to 'detach himself from the feeling, to move towards the object, and fix it according to his first impression' (p. 17)—a suggestion carried a stage further by Wlassics, according to whom events in the *Comedy* are represented as they would be seen by a spectator, and according to the normal order of human perception.[23] All of these formulations clearly point to an important aspect of the *Comedy*'s poetry, but in a more or less imprecise and impressionistic manner. Here, once again, systematic comparative study could lead to a better understanding of the text.

Concerning the thematic structure of the canto, Rocco Montano suggested briefly in his *Storia della poesia di Dante* (1962–3) how the geographical or temporal openings to certain canti 'mark as it were the verbal and spiritual theme from which the whole *canto* develops', (vol. i, pp. 482–4), and that each canto possesses a unity comparable to that of a *canzone*. This aspect of the canto's structure is one that could well be explored further, in the first instance, perhaps, through a synthesis of the conclusions offered concerning it in the many *lecturae* of individual canti offered by traditional Dante critics. In the investigation of plot structure, on the other hand, more radically novel methods have been adopted in the last few years, though with rather questionable results. In his *Modelli semiologici nella Commedia di Dante* (1975) D'Arco Silvio Avalle argues that some plot structures in the *Inferno* may be represented in terms of a series of 'functions' derived from the pioneering work of the Russian formalist Propp, with some additions of his own. Avalle's 'functions' include such categories as the 'disruption of the equilibrium of the family', the 'intervention of the helper', the 'breach of the matrimonial taboo', the 'tragic chase'. But while these allow the identification of analogies between plots in the *Comedy* and those of earlier literary texts, they can scarcely be accepted, as Avalle suggests they should be, as parts of the literary 'system'; the analysis stops at far too superficial and arbitrary a level for that. The interest of Avalle's proposals (which to do him justice he advances very tentatively) is thus mainly historical, in that it indicates possible (indirect) sources of the *Comedy*. But it tells us scarcely anything about the intrinsic literary properties of the poem. The same criticism applies to F. Gabrielli's contribution to the second of the three volumes published in 1972 under the title of *Psicanalisi e strutturalismo di fronte a Dante*, which proposes another 'function' in the plot structure of the *Comedy*, the *traghetto* (pp. 65–89). From a theoretical point of view a more satisfactory essay is that of C. Paolazzi in the same volume (pp. 161–81), which attempts to apply to the first canto of the *Purgatorio* the 'actantial' analysis of Greimas.[24] Here the objection is one to which much structuralist literary analysis is open: it tells us nothing at all about the distinctive character of the text, nor, indeed, does it set out to do so.

The reader may be tempted to conclude from this discussion that the exact work on Dante's poem tends to be uninteresting and the interesting work, perhaps, inexact. It may indeed be that what many find most beautiful or moving about the *Comedy* is, by its very nature, unexplainable by any kind of academic study. It is also true, on the other hand, that the sort of analysis surveyed here is not very far advanced, and is clearly capable of further progress. One obstacle does seem at present to be insuperable: stylistics often makes much use of the notion of deviation from the norm, or at least defines the structure of forms of expression by reference either to established literary usage, or to the standard contemporary language. Neither of these points of reference are available to students of the *Comedy* in any but the most fragmentary way. But stylistic analysis has other possibilities. Comparative literary studies of a more broadly based kind could also contribute to the exact description of the *Comedy*'s style, and of its structures of content, by relating aspects of these to a wide range of representative texts from other periods and literatures. This sort of approach could improve our understanding of Dante's imagery and other poetic figures, as I have suggested, and would probably also help that of his syntax; but at the moment it is limited by the undeveloped state of comparative literature and the related subject of poetics.

Moreover the prestige of the historical approach has caused some stylistic studies to be limited by their interest in genetic explanation. Marzot's *Il linguaggio biblico nella Divina Commedia*, for instance, has some interesting and original things to say about Dante's style; but what it says is fragmentary, imprecise, and frequently exaggerated, because its author's principal concern is to show the extent to which Dante owes his inspiration to biblical sources. Much the same could be said of numerous studies of the relationship between the *Comedy* and medieval poetic theory, including Dante's own, though here the emphasis is as much on differences as on similarities. Such more or less genetic studies indicate the need for a more extensive and precise description of the 'intrinsic constituent elements', as Beccaria puts it (p. 90), of Dante's text. Much effort has been spent on the historical interpretation and explanation of a work whose objective qualities are so little understood; some re-direction of academic energies would not come amiss. However minute and inconclusive some of the stylistic studies considered here may be, there can be no doubt that in one way or another they all must contribute to our understanding of the *Comedy*'s poetic effect.

But how exactly do they contribute? It would be wrong to suppose that the exact and systematic analysis of the *Comedy*—or of any literary work—is a purely cumulative process. Even if it were practically possible, the exhaustive application to all levels of the poem's style of an objectively analytical approach, such as that of Schwarze's massive study, would certainly not be sufficient for literary understanding. In its more interesting and illuminating forms, stylistics is not a purely objective or analytical discipline, as linguistics possibly can be. It differs from linguistics not merely through an interest in deviation, but, more importantly, by drawing on theories or models of the literary work of a subjective or philosophical kind, in order to select its objects of study, organize them in an order of priority, and above all define their significance within the text. Objective studies such as Schwarze's remain relatively uninteresting from a literary point of view, unless, by relating them to an idea of the nature of the literary work, we can say what the aesthetic function is of the facts that are described. The more interesting studies of the *Comedy*'s style, on the other hand, have on the whole been strongly influenced by ideas of a subjective or philosophical kind, and have, as a result, been open to all sorts of theoretical objections. But no form of literary study, it hardly needs saying, is a wholly exact and systematic science.

NOTES

1. e.g. Ewert, p. 77; Hatzfeld, 'The Art of Dante's *Purgatorio*', p. 64. Full bibliographical references for these and subsequent items cited in the text will be found in the Appendix at the end of this essay. I must here thank Dr. P. Boyde and Mrs. P. James for their helpful advice about what I have written.
2. Benedetto Croce, *La poesia di Dante* (Bari, 1921).
3. Id., *Estetica come scienza dell'espressione e linguistica generale* (Bari, 1922) (first published in 1902).
4. G. Getto (*Aspetti della poesia di Dante* (Florence, 1947), p. 6), a Crocean critic, accuses the 'critica dantesca ufficiale' of avoiding any authentic evaluation of the *Comedy*'s poetry.
5. See M. Hatwell, 'Dante', in *The Year's Work in Modern Languages*, xxvii (1965), 289 ff.
6. e.g. Getto, op. cit.; A. Momigliano, 'Il paesaggio della *Divina Commedia*' in his *Dante, Manzoni, Verga* (Città di Castello, 1944), pp. 9–33 (originally published in 1932).
7. Malagoli, *Linguaggio e poesia nella Divina Commedia*, p. 173.
8. P. Boyde, *Dante's Style in his Lyric Poetry* (Cambridge, 1971).
9. The page numbers refer to the editions cited in the bibliography at the end of this essay.
10. Montano, 'Dante's Style and Gothic Aesthetic', pp. 21 f.; Bigi, *passim*.
11. Rather than offering a descriptive survey of the language of the *Comedy*, this essay also deliberately (p. 603) limits attention to points of obscurity in the text. A sixth volume of the *Enciclopedia dantesca* is to be published as an Appendix at the end of 1978, and will include a detailed description of the language of the *Comedy*, as well as a briefer

230   *The Stylistic Analysis of the* Divine Comedy

section on its style (by F. Agostini, I. Baldelli, and F. Brambilla Ageno).

12. Cf. Rossi, *Problematica della Divina Commedia*, pp. 187 ff.

13. Cf. Valesio, p. 347, who refers to Taylor.

14. 'Man hört den Körper gleichsam auf den Boden aufschlagen' (p. 20).

15. Lisio's introduction also contains an interesting early statement of a formalist approach to the Comedy (pp. 1 ff.), which anticipates C. De Lollis's criticism of Croce's book ('La fede di Dante nell' arte', *Nuova antologia*, ccxiii (August 1921), pp. 208–17).

16. Croce thought Lisio's analysis pointless because it fragmented Dante's work, and divided the fragments into rhetorical categories 'each of which in itself says too much or too little, or says nothing at all' (in his *Conversazioni critiche*, ii (Bari, 1924), pp. 180–1).

17. While Lisio's, Fubini's, and Beltrami's studies all point to the decisive importance of the *terzina* as a syntactical unit, Gifford has proposed that on occasions there is a shift in the Comedy from a ternary to a binary rhythm, in the sense that breaks in meaning come at the end of every second rather than every third line. The effect of this is to enhance the impression of detachment created by the last line of the canto.

18. W. Empson, *Seven Types of Ambiguity* (London, 1930).

19. Centro Pisano dell'I.B.M., *La Divina Commedia. Testo, concordanza, indici* (Pisa, 1965).

20. A detailed study of Dante's syntax should be found in the forthcoming Appendix to the *Enciclopedia dantesca* (see n. 11).

21. G. Contini, 'La lingua del Petrarca', in Libera cattedra di storia della civiltà fiorentina, *Il Trecento* (Florence, 1953), pp. 97 f.

22. *Dante narratore*, pp. 69–90. I use the word 'paronomasia' here to include all repetitions of cognate and homophonous, but not of identical, words.

23. Ibid., pp. 165 ff.

24. A.–J. Greimas, *Sémantique structurale* (Paris, 1966).

Bibliography

Stylistic Studies of the *Divine Comedy*

I have tried to make the following list as comprehensive as possible, but have not included studies of individual passages in the *Comedy*, unless they have clear implications concerning the structure of the poem as a whole. Studies to which reference has been made in the foregoing essay—and I have tried to include all those that offer useful or interesting contributions to the type of analysis with which I have been concerned—have been marked with an asterisk(*), those which I have not myself seen with a cross(‡).

AKIYAMA, Y., ‡'Vocaboli in rima nella *Divina Commedia*', *Studi italici*, xii (1964).

ALAERTS, Y., *'Essai sur l'épithète dans la *Divine Comédie*', *Lettres romanes*, viii (1954), 3–18.

ALLAVENA, O., *Stile e poesia nelle similitudini della 'Divina Commedia*' (Savona, 1970).

AMREIN-WIDMER, M., *Rhythmus als Ausdruck inneren Erlebens in Dantes 'Divina Commedia*' (Zürich, 1932).

ANTONETTI, P., 'Essai de lecture structurelle du chant I de l'*Enfer*', *Studi danteschi*, xlix (1972), 27–41.

APPLEWHITE, J., *'Dante's Use of the Extended Simile in the Inferno*', *Italica*, xli (1964), 294–309.

AUERBACH, E., *Mimesis* (Princeton, N.J., 1971); *Literary Language and its Public in Late Latin Antiquity and the Middle Ages* (London, 1965) (original versions published in 1946 and 1958).

AUSTIN, H. D., *'Multiple Meanings and their Bearing on the Understanding of Dante's Metaphors', *Modern Philology*, xxx (1932), 129–40.

AVALLE, D'A. S., *Modelli semiologici nella Commedia di Dante* (Milan, 1975).

BALDELLI, I., *'endecasillabo', *'rima', *'terzina' in *Enciclopedia dantesca*, 5 vols. (Rome, 1970–6).

BATARD, Y., *'Sur quelques métaphores de Dante', *Cahiers du Sud*, xxxiv, no. 308 (1951), 20–4; *Dante, Minerve et Apollon: les images de la Divine Comédie* (Paris, 1952).

BECCARIA, G. L., ‡*Appunti di metrica dantesca* (Turin, 1969);

*‘cesura’, *‘dialefe’, *‘dieresi’, *‘ritmo’ in *Enciclopedia dantesca*, 5 vols. (Rome, 1970–6); *‘Alliterazioni dantesche’ and *‘Figure dantesche’ in id., *L’Autonomia del significante* (Turin, 1975), pp. 90–113 and 114–35.

BELTRAMI, P. G., *‘Primi appunti sull’ arte del verso nella *Divina Commedia*’, *Giorn. stor. d. lett. it.* clii (1975), 1–32; *‘Sul metro della *Divina Commedia*: sondaggi per un’analisi sintattica’, *Studi mediolatini e volgari*, xxiv (1976), 7–72.

BERTINETTO, P. M., ‘iato’ in *Enciclopedia dantesca*, 5 vols. (Rome 1970–6); *Ritmo e modelli ritmici. Analisi computazionale delle funzioni periodiche nella versificazione dantesca* (Turin, 1973).

BERTONI, G., ‘La lingua di Dante’ in id., *Lingua e poesia* (Florence, 1937), pp. 25–50.

BIANCHI, D., ‘Rima e verso nella *Divina Commedia*’, *Rend. dell’Ist. Lombardo*, xcv (1961), 127–40; ‘Appunti sulla lingua usata da Dante nel poema sacro’, *Atti dell’Accad. Ligure*, xx (1964), 20–31.

BIGI, E., *‘Caratteri e funzione della retorica nella *Divina Commedia*’, *Letture classensi*, iv (1973), 183–203.

BLASUCCI, L., *‘L’esperienza delle “petrose” e il linguaggio della *Divina Commedia*’, *Belfagor*, xii (1957), 403–31.

BRAMBILLA AGENO, F., ‘Osservazioni sull’ aspetto e il tempo del verbo nella *Commedia*’, *Studi di grammatica italiana*, i (1971), 61–100.

BRANDEIS, I., *The Ladder of Vision. A Study of Images in Dante’s Comedy* (London, 1960).

BUONOCUORE, O., ‡*La similitudine nella ‘Divina Commedia’* (Naples, 1940).

CAMBON, G., *Dante’s Craft. Studies in Language and Style* (Minneapolis, 1969); *‘Synaesthesia in the Divine Comedy’, *Dante Studies*, lxxxviii (1970), 1–16.

CASELLA, M., *‘Studi sul testo della *Divina Commedia*’, *Studi danteschi*, viii (1924), 5–85.

CASETTI, F., ‘Per un approccio strutturalista a Dante’, *Lectura Dantis mystica* (Florence, 1969), 519–30.

CHIAPPELLI, F., ‘The Structure of Dante’s *Purgatory*’, *Italian Quarterly*, viii (1964), 3–13; ‘La struttura figurativa del *Paradiso*’, *Deutsches Dante-Jahrb.* xliii (1965), 25–41.

CHIAVACCI LEONARDI, A. M., *Lettura del Paradiso dantesco* (Florence, 1963).

CIPOLLA, F., *‘Risuonanze nella *Divina Commedia*’, *Atti dell’Ist. Veneto di Sc., Lett. ed Arti*, lx (1900–1), 31–42.

CONTINI, G., *‘Un’interpretazione di Dante’, in id., *Un’idea di Dante* (Turin, 1976), 69–111 (first published in 1965).

COSTANZO, L., *Il linguaggio di Dante nella ‘Divina Commedia’* (Naples, 1968).

CURTIUS, E. R., *'Neue Dante Studien', *Rom. Forschungen*, lx (1947), 237–89.

DEBENEDETTI, S., *'Intorno ad alcuni versi di Dante', *Giorn. stor. della lett. it.* lxxxvii (1934), 74–99.

DELLA TERZA, D., 'I canti del disordinato amore.osservazioni sulla struttura e lo stile del *Purgatorio'*, *Belfagor*, xxi (1966), 156–79.

DE MAURO, T., 'Alcuni aspetti quantitativi della lingua della *Commedia'*, in *Atti del Conv. di Studi su Dante e la Magna Curia* (Palermo, 1967), pp. 519–23.

DE SALVIO, A., *The Rhyme Words in the 'Divine Comedy'* (Paris, 1929).

DEVOTO, G., 'Dalla lingua latina alla lingua di Dante', in Libera cattedra di storia della civiltà fiorentina, *Il Trecento* (Florence, 1953), pp. 39–54; 'La langue de Dante', *Bull. de la Fac. de Lettres de Strasbourg*, xliv (1965–6), 557–65.

DI CAPUA, F. 'Lo stile isidoriano nella retorica medievale e in Dante', in *Studi in onore di F. Torraca* (Naples, 1922), pp. 233–59.

DI GIROLAMO, C. *Teoria e prassi della versificazione* (Bologna, 1976).

DI PINOk G., 'Unità di racconto e quoziente narratigo nell'opera dantesca', *Italianistica*, iv (1975), 247–72.

ELIOT, T. S., *Dante* (London, 1965) (first published in 1929).

EWERT, A., *'Art and Artifice in the Divine Comedy', in *Centenary Essays on Dante* by members of the Oxford Dante Society (Oxford, 1965), pp. 77–90.

FITZGERALD, T. A., *'Dante's Figures of Speech', *Italica*, xviii (1941), 120–3.

FORTI, F., 'La "transumptio" nei dettatori bolognesi e in Dante', in *Dante e Bologna nei tempi di Dante* (Bologna, 1967), 127–49.

FRANZ, A., *'Sinn und Rhythmus in Danteversen', *Deutsches Dante-Jahrb.* xxxvi–xxxvii (1958), 13–39.

FRASCINO, S., *'Suono e pensiero nella poesia dantesca', *Giorn. stor della lett. it.*, suppl. no. 24 (Turin, 1928), 1–138.

FUBINI, M., *'Il metro della Divina Commedia', in id., *Metrica e poesia* (Milan, 1962), 185–221 (slightly revised in 'La terzina della *Commedia'*, *Deutsches Dante-Jahrb.* xliii (1965), 58–89); *review of Wlassics, *Interpretazioni di prosodia dantesca*, in *Giorn. stor. della lett. it.* cxlix (1972), 576–84.

GARLANDA, F., *Il verso di Dante* (Rome, 1907).

GENINASCA, J., ‡'Note per un'analisi strutturale del primo canto della *Divina Commedia'*, in G. B. Palumbo (ed.), *Problemi*, xiii (1969), 572–7.

GHINASSI, G., 'idiotismi', in *Enciclopedia dantesca*, 5 vols. (Rome 1970–6).

GIFFORD, G. H., *'Metrical Patterns in the Divine Comedy', in W. De Sua and G. Rizzo (eds.), *A Dante Symposium* (Chapel Hill, N.C., 1965), pp. 75–85.

GILBERT, A. H., 'Dante's Rimario', *Italica*, xliv (1967), 409–24.

GMELIN, H., *'Die Sprache des Transzendenten in Dantes *Paradiso*', in *Stil- und Formprobleme in der Literatur* (Vorträge des VII. Kongresses der Internationalen Vereinigung für moderne Sprachen und Literaturen in Heidelberg), ed. P. Böckmann (Heidelberg, 1959), pp. 169–95.

GOFFIS, C. F., *'Il linguaggio mistico del *Paradiso*', in *Miscellanea di studi danteschi* (Genoa, 1966), pp. 133–65.

GROULT, P., 'Musicalité de la Divine Comédie', *Lettres romanes*, xix (1965), 303–34.

HARDT, M., 'Textstrategie in der *Divina Commedia*. Beobachtungen zur dichterischen Sprache Dantes', *Rom. Forschungen*, lxxxiv (1972), 489–516.

HATZFELD, H., 'Das Heilige im dichterischen Sprachausdruck des *Paradiso*', *Deutsches Dante-Jahrb*. xii (1930), 41–70 (tr. in id., *Saggi di stilistica romanza* (Bari, 1967), pp. 203–37); 'Features of the Poetic Language of the Divine Comedy' in *A Dante Symposium* cit. (see Gifford); 'The Art of Dante's *Purgatorio*', in R. J. Clements (ed.), *American Critical Essays on the Divine Comedy* (New York, 1967), pp. 64–88.

HERCZEG, G., 'Appunti per una sintassi delle proposizioni temporali nel Trecento', *Lingua nostra*, xxii, 4 (1961), 103–10.

HINSHELWOOD, SIR CYRIL, 'Dante's Imagery' in *Centenary Essays on Dante*, cit. (see Ewert), pp. 39–53.

JERNEJ, J., 'Osservazioni sul predicativo libero e la struttura interna della frase in Dante', in *Atti del Congresso Internazionale di Studi Danteschi*, 2 vols. (Florence, 1965–6), ii, 231–5.

KIRKPATRICK, R., *Dante's Paradiso and the Limitations of Modern Criticism. A Study of Style and Poetic Theory* (Cambridge, 1978).

LANCI, A., 'Sul linguaggio della *Commedia*. Situazione della critica e una proposta di esegesi', *Il Protagora*, ix (February 1968 and April 1968), 34–74 and 14–58.

LANSING, R. H., 'Submerged Meanings in Dante's Similes (*Inferno* xxvii)', *Dante Studies*, xciv (1976), 61–9; *From Image to Idea. A Study of Simile in Dante's Comedy* (Ravenna, 1977).

LEO, U., *'Sehen und Schauen bei Dante. Eine Stil-Untersuchung', *Deutsches Dante-Jahrb*., xi (1929), 183–221.

LEWIS, C. S., 'Dante's Similes', in id., *Studies in Medieval and Renaissance Literature* (Cambridge, 1966).

LISIO, G., *L'arte del periodo nelle opere volgari di Dante Alighieri e del secolo XIII* (Bologna, 1902).

MAGGINI, F., *Dalle 'Rime' alla lirica del 'Paradiso'* (Florence, 1938); *'Associazioni etimologiche nelle immagini di Dante', *Lingua nostra*, vi (1944–5), 25–8.

MALAGOLI, L., **Linguaggio e poesia nella 'Divina Commedia'* (Genoa, 1949); *Storia della poesia nella 'Divina Commedia'* (Genoa, 1950); ‡'Lo stile dantesco', *Ausonia* (Siena), x, 3 (1955), 3–6; *Saggio sulla 'Divina Commedia'* (Florence, 1962); 'Il linguaggio del *Paradiso* e la crisi dello spirito cristiano medievale', *L'Alighieri*, vii (1966), 40–52; 'Lo stile della Commedia e lo stile dei Siciliani', in *Atti del Convegno di Studi su Dante e la Magna Curia* (Palermo, 1967), pp. 185–91; 'La pittoricità del *Paradiso*', in id., *Strutturalismo contemporaneo* (Bologna, 1969), pp. 55–66.

MARZOT, G., *Il linguaggio biblico nella 'Divina Commedia'* (Pisa, 1956).

MAZZELI, E., 'Appunti sul ritmo e sui modi narrativi dell' *Inferno* (Canti i–viii)', *Convivium*, xxxiv (1966), 184–209.

MIGLIORINI, B., **Storia della lingua italiana* (Florence, 1961), pp. 169–85; 'latinismi', in *Enciclopedia dantesca*, 5 vols. (Rome, 1970–6).

MONTANO, R., *Storia della poesia di Dante*, 2 vols. (Naples, 1962–3); *'Dante's Style and Gothic Aesthetic', in *A Dante Symposium*, cit. (see Gifford), pp. 11–33.

NAUMANN, H., 'Der Vergleich bei Dante in antiker, mittelalterlicher und moderner Sicht', *Wirkendes Wort*, xiv (1964), 314–32.

NAUMANN, W., 'Hunger und Durst als Metaphern bei Dante', *Rom. Forschungen*, liv (1940), 13–36.

NENCIONI, G., *'Dante e la rettorica', in *Dante e Bologna nei tempi di Dante* (Bologna, 1967), pp. 91–112.

NOYER-WEIDNER, A., *Symmetrie und Steigerung als stilistisches Gesetz der Divina Commedia* (Cologne, 1961).

OLIVERO, F., **La rappresentazione dell'immagine in Dante* (Turin, 1936).

OXILIA, A., *'L'endecasillabo con accento sulla settima usato in coppia nella *Commedia*', in *Atti del Congresso Internazionale di Studi Danteschi*, 2 vols. (Florence, 1965–6), ii. 221–9.

PAGLIARO, A., ‡'Sul linguaggio poetico della *Commedia*', *Il veltro*, ix (1965), 589–630; 'La lingua di Dante oggi', in U. Parricchi (ed.), *Dante* (Rome, 1965), pp. 191–209; *'Il linguaggio poetico', in A. Pagliaro, *Ulisse. Ricerche semantiche sulla Divina Commedia*, 2 vols. (Messina/Florence, 1966), pp. 585–697; *'similitudine', in *Enciclopedia dantesca*, 5 vols. (Rome 1970–6).

PALGEN, R., 'Due particolarità dello stile epico di Dante', *Convivium*, xxxi (1963), 10–18.

PARODI, E. G., 'Il comico nella *Divina Commedia*', in id., *Poesia e storia nella 'Divina Commedia'* (Naples, 1921), pp. 105–209; *'La rima

236   *Stylistic Studies of the* Divine Comedy

e i vocaboli in rima nella *Divina Commedia*', in id., *Lingua e letteratura*, ed. G. Folena, 2 vols. (Venice, 1957), ii, 203–84 (first published in 1896); *review of Lisio's *L'arte del pwriodo* . . . , ibid., 305–28.

PEIRONE, L., 'Il secondo stile tragico di Dante', *Giorn. it. di filologia*, xviii (1965), 71–7.

PÉZARD, A., ‡'Allusions, demi-mots et silences de la *Comédie*', *Bull. de la Soc. d'Études Dantesques* (Centre Universitaire Méditerranéen), xvi (1967), 169–99.

PIEROTTI, G. L., *'Le ripetizioni nella *Divina Commedia*', *L'Alighieri*, xviii (1977), 3–28.

PISTELLI RINALDI, E., *La musicalità di Dante* (Florence, 1968).

PORCELLI, B., *'Appunti sul linguaggio del Paradiso', *L'Alighieri*, ix (1968), 37–54.

Psicanalisi e strutturalismo di fronte a Dante, 3 vols. (Florence, 1972).

RABUSE, G., ‡'Dantes Bilder und Vergleiche', *Orbis Litterarum*, xv (1960), 65–94.

RICCI BATTAGLIA, L., *'Tradizione e struttura narrativa nella *Commedia*', *Giornale storico della letteratura italiana*, cliii (1976), 481–522.

RICHTOFEN, E. von, 'Dantes Verwendung von gleichgerichteten und gegensätzlichen Sinnbildern', *Deutsches Dante-Jahrbuch*, xxxi–xxxii (1953), 24–41; *Veltro und Diana. Dantes mittelalterliche und antike Gleichnisse nebst einer Darstellung ihrer Ausdrucksformen* (Tübingen, 1956).

RODOTÀ, L., ‡*Immagini e similitudini nella 'Divina Commedia'* (1964).

ROHLFS, G., 'La lingua di Dante nelle rime della *Divina Commedia*', in id., *Studi e ricerche su lingua e dialetti d'Italia* (Florence, 1972), pp. 132–8.

ROSSI, M., 'Poesia e struttura nelle similitudini della terza cantica', in id., *Gusto filologico e gusto poetico* (Bari, 1942), pp. 149–65; *'La musicalità della *Divina Commedia*', in id., *Problematica della 'Divina Commedia'* (Florence, 1969).

SACCHETTO, A., *Letture e note dantesche* (Padua, 1935); *Il gioco delle immagini in Dante* (Florence, 1947).

SALINARI, G., 'Il comico nella *Divina Commedia*', *Belfagor*, x (1955), 623–41.

SCAGLIONE, A., *'Periodic Syntax and Flexible Meter in the *Divine Comedy*', *Romance Philology*, xxi (1967), 1–22; *'Imagery and Thematic Patterns in *Paradiso* xxiii', in T. Bergin (ed.), *From Time to Eternity* (New Haven, Conn., 1967), pp. 137–72.

SCHEEL, H. L., 'Die volkssprachliche-lyrische Tradition in Dantes *Commedia*', *Deutsches Dante-Jahrbuch*, xli–xlii (1964), 9–34.

1. Janmot, *Le vol de l'âme*

2. Delacroix, *Dante and Virgil watching the Acheron crossing*

3. Delacroix, *Dante introduced to Homer by Virgil*

4. Delacroix, *Paolo and Francesca reading*

5. Delacroix, *Dante and Virgil in Phlegias' bark*

6. Reynolds, *Ugolino and his sons*

7. Delacroix, *Ugolino and his sons*

8. Delacroix, *The justice of Trajan*

SCHIAFFINI, A., 'Note sul colorito dialettale della *Divina Commedia*', *Studi danteschi*, xiii (1928), 31–45; *'A proposito dello "stile comico" di Dante', in id., *Momenti di storia della lingua italiana* (Rome, 1953), pp. 43–56.

SCHWARZE, C., *Untersuchungen zum syntaktischen Stil der italienischen Dichtungssprache bei Dante* (Bad Homburg, 1970).

SICARDI, E., *La lingua italiana in Dante* (Rome, 1928).

SPITZER, L., *'Speech and Language in *Inferno* xiii', *Italica*, xix (1941), 81–104; *'Two Dante Notes', *Romanic Review*, xxxiv (1943), 248–56.

SPOERRI, T., *Dante und die europäische Literatur* (Stuttgart, 1963), 22–30.

STAEDLER, E., 'Das rhetorische Element in Dantes *Divina Commedia*', *Deutsches Dante-Jahrbuch*, xxi (1940), 107–51.

TATEO, F., 'anadiplosi', *'anafora', *'antitesi', 'antonomasia', *'chiasmo', 'epanalessi', 'epifonema', 'ipotiposi', 'ironia', 'litote', *'metafora', *'metonimia', *'parallelismo', *'paronomasia', *'perifrasi', *'replicazione', *'sinecdoche', *'tautologia', *'transumptio', *'variatio', 'zeugma' (also 'alliterazione'), in *Enciclopedia dantesca*, 5 vols. (Rome, 1970–6).

TAYLOR, R. L., *Alliteration in Italian* (New Haven, Conn., 1900).

TOLLEMACHE, F., 'I parasinteti verbali e i deverbali nella *Divina Commedia*', *Lingua nostra*, xxi (1960), 112–15.

TONELLI, L., *Dante e la poesia dell'ineffabile* (Florence, 1934).

VALESIO, P., *Strutture dell'alliterazione* (Bologna, 1967).

VALLONE, A., 'Altri aspetti della sintassi poetica di Dante', in *Scritti in onore di Cleto Carbonara* (Naples, 1976), pp. 997–1006.

VAZZANA, S., ‡'Le similitudini nella *Divina Commedia*', *Ausonia* (Siena), xiii, 4 (1958), 3–10.

VENTURI, L., *Le similitudini dantesche ordinate, illustrate e confronntate* (Florence, 1874).

VEZIN, A., *'Die Periphrase in der *Divina Commedia*', *Deutsches Dante-Jahrbuch*, xxxiii (1954), 120–41.

VINASSA DE REGNY, P., 'Note sulla Commedia', *Rendiconti dell'Istituto Lombardo*, lxvi (1933), 115–22.

VINCENT, E. R., 'Dante's Choice of Words', *Italian Studies*, x (1955), 1–18.

VIOLA, P. M., *Ricerche di metodo e struttura su Dante e Manzoni* (Cagliari, 1969).

WLASSICS, T., *Interpretazioni di prosodia dantesca* (Rome, 1972); *Dante narratore* (Florence, 1975).

ZINGARELLI, N. *'Parole e forme della *Divina Commedia* aliene dal dialetto fiorentino', *Studi di filologia romanza*, i (1885), 1–202.

10

Dante and Delacroix

JEAN SEZNEC

One of the very first entries in Delacroix's *Journal*, dating from September 1822 (he was then twenty-three) is the following:
'I was reading this morning in the garden some passages from CORINNE on Italian music: I enjoyed it very much.' 'CORINNE' is of course Madame de Staël's novel—a novel which is, at the same time, a guide-book to Italy. One chapter is dedicated to music. 'Whoever has not heard an Italian singing cannot conceive what music is. Voices, in Italy, have a softness, a mellowness, that recall the perfume of flowers, and the purity of the sky.'
Now comes the page which Delacroix copied in his diary:

The Italians, for centuries, have had a passion for music. Dante, in his *Purgatory*, meets one of the best singers of his day; he asks him to sing one of his delightful tunes, and the penitent souls are so enraptured that they forget their condition and stay on to listen, until their keeper calls them back [*an admirable subject for a painting* is Delacroix's comment].

The episode occurs in the second canto. Dante meets Casella, and makes his request: 'If no law deprives you of use and memory of those songs of love which used to quiet all my troubles, with them give comfort to my soul, which—since yet it is burdened with its body—is now so sore fatigued by coming here.'
Casella then begins:

> '*Amor che nella mente mi ragiona*'
> cominciò elli allor sì dolcemente,
> che la dolcezza ancor dentro mi suona.
> Lo mio maestro e io e quella gente
> ch'eran con lui parevan sì contenti,
> come a nessun toccasse altro la mente.

Noi eravam tutti fissi e attenti
a le sue note . . .
(Purg. ii. 112–19)

But the keeper now appears on the scene, and upbraids the souls, who immediately flee like so many frightened doves, and rush toward the mount where they have to resume their penance.

. . . . ed ecco il veglio onesto
gridando: 'Che è ciò, spiriti lenti?
qual negligenza, quale stare è questo?
Correte al monte a spogliarvi lo scoglio . . .'
(Ibid. 119–22)

The souls then disperse; they scatter

Come quando, cogliendo biado o loglio,
li colombi adunati a la pastura,
queti, sanza mostrar l'usato orgoglio,
se cosa appare ond' elli abbian paura,
subitamente lasciano star l'esca,
perch' assaliti son da maggior cura;
(Ibid. 124–9)

Delacroix quotes these last lines, in the original, in another part of his diary (9 May, 1824), to illustrate what he calls Dante's sublime *naivete*. On that evening he had been listening to a nightingale, and he wonders:

How many among the poets have been able to express what one feels when hearing the nightingale? Most of them write about it as they write about love; to them it is just a conventional, artificial motif; not so with Dante. He is as new and fresh as nature itself. He makes you shudder as if you were in front of the immediate reality: 'Come colombi adunati alla pastura . . . Come a gracidar si sta la rana . . . Come il villanello . . .' This exquisite humility in the choice of details was alien to our classical writers. Yes, *this is precisely what I am after*, what I have always been dreaming of, without defining it.

Read and re-read Dante [he concludes]. Shake yourself. He will lead you back to greatness. Be in painting what he is as a poet.

Delacroix then, at an early stage in his career, looks to Dante as a teacher, and discovers, between the master and himself, a deep affinity.

Now, what are the particular aspects of Dante's genius which he finds so congenial? From the examples which he has been quoting, you might think that he is, above all, sensitive to the *dolci note*—I mean the grace and suavity of the poet's imagination; this seems to be confirmed in a surprising and almost alarming way by his comment on a would-be mystical picture by Janmot, one of those 'lyonnais' painters whose brains, according to Baudelaire, are as misty as the sky of their native city.

That picture is part of a series illustrating a poem composed by the painter himself, *le Poème de l'Ame* (pl. 1). Delacroix detects in it what he calls a Dantesque flavour, 'un parfum dantesque remarquable'. As I look at it, he says, 'I think of the angels in the *Purgatory* of the famous Florentine. I love the green robes, green as the grass in the meadows in May; I love these heads which seem to come out of a dream, like reminiscences of another world.' Delacroix is obviously reminded of that episode where Virgil and Dante, led by Sordello, discover the vale, as serene and flowery as the Elysian fields, which serves as an antechamber to Purgatory. This is the residence of the souls of those negligent princes who were late in thinking of their salvation. They are now singing to implore the intercession of the Madonna:

> Non avea pur natura ivi dipinto,
> ma di soavità di mille odori
> vi facea uno incognito e indistinto.
>   '*Salve, Regina*' in sul verde e 'n su' fiori,
> quindi seder cantando anime vidi . . .
> (Purg. vii. 79–83)

As for the angels, messengers of hope, who descend upon the vale at sunset, when the singing is over, Dante perceives their blonde hair and the colour of their wings, green as the first leaves in the spring . . .

> e vidi uscir de l'alto e scender giùe
> due angeli. . . .
>   Verdi come fogliette pur mo nate
> erano in veste, che da verdi penne
> percosse traean dietro e ventilate.
> (Purg. viii. 25–30)

Delacroix is generous indeed in recalling such lines in front of Janmot's graceful, but rather anaemic, production. Suavity, however, is neither the only nor the major aspect of the *Commedia* that fascinates him. Another side appeals to him far more strongly, as it fully satisfies the requirements of his sensibility. The accent that strikes him, as he reads Dante, is the mournful one—what he calls 'the sombre turbulence of the Middle Ages'; the songs that reverberate in his heart are the songs of anguish and misfortune. In his own works, through the apparent variety of subjects and the diversity of times and places, the same basic theme is running: the ill-starred genius as a martyr is of course a romantic commonplace, but Delacroix gives it his personal stamp. The tragic sense of life pervades the whole of his compositions, whether they picture individual destinies or episodes of history: they testify, in Baudelaire's words, against man's eternal, incurable inhumanity to man; but they also seem to betray a cruel, sadistic imagination for which Baudelaire again coined a word, Delacroix's *molochism*, his taste for scenes of violence and slaughter. Just think of these women about to be sacrificed on Sardanapalus' funeral pyre; of these other women raped, or crushed under the hoofs of the conqueror's horses— whether the conquerors are the Crusaders or the Turks. Remember the *Massacre at Chios*, which Delacroix complacently called: 'mon massacre numéro 2'.

In short, what Delacroix's works illustrate is more than the martyrdom of genius: it is that of mankind itself—'le martyrologe de l'humanité'. Such is indeed his vision of the world; he sums it up in one word: 'fatality'—the helplessness of man. 'Hence', he says, 'the solemn, baneful sense of human weakness —a feeling however which is deeply poetic, and which generates an inexhaustible flow of powerful emotions.'

The powerful emotions he is longing for have been expressed most forcefully by these noble poets who were, *par excellence*, the bards of fatality: Shakespeare, Goethe, Byron—and, supreme among them, Dante.

One could then forecast what figures, and what episodes, Delacroix would borrow from the *Commedia*. He did not attempt a continuous illustration of the poem; yet we may take him as a guide for the great journey among the shadows, 'le voyage parmi les ombres', as he puts it. Let us follow him from the vestibule of Hell to the first *Girone*, the first terrace of Purgatory. Significantly perhaps, he did not ascend any higher.

He had planned, at one point, to draw a frontispiece for the poem; he would have pictured Dante walking in the Colosseum by moonlight.

Did he read the *Commedia* in the original? He certainly did. He knew Italian, as we know from the quotations in his diary; he even used an Italian expression to record his amorous performances (Victor Hugo used Spanish for the same purpose). He claimed, furthermore, that Dante was almost impossible to translate. The difficulty, he explained, does not lie so much in the language itself as in the spirit of the time, which imbues an archaic poem with a peculiar flavour. Dante's poem, in spite of so many attempts, will never be rendered in its pristine beauty. In May 1824 Delacroix does mention a verse version of the *Inferno*; but before that date he had copied a fragment of a prose one; this was in 1822, when he was preparing his first exhibition. He had thought of several possible passages to illustrate; one was Dante's meeting with Virgil, and their waiting to cross the Acheron in Charon's boat. On one single page was Delacroix's copy of the translation—and a first sketch for the illustration of the passage (pl. 2).

The translation, although reasonably accurate, is weak. The sketch shows Virgil and Dante watching the damned boarding the barge that will ferry them across, while Charon beats with his oar the laggard ones. 'Caron dimonio . . . batte col remo qualunque s'adagia' (*Inf.* iii. 109–111).

One can detect in Delacroix's drawing a reminiscence of Michelangelo's *Last Judgment*. We find, later on, Dante and his guide being carried themselves in another boat, by another oarsman, Phlegias; but first a luminous interval takes place, as the two pilgrims pass through the limbo where they meet the great men of Greece and Rome. In the magnificent cupola of the Senate Library in Paris, Delacroix has evoked the radiant scene (pl. 3).

Dante suddenly perceives, coming toward him and his guide, four great shadows:

> vidi quattro grand' ombre a noi venire:
>
> (*Inf.* iv. 83)

Virgil names these four ghosts; they are Horace, Ovid, Lucan
—and, leading them and towering over them, Homer, to whom
Virgil introduces Dante:

> 'Mira colui con quella spada in mano,
> che vien dinanzi ai tre sì come sire:
> quelli è Omero poeta sovrano . . .'
>
> (Ibid. 86–8)

Thus, Dante reports, did I see the gathering of this beautiful
group—the disciples of this master who, like the eagle, flies high
above the others. These last words have been reproduced by
Delacroix on a scroll, above the scene where Dante, with an
ecstatic expression on his face, is introduced to Homer.

Delacroix, incidentally, never took his inspiration directly
from Virgil. He noted in his diary two episodes from the
Aeneid—and, typically, two gruesome ones, two scenes of rape
and murder; but he never painted them. The same is true of
Lucan; there again Delacroix had planned to illustrate three
scenes from the *Pharsalia*—three terrifying, nightmarish scenes;
but again he failed to bring this project to completion.

Dante and Virgil now enter the second circle of Hell, where
the realm of perpetual gloom begins, 'in parte ove non è che
luca'. There, among the lascivious and the adulterers, they
meet the famous lovers of Rimini, Paolo and Francesca. Francesca tells them how she and Paolo became aware of their
mutual passion while reading a book—the romance of Lancelot
and Queen Guinevere—a tale so poignant that at the end
Dante faints with compassion.

Delacroix illustrated these immortal lines:

> '. . . Noi leggiavamo un giorno per diletto
> di Lancialotto come amor lo strinse . . .'
>
> (*Inf.* v. 127–8)

One must confess, however, that for once he was in danger of
erring on the side of suavity (pl. 4). This is a troubadour scene,
although not quite as sweetish as Ingres's rendering of the same
passage. There is of course in both Ingres and Delacroix the
suggestion of the imminent murder—for Paolo and Francesca
were not alone; behind the curtain the husband, Gianciotto, is
ready with his sword.

One may also regret that Delacroix did not select rather the epilogue of the story—the part that takes place in Hell, where the two guilty lovers, inseparable for eternity, are buffeted and tossed about by the raging wind which blows incessantly,

La bufera infernal, che mai non resta . . .

(Inf. v. 31)

That scene, alas, was left for Ary Scheffer to illustrate.

The pilgrims have now descended into the lower Hell, the fifth circle. They are crossing the lake that surrounds the infernal city of Dite, in a boat steered by Phlegias. Some of the damned, floating in the lake, are clinging to the boat, trying desperately to get aboard. Dante recognizes among them one of his fellow-citizens, Filippo Argenti, who implores his help—in vain. Both Dante and Virgil repel him with the utmost brutality;

As we were running through the dead channel, there appeared before me one covered with mud, and he said: 'Who are you that come before your time?' And I to him: 'If I come, I do not remain, but you, who are you who have become so foul?' He answered: 'You see that I am one who weeps.' And I to him: 'In weeping and in sorrow do you remain, accursed spirit, for I know you, even if you are all filthy.'

Then he stretched both his hands to the boat, whereat the wary master thrust him off, saying: 'Away there with the other dogs!' ('Via costà con li altri cani!').

As he was painting this episode, Delacroix had the Italian text read aloud to him by a friend—not so much because he wanted to be accurate, but rather, he explains, because he was eager to recapture the music, the particular tonality of that sinister passage: 'The best head in my Dante picture was painted with extraordinary ease as I was listening to my friend reading the Canto; his accent electrified me. That head is that of the man who is facing the spectator, and whose arm is inside the boat' (pl. 5).

Delacroix comes back again and again to this inspiring effect of sound, of music; better still, he claims that the painter himself should strive at musical effects; but how is he going to produce them with line and colour?

If [he answers] you add to a composition which is already interesting by its subject a disposition of lines which reinforces the impression, a striking chiaroscuro, *a colour that fits the character of the scene*—then you will have solved the most difficult problem, the problem of harmony, the combination of several elements into a single tone; this is what I call *la tendance musicale*.

In this particular case, he succeeded in reaching that single tone he was seeking, a lugubrious one. He left it to colour to express violence, horror, and despair. Among his preparatory studies there is a watercolour with no figures—just colour spots, a sort of colour scheme.

The glimmers of the city of Dite illuminated by the infernal fire,

vermiglie come se di foco uscite . . .;

the black sky, the greenish bodies of the damned; the red of Dante's hood, the brown of Virgil's mantle, the blue of Phlegias' scarf—all this results in an over-all impression—a musical one. 'Les couleurs et les sons se répondent.'

Another grisly episode, one which has been treated by many artists, all the way from Reynolds to Carpeaux, is the story of Ugolino, whom Dante and Virgil find in the ninth circle, gnawing the skull and brain of archbishop Ruggieri like a dog crushing a bone. This bestial meal—'quel fiero pasto'—he consumes out of hatred and for revenge, as he tells his horrified listeners.

Archbishop Ruggieri once had him locked in a tower with his four sons. The children, one after the other, died of hunger; and, ultimately, the father devoured the corpses. This passage is the one which both Reynolds and Carpeaux illustrated. Michelet, who saw Reynolds's picture in London, in Chantrey's studio in 1834, found it 'sublime', as the father seems to be raised above himself by the realization of his supreme wretchedness (pl. 6). Carpeaux's sculpture is a literal rendering of the text. As they see their father biting his fingers, out of despair, the children believe that he does it out of hunger—and this is when they offer themselves as nourishment.

> ambo le man per lo dolor mi morsi;
> ed ei, pensando ch'io 'l fessi per voglia
> di manicar . . .
> . . . disser: 'Padre, assai ci fia men doglia
> se tu mangi di noi:
>
> (*Inf.* xxxiii. 58–62)

On that day, and the next, says Ugolino, we all stayed silent. 'When we had come to the fourth day. Guido threw himself outstretched at my feet, saying: "Father, why don't you help me?" ("Padre mio, ché non m'aiuti?").' This is the moment which Delacroix chose to depict—the petrified father, the pathetic gesture of the child who dies immediately after crying for help. This calls for a comparison with another gruesome story, also illustrated by Delacroix: Byron's *Prisoner of Chillon.* We are again in a 'Torre della Fame'. A Swiss patriot has been jailed with his two brothers; each of them is chained to a pillar. Then one of the brothers dies of hunger; and the eldest one—who tells the story—watches him expire without being able to reach him. The younger of the three is now about to die; this time, however, the eldest succeeds in breaking his chain.

> I burst my chain with one strong bound
> and rushed to him.

Delacroix, again, selected the climactic moment—the desperate effort (pl. 7).

The two pilgrims have now reached the confines of Purgatory. This is where, as you remember, they meet Casella and listen to his song—a song so delicious that the souls doing their penance forget that they are still on probation. You may also remember that Delacroix had noted in his diary: 'an admirable subject for a painting'; yet he did not paint it, nor did he paint the serene vision which he knew and liked so well; the souls praying to the Madonna at sunset.

He picked up instead the splendid episode of the Emperor Trajan. Those who in their lifetime have committed the sin of pride have to be taught humility; this is achieved by contemplation. They have to look at outstanding examples of humility. These examples are carved on marble reliefs which are displayed precisely for that purpose. One of these models of virtue is Trajan who, as he was on his way to a military expedition, was stopped by a widow whose child had been killed, and who implored justice.

Depicted was the glorious deed of the Roman prince ... A poor widow was at his bridle in a posture of grief ... and she seemed to say: 'Lord, avenge me for my son ...' and he to answer: 'Wait till I return': and she: 'My Lord, ... if thou return not?': and he: 'He that is in my place will do it for thee': and she: 'What shall another's goodness avail thee, if thou art forgetful of thine own?'—He, therefore: 'Now, take comfort, for I must fulfil my duty before I go; justice requires it, and compassion bids me to stay' (giustizia vuole e pietà mi ritene). *Purg.* x. 73ff.

The Emperor then dismounted from his horse and did justice to the poor woman.

Delacroix's picture is magnificently animated, bursting with life and splendour (pl. 8). It conjures up one of those great Venetian compositions—Veronese or Tiepolo—full of prancing horses and waving standards. All this, however, was already in Dante's text; for although Dante is supposed to describe a marble relief, he actually suggests a grandiose and colourful scene, full of pomp and tumult—'The place around Trajan seemed trampled and thronged with knights, and the eagles on the gold above them moved visibly in the wind.'

> Intorno a lui parea calcato e pieno
> di cavalieri, e l'aguglie ne l'oro
> sovr' essi in vista al vento si movieno.
>
> (Ibid. 79–81)

Delacroix's supreme merit was to perceive and to develop the indications of the text, and to visualize the scene just as Dante had; an achievement far beyond the reach of a mere illustrator.

I have been accused [Delacroix writes in his diary] of being a *literary* painter; my critics have claimed that if I borrow my subjects for books, this is because I lack imagination; it is a sign of sterility.

But [he answers] books to me are not simply models to copy from; I do not *imitate* them—for what I look for in them is an echo, a confirmation of my own feelings and of my own dreams. My choice of books is not dictated by the necessity of finding subjects, but by a secret sympathy. What I take from them is only what I already had in me—I mean the figures and the themes that correspond to my personal moods. If I use Byron and Shakespeare *and Dante*, it is because I sense, between them and me, an affinity. I am attuned to their works, and they never fail to move me.

Remember Delacroix's self-exhortation: 'Read and re-read Dante, you will find in him what you have always felt in yourself.'

Index